W9-CKI-143

LITERATURE AS HISTORY

MARIO T. GARCÍA

LITERATURE AS HISTORY

*Autobiography, Testimonio, and the Novel
in the Chicano and Latino Experience*

THE UNIVERSITY OF
ARIZONA PRESS

TUCSON

The University of Arizona Press
www.uapress.arizona.edu

© 2016 The Arizona Board of Regents
All rights reserved. Published 2016

Printed in the United States of America
21 20 19 18 17 16   6 5 4 3 2 1

ISBN-13: 978-0-8165-3355-8 (cloth)

Cover design by Nicole Hayward

Publication of this book is made possible in part by the proceeds of a permanent endowment created with the assistance of a Challenge Grant from the National Endowment for the Humanities, a federal agency.

Library of Congress Cataloging-in-Publication Data
Names: García, Mario T., author.
Title: Literature as history : autobiography, testimonio, and the novel in the Chicano and
    Latino experience / Mario T. García.
Description: Tucson : The University of Arizona Press, 2016. | Includes bibliographical
    references and index.
Identifiers: LCCN 2016007476 | ISBN 9780816533558 (cloth : alk. paper)
Subjects: LCSH: Literature and history—United States. | Mexican Americans—History. |
    Hispanic Americans—History.
Classification: LCC E184.M5 G3746 2016 | DDC 973/.046872—dc23 LC record available at
    http://lccn.loc.gov/2016007476

♾ This paper meets the requirements of ANSI/NISO Z39.48-1992 (Permanence of Paper).

*To Ellen, with love and thoughts
for all the good times in Spain*

Our own fate as Latin American writers is linked to the need for profound social transformations.

—EDUARDO GALEANO

CONTENTS

ACKNOWLEDGMENTS

I FIRST WANT TO THANK Kristen Buckles at the University of Arizona Press for her support of my book manuscript and for professionally guiding it through the review process. I also want to thank the two reviewers of the manuscript, who fully engaged with it in an unbiased manner and who provided excellent suggestions for changes. Thanks also to Melanie Mallon for her professional copyediting. Of course, for the wonderful texts and stories I interpret from a historical perspective in this book, I am grateful to Ramón Eduardo Ruiz, Frances Esquibel Tywoniak, Mary Helen Ponce, Richard Rodriguez, John Rechy, Yamileth López, Evelyn Cortez-Davis, Dianne Walta Hart, Alejandro Morales, Ruben Salazar, and Stella Pope Duarte. I am likewise appreciative of Professor María Herrera-Sobek and Professor Francisco Lomelí, who encouraged me to participate in the Chicano literature conferences in Spain that gave birth to the idea of this book. Thanks also to Professor Katherine Leen, who gave me the opportunity to present some of this work at the National University of Ireland, Maynooth. I am likewise grateful to the Freshman Seminar Program at University of California, Santa Barbara, for the research funding that facilitated my travel to Spain and Ireland. My love and thanks to Professor Ellen McCracken, who also encouraged this work and with whom I spent delightful days in Spain and Ireland, where I showcased some of this work. Finally, my love to my wonderful children and now young adults, Giuliana and Carlo.

LITERATURE AS HISTORY

INTRODUCTION

Literature as History

I

WHAT IS NARRATIVE? While there are complex literary definitions of narrative, or narratology, I define narrative or literature, at least for this study, as fictional texts, autobiographies, and testimonios (oral history). Of course, all written texts are narratives. Narrative is the attempt by writers to communicate with others through the written language. Narrative has a purpose—communication. Although I am not steeped in narrative theory, I do agree with Didier Coste, who writes, "An act of communication is narrative whenever and only when imparting a transitive view of the world is the effect of the message produced."[1] In imparting a transitive view of the world, narrative is more than communication; it is also history. All narratives possess a historical context and therefore directly and indirectly speak to their historical period. Novels and autobiographies are historical narratives. While I don't fully agree with Louis Gerard Mendoza, who argues that Chicano fiction writers are better historians than Chicano historians, I do agree with him that fictional and autobiographical narratives, for example, can represent very well their historical moment.[2] My difference with Mendoza is that he believes it has to be one and not the other. The fact is that both can capture that experience. As a historian I am examining the narratives in this book as historical documents and for what they convey about Chicano/Latino history. This is a study about how historians can use narrative in the form of autobiographies and novels as history. This is not an exercise in literary studies or literary theory, which I am not equipped to do. Rather, I use my strengths as a historian to examine various autobiographies, testimonios, and novels from a historical perspective.

I should note that the genre of testimonio comes out of the Latin American tradition, commencing in the 1960s, of producing an oral history through collaboration between a journalist or an academic and a political activist or a revolutionary. It is the political protagonist's story, but it is written and produced by the journalist or academic. The best-known Latin American testimonio is *I, Rigoberta Menchú: An Indian Woman in Guatemala*, produced by the collaboration between Menchú, a Guatemalan indigenous activist, and Elisabeth Burgos-Debray, a French anthropologist.[3] The testimonio is an autobiographical text written in the activist's words, but unlike an autobiography, which is written by the subject, in the testimonio the story is written by the journalist or academic.

Historical documents, or historical sources, for that matter, exist in different forms. Archival sources are the more traditional ones historians use, and they include official documents, newspapers, correspondence, diaries, and other printed forms that have been deposited in public or private archives. Family or personal archives are sometimes available to researchers. Oral history is still another important form of historical evidence, since libraries and archives have traditionally not been interested in collecting and housing sources for working-class people, including minorities such as Chicanos, and fewer documents exist for these groups. Oral history helps fill in these gaps. In addition, other forms of historical sources are more literary. Novelists and autobiographers also document history, and so their writings can be used by historians to illuminate the past. These literary texts can sometimes reveal even more about ordinary people's lives—a people's history. This is certainly the case in these eight chapters. My chapter essays are a way of bridging what is often seen as separate spheres. There is history, and then there is literature. But from an interdisciplinary perspective, the two can come together. It is interesting that with all the recent emphasis on interdisciplinarity in the academy, many scholars, including historians and literary critics, don't come together. I have written several testimonios, which certainly in Latin America is accepted as a literary genre, and even among Latin Americanists in this country. Yet, none of my testimonios have been engaged with by Chicano literary scholars. This includes my Bert Corona and Sal Castro testimonios, which have never been reviewed by or written about by Chicano literary critics.[4] It's as if these testimonios don't exist. But Chicano historians have also not engaged with literary sources as historical documents. A literary writer not only can provide us with historical evidence, but also can provide a personal insight into history that more formal documents cannot. This is what I attempt to do in this book: to bring history and different forms of narrative together to help provide new windows into the past.

Each of my chapters is intended to do this. I use my skills and knowledge as a historian to seek historical understanding through these narratives I engage with. I see these sources as more than literary narratives, but as forms of historical archives. In this study, I engage with five autobiographical texts and three novels. On the surface, these are not historical narratives, and yet they are, and I attempt to show how they provide historical knowledge and analysis. The chapters are organized according to genre. In part 1, I include my historical analysis of three personally written autobiographies and two testimonios, or oral histories. The autobiography, of course, has a long history and tradition, and Chicano/Latino writers have contributed to this genre. While these personal and introspective texts are not necessarily written with the historian in mind, they are still written within the historical context of the period these writers reference. Because so much of Chicano/Latino literature, including the autobiography and testimonio, has been influenced by political struggles, these types of texts encourage a historical reading. In part 2, I write about three novels that also possess a historical context. Moreover, each novel has a connection with part 1 in that the novelists each position their stories within a familiar personal or family setting. The Chicano/Latino novel, of course, has impressively developed over the last fifty years and has come to influence the American literary canon, although the novels I examine have not been given the attention they deserve, and one is an unfinished novel. In both parts, I have arranged the texts chronologically based on the historical period they encompass.

In part 1, chapter 1, I examine the autobiography by Professor Ramón Eduardo Ruiz Urueta, one of the few autobiographies written by a Mexican American intellectual, which reveals the mindset of an earlier generation of scholars of the post–World War II era, prior to the Chicano Movement. In chapter 2 I interpret Frances Esquibel Tywoniak's testimonio from the perspective of her struggle with identity and gender. In chapter 3 I treat the coming-of-age autobiography of writer Mary Helen Ponce, who depicts what it meant to grow up Mexican American in Pacoima, California, in the San Fernando Valley during

World War II. In chapter 4, I draw from the autobiographies of Richard Rodriguez and John Rechy and their memories of dealing with what I call a "triple consciousness"—that is, three distinct parts of their identities: their Mexican descent, their American lives as U.S.-born citizens, and their early sexual sensibilities concerning homosexuality. The lens of triple consciousness I adapt from the great African American writer, historian, and activist W. E. B. Du Bois and his concept of "double consciousness." While I modify this perspective to my analysis of Rodriguez and Rechy, it could actually apply to many of the texts I analyze. Chicanos and Latinos, like African Americans, have always wrestled or negotiated with the dual pressures of being Mexican, for example, and being American, but many also contend with a third pressure related to their gender and sexuality—hence a triple consciousness. In the final chapter of part 1, I look at Central American migration to the United States in the 1980s, driven by civil wars, specifically in El Salvador and Nicaragua, as forcefully narrated in the autobiography of Evelyn Cortez-Davis and in the testimonio of Yamileth López. I have included these two Central American texts not only because they are powerful works that speak to the significant role women play in the migration and adaptation process of immigrants and refugees, but also because they complement the mostly Mexican American, or Chicano, texts by adding a broader Latino context to this study.

In part 2, "The Novel," I engage in chapter 6 with Alejandro Morales's *The Brick People*, set in 1920s and 1930s Los Angeles, which reveals the working conditions of Mexican immigrant workers and U.S.-born Mexican Americans in the brick industry of this area. Chapter 7 concerns an unfinished novel by Ruben Salazar about his coming-of-age years in El Paso in the 1930s, 1940s, and early 1950s, including the movement of his immigrant parents out of the barrio into a lower-middle-class, ethnically mixed neighborhood. Salazar, of course, would go on to become a pioneer Chicano journalist with the *Los Angeles Times* in the 1960s, only to be tragically killed covering the large National Chicano Moratorium against the Vietnam War in East Los Angeles on August 29, 1970. His death at the hands of a county sheriff elevated Salazar to martyr status in the Chicano Movement. And in chapter 8, I analyze Stella Pope Duarte's novel *Let Their Spirits Dance* as a historical depiction of the Chicano antiwar movement associated with the Chicano Movement of the late 1960s and 1970s. These different examples of narrative genres—autobiographies, testimonios, and novels—are filled with historical references that are highly useful to historians, as I try to exhibit in my analysis and engagement with each of them.

II

These narratives reference several themes of the Chicano/Latino historical experience that are important to understand to better appreciate each chapter and the text as a whole. As a historian, I have incorporated these references in many of my own studies.

Immigration, of course, is a major theme in Chicano/Latino history. While some Mexican Americans can trace their ancestry to the early Spanish and mestizo settlements first in New Mexico and then in other parts of what would become the Southwest, including California, most Chicanos and other Latinos are the products of immigration from Mexico, Central America, the Caribbean, and South America. The Southwest used to be El Norte under both Spain and Mexico (1598–1848), but after the United States defeated Mexico in the U.S.-Mexico War (1846–48), the northern part of Mexico became a U.S. possession in a war of choice and conquest. Geography followed history. Geography is not innocent or just a matter of topography. It is political, reflecting political changes, which are often the result of one nation's conquest of another's territory. The Mexicans in that territory, now the U.S. Southwest, some one hundred thousand people, were granted U.S. citizenship if they chose it, which meant that they were indirectly recognized as "white" since only whites of European extraction could become naturalized citizens; in time, however, they were deprived of their lands and subjected to second-class citizenship accompanied by American racism. They became what I call the conquered generation in Chicano history.[5]

Mexican Americans in the second half of the nineteenth century might have simply become a footnote in American history except that something happened by the end of that century and into the beginning of the twentieth. That something was the rise of industrialization and the incorporation of the Southwest as a region that could provide new sources of food for the industrial armies being assembled in the East and Midwest through domestic migration and, more important, the "New Immigrants" from eastern and southern Europe. In the Southwest, the extension of the railroad system, agribusiness, mining, and ranching also necessitated new sources of labor, especially cheap labor, and Anglo-American captains of industry found this south of the border. Between 1900 and 1930, perhaps as many as one million Mexican immigrants entered the United States to work in these industries. They are what I call the immigrant generation in Chicano history, since in no other period will immigrants so totally dominate the Mexican experience in the United States. They became the labor foundation of the Southwest, toiling in racialized "Mexican jobs" and being paid "Mexican wages." Their hard labor, despite the racist labeling of the "lazy and sleepy Mexican," contributed tremendously to the wealth of the nation.[6] The beginning of mass Mexican immigration would continue throughout the century and into the new millennium, with the exception of the Great Depression years of the 1930s, when Mexicans were blamed in some circles for the economic crisis, leading to the largest deportation and repatriation of any American ethnic group, with perhaps as many as half a million people of Mexican descent forced into Mexico. Many, some suggest a majority, should have never been sent since they were U.S.-born children.[7] But there is no question that immigration has been a central feature of Chicano/Latino experiences, and almost all the chapters in this book reference it, since the writers are either immigrants or children of immigrants.

The second-generation experience is another important theme that appears in some of the chapters. This experience began with the children of the immigrant generation who were born or largely raised in the United States. They became what I further term the Mexican American generation, which came of age from the 1930s through the 1950s. They, as members of a biological as well as historical generation, are characterized by their process of acculturation or better transculturation than previous generations. They were the products of dual and sometimes multiple cultures. They lived in a Mexican world at home with their Spanish-speaking immigrant parents, but they also lived in an English-speaking environment outside the home and especially in the schools. They bridged cultures and became bilingual and bicultural, although not devoid of cultural tensions. They were the new mestizos. This generation also experienced the Great Depression and World War II, plus the political pressures of the Cold War. The Mexican American generation became the prototype for later Chicano and Latino second-generation experiences in the latter part of the twentieth century and into the new millennium. Indicative of these experiences are the chapters on Ramón Ruiz, Mary Helen Ponce, Richard Rodriguez, John Rechy, Ruben Salazar, and the two Central American autobiographies of Evelyn Cortez-Davis and Yamileth López.[8]

The second-generation experience further translates into changing identities, which characterizes a number of the chapters. Identity is always fluid and never static. Immigrants, for example, undergo their own transculturation, although not as noticeably as their U.S.-born children. Still, being an immigrant already represents an adjustment to living, in this case, in the United States. In the immigrant generation, transculturation took the form of immigrants becoming more *mexicano* on this side of the border. They began to shed their localized or regional Mexican identities as, especially in urban areas in the United States, they associated with Mexicans from different regions in Mexico. This resulted in a greater Mexican nationalist identity, but one that was affected by their being in another country. Still, the immigrants were not immune to some Americanization as they began the process, as George Sánchez notes, of becoming Mexican Americans.[9] Their children were Mexican American, whose evolving identities would be affected by their parents' immigrant backgrounds, but also by the second generation's socialization into American culture. Being Mexican American is also a fluid identity, and some will lean more toward the Mexican, some more toward the American, with most in between. At the same time, generational change also affects identity. In the 1960s and 1970s a new generation shunned being Mexican American and instead chose to become Chicano, an older immigrant term transformed first in the 1940s and 1950s by its use by pachucos and zoot-suiters among hardcore barrio youth, and then by those who would become the Chicano generation of the 1960s and 1970s. Being Chicano involved rediscovering one's Mexican heritage and history, especially the indigenous and mestizo side, as well as the revolutionary heritage of the Mexican Revolution of 1910.[10] In the post–Chicano Movement era of the late twentieth and early twenty-first centuries, the children of the immigrants and political refugees who had arrived in the 1970s and 1980s constitute what I am calling the Latino generation. This millennial generation sees its identity in more pan-Latino terms as a result of globalization, new communication technologies, the demographic explosion of Latinos in the United States, and the growing political power of Latinos. All this and more have made for an expansive identity beyond the nationality of their immigrant parents.[11] Throughout these changes remains the pressure of securing an identity that reflects one's historical and generational experiences. This tension, or the search for identity, is visible in almost all the chapters in this volume, from Ramón Ruiz's effort to somehow, as a Mexican American, propose that he is more Mexican than American, to Ruben Salazar's quest for his identity growing up in El Paso, rejecting his parents' identity as immigrants and yet being rejected by Anglo-Americans. The search for identity is very much an American process, and this includes Chicanos and Latinos.

Class, race, and gender are additional factors that these chapters touch on in one way or another. Alejandro Morales's *The Brick People* reminds us that

Mexicans and most other Latinos have historically been working people. As immigrants, they have come to this country to work, work, and work. They have not come to get on welfare or to have their kids—so-called anchor babies—in this country. While some Americans acknowledge that Mexicans and other Latinos have contributed culturally, and they certainly have, to me the most significant contribution has been their blood, sweat, and tears as a laboring people. The immigrants have done this, but so have many of their offspring, who, because of a racialized educational system, have been funneled into the cheap labor force like their parents. Class discrimination, in turn, has been bolstered by racism and racialization. Mexicans and other Latinos have been painted as an inferior "race." In the early twentieth century, to be Mexican was to be considered by whites as racially inferior. Yet when one thinks about it, the term Mexican has nothing to do with race; it is a term of nationality and ethnicity, but it is not a racial one. Can we really speak of a Mexican race? Even if one defines race biologically, Mexicans and Latinos cover the gamut from very dark to very white. There is no Mexican or Latino race. Race, and racialization, in this context is an invention to justify the exploitation of Mexicans and other Latinos by suggesting that they are not capable of rising above menial working status.[12] Mexican and other Latina women, in turn, have been triply oppressed as women, as Mexicanas and Latinas, and as predominantly working-class people. Historically, besides their roles as wives and mothers, they have worked as domestics, in laundries, in the fields, and in low-skilled jobs such as in the garment industry.[13] Together class, race, and gender discrimination have limited the economic and social mobility of Mexicans and Latinos in the United States and have kept many of them as a permanent minority. By "permanent minority," I mean that many Mexican immigrants, Mexican Americans, and other Latinos have been negatively affected by institutional racism in jobs, wages, housing, and education, which has historically restricted economic and educational mobility. In the early twentieth century, this permanent minority status can be seen in the "Mexican jobs," "Mexican wages," "Mexican barrios," and "Mexican schools" of that period. These terms have changed over the years, but the reality of permanent second-class status has not. Issues of class, race, and gender manifest themselves in all the chapters of this study.

Yet the Mexican/Latino population has never been homogeneous. While many have been working class, there has been class differentiation as well. Some Mexican immigrants, for example, have come with enough capital to start small businesses in the barrios, catering to the working class. Some have been able to accumulate sufficient funds to start their own establishments. Moreover, some children of immigrants have been able to overcome educational discrimination to go to college, earn degrees, and become professionals. As a result, there has always been a small but increasingly growing Mexican/Latino middle class.[14] This is evident, for example, in some of the writers I study in this book. Ramón Ruiz became a university professor; Frances Esquibel Tywoniak was a teacher and administrator in San Francisco; Mary Helen Ponce, besides being a recognized writer, also obtained a PhD in anthropology; Richard Rodriguez is a widely read writer; John Rechy is a best-selling novelist; and Ruben Salazar became a major journalist.

The role of education is likewise an issue in several chapters. Beginning in the early twentieth century, public schools served the children of the immigrant generation in what were called "Mexican schools." These segregated schools were mandated by local school boards, in effect making such segregation a form of legal separation. Not only were these schools segregated, but they were also inferior. Up to the 1920s, Mexican American children could receive at most a sixth-grade education, and this was possible only in larger cities, such as El Paso, San Antonio, and Los Angeles. The schools were poorly equipped, with not enough classrooms, books, cafeterias, and playgrounds. Teachers and administrators exhibited little sensitivity to the language and cultural background of the children and enforced a strict English-only policy. Students caught speaking in Spanish were punished, including corporal punishment. On top of this, and perhaps the most egregious characteristic of these schools, too many teachers and principals possessed a low expectation of the Mexican American students' ability to perform demanding schoolwork. Much if not all of this attitude was racialized, based on the perception that biologically and mentally, the students were not very bright and could not handle more rigorous studies. Early IQ tests, with their cultural biases, administered only in English, were then used to substantiate these low expectations because Mexican American students did poorly on them. Consequently, the schools stressed vocational work for the students, a paternalistic approach that complemented the southwestern economic system, which relied on cheap labor from the Mexican population. Into the century, while Mexican Americans were able to acquire more education, including high school, the characteristics of the early Mexican schools remained, although now they were referred to as inner city schools. The lack of educational mobility for most Mexican Americans and other working-class Latinos has unfortunately remained a factor in Chicano/Latino history, as observed in some of the works I discuss in this book, such as Mary Helen Ponce's autobiography, Ruben Salazar's novel, and John Rechy's autobiography. Each author comments on either the conditions of the Mexican schools or the racism Mexican Americans encountered in mixed public schools.[15]

Barrio life is another theme that appears in Chicano/Latino history. Mary Helen Ponce's autobiography is set in the barrio of Pacoima; John Rechy grew up in El Segundo Barrio (Second Ward) of south El Paso, as did Ruben Salazar for part of his early life; Stella Pope Duarte's novel takes place partly in the south Phoenix Mexican barrio of El Cielito, and barrio life is also the backdrop of the two Central American stories. Mexican/Latino barrios have existed for many years, but they took on various features as mass immigration commenced from Mexico in the early twentieth century. One of these has to do with what Albert Camarillo calls "barrioization." By this he means that barrios exist not just because, for example, Mexicans want to live among themselves, but because of housing segregation. Mexicans may have wanted to live among themselves, but the point that Camarillo makes is that they had no choice anyway. As a result of racialization, including job and wage discrimination, Mexican immigrants then and today could not and cannot afford to live anywhere else other than the substandard housing available in the barrios. As a result, barrios are part of the institutionalized racism that Mexicans and other Latinos have experienced.[16]

Barrioization contains another dialectic, or Du Bois's double consciousness, which is especially noticeable in Esquibel Tywoniak's depiction of barrio life in Visalia and in Ponce's Hoyt Street narrative. This dialectic is between what can be called Mexicanization and Americanization. While the barrio, at one level, is part of the community building associated with immigrants, where they retain and continue to practice familiar forms of Mexican cultural traditions, including speaking Spanish, the barrio is also porous and reflects a certain process of Americanization. This dialectic further suggests that barrios are not inward looking per se but represent a process of immigrant adjustment to life in the United States that is outward looking. Barrios are part of the acculturation, or transculturation, of immigrants rather than a defiance of such changes. Mexican immigrants and their children practice their culture in the barrio, but they are not immune to Americanization. Learning some English, especially at workplaces; purchasing American household items; and sending their children to public or even Catholic or Protestant schools are part of this process. Children especially prove to be Americanizing agents. Learning English at school as well as American mores and traditions, plus being more affected by American mass culture through films, radio, and later television, the children of immigrants prove to be part of this dialectic as they bring their acculturation into the home. They retain certain aspects of their immigrant Mexican or Latino culture, but they also absorb various American ways as they become bilingual and bicultural. They become Mexican Americans, although they still live in the barrios. Indeed, the barrios become Mexican American barrios.[17]

In the various narratives I analyze in this text, one of the other themes that stands out to me is what I call historical agency. Mexicans and other Latinos have not just been victims of history; they have also made history. They possess agency. They attempt to control their own destinies, whether in barrio life, at the workplace, or in their dreams of a better life. Immigrant adjustment is part of this agency. Mexican and Mexican American workers, such as those in *The Brick People*, react against exploitative conditions by going on strike and joining labor unions. Ramón Ruiz took advantage of the GI Bill after World War II to go to college, eventually becoming a university professor. Ruben Salazar struggled against the racism he experienced in his school by attempting to reconcile his sense of identity. John Rechy likewise reacts against racism toward other Mexicans. Historical agency is further seen in the other narratives when the narrators themselves or the subjects they write about are not just passive and accepting of their conditions. On the contrary, they attempt to defy them and struggle in their own ways to change them. Chicano history is not nor should be victimization history; rather, it is the story of Chicanos making history through their personal and collective struggles.[18]

Historical agency also includes the role of women in Chicano/Latino history. Women have displayed their agency in keeping families together in the migration process as well as in the resettlement of their families. As wives and mothers, they have nurtured their families in the home and been the keepers of cultural, including religious, traditions. But over the years, many Chicana and Latina women have also labored outside the home. Mothers and daughters have traditionally worked various jobs, including farm labor as well as service and industrial occupations, which contribute to their household incomes and provide them, through their pay, more leverage within a patriarchal family. Some women have also emerged as labor and community leaders. They have displayed leadership where, in the barrios, they have been given an opening to do so, such as in their religious sodalities. Women authoring their own stories is another form of historical agency. In this book, I deal with such examples.

Fran Esquibel Tywoniak displays her agency by crossing different cultural and identity borders, within and outside the barrio, as well as by applying herself in her schoolwork to ensure she will be placed in the academic track, not the vocational one, where the school channeled most Mexican American students. In Stella Pope Duarte's novel, the key character is Teresa, who helps hold her family together after her brother, Jesse, is killed in Vietnam and who plays a prominent role in her family members' efforts to reconcile their long-lasting grief. Teresa is a survivor. In the two Central American autobiographical texts, the narrators, Evelyn Cortez-Davis and Yamileth López, both show their agency by surviving the ordeals of migrating to the United States with their families as undocumented immigrants and by being able to adjust to their new lives in the United States. All these women, both real and fictional, do not call themselves feminists, but they all display strong feminist characteristics. Women in the Chicano/Latino experiences have always played a major role, as they continue to do today.[19]

Another aspect of historical agency is a sense of collective history, which is evident in these narratives. Though the authors I analyze focus on their individual stories, at the same time, they are writing within the context of a collective experience. No man (or woman) is an island, and this applies as well to these subjects. No story is just an individual one. History is the context of anyone's tale, since we all live in history. We may not be aware of this, but we are all the products and the subjects of our historical periods. What Edward Hallett Carr states about historians is equally applicable to writers. "The historian [writer] being an individual," he writes, "is also a product of history and of society; and it is in this twofold light that the student of history must learn to regard him [her]."[20] This is certainly true of the authors I discuss in this volume. Of course, this context begins with one's family. The family is part of the collective framework of any story. *La familia* is at the heart of Chicano/Latino life. Nuclear and extended families are at the center of the culture and barrio life. Indeed, the Chicano Movement expanded the meaning of la familia to include not just one's family but the entire Chicano community.[21] All Chicanos were part of one familia, and the movement was La Familia. The barrio context is another form of collective history that some of these authors directly and indirectly reference. Collective movements to change history and conditions are still another, whether they be in Morales's story of brick workers or in the struggles of the Chicano Movement as part of Duarte's novel. Ramón Ruiz as a historian clearly and consciously places his autobiography within different historical communities. Cortez-Davis and López locate their stories within the civil wars in Central America as well as in the diaspora to the United States that is part of these conflicts. But even in the more introspective stories, a collective history is part of the background, such as in the farm worker context of Tywoniak and in the urban barrios of Rechy and Rodriguez. All these narratives speak in one way or another to a collective experience.

Several other historical themes are enveloped in the different chapters, which I just comment on briefly here, and in no particular order of importance.

Popular culture in its Mexican and Mexican American forms is one such theme. By "popular culture," I mean the culture of the people that is part of their daily lives and not mediated by the mass culture perpetuated by commercial interests. The theme of popular culture is especially pronounced in Mary Helen Ponce's autobiography. She notes several forms of popular culture related to home medical remedies, religious rituals at home, and Mexican popular religiosity in the local parish church, such as processions and the devotion to Our Lady of Guadalupe.[22]

The Mexican American experience in U.S. wars is also a theme that is alluded to in some of the chapters. Mexican Americans and other Latinos have always participated in the wars of the United States. In the Civil War, Mexican Americans in the Southwest, including Texas, fought on both sides of this tragic conflict. Many of Theodore Roosevelt's Rough Riders in the Spanish-American War of 1898 were Mexican American, as were others who fought in Cuba during that conflict. World War I saw an increasing number of Mexican Americans and some Mexican immigrants in the U.S. military, fighting in the trenches in Europe. Some never returned, and some won honors for their bravery.[23] But these earlier Chicano/Latino military contributions paled beside their service in World War II. Estimates range from 350,000 to 500,000 Chicano/Latino soldiers—mostly Mexican Americans but also Puerto Ricans—who fought bravely in the war. More Congressional Medals of Honor were awarded to Latinos per capita than to U.S. soldiers of any other ethnicity. Many, of course, never came back or came back physically or emotionally wounded, and probably both. Although their service has not been significantly recognized by mainstream historians, Latinos are in fact part of the so-called greatest generation.[24] In America's later wars, including those in Korea, Vietnam, Iraq, and Afghanistan, Latinos have participated and with distinction.[25] This military contribution by Mexican Americans/Latinos is touched on in several chapters. Ramón Ruiz served in World War II, as did Ponce's brother and Rechy's two older brothers; Rechy was in the U.S. Army in the early 1950s, as was Ruben Salazar; and in Duarte's novel, Jesse Ramírez served and was killed in Vietnam. War has not been a stranger to the Latino experience, despite continuing stereotypes that Latinos don't really want to become part of this nation. This is nonsense, and the military history of Latinos shows this.

The Chicano Movement is a topic touched on, for example, in Ruiz's autobiography and in Duarte's novel. The Chicano Movement was the largest and most widespread civil rights and community empowerment movement in the history of Mexican Americans. Reappropriating an older barrio term of identity, a new generation of Mexican Americans now called themselves Chicano. The Chicano generation, influenced by the political militancy of the 1960s as well as third world movements of liberation, rejected the melting pot and American liberalism, instead adopting a challenging and oppositional politics based on a rediscovery of the "authentic" history and identity of Chicanos, centered on their indigenous and mestizo backgrounds. Chicanos now saw themselves as an internally colonized people with a historical and conquered homeland in the Southwest called Aztlán. The cry of "Chicano Power" meant self-determination.[26] Despite the movement's militancy and call for "revolución," it also accomplished many concrete reforms in education and in government programs to better serve Mexican Americans. These reforms included affirmative action, which led to many more Chicanos attending college and to the establishment of Chicano studies. Politically, the two-party system reacted to the movement by running more Chicano candidates and appealing to the Chicano vote. The movement established for the first time Chicanos and other Latinos as national political actors. The movement laid the basis for the significant Latino political power that exists today. Ruiz in his autobiography notes that the power of the movement helped create conditions for hiring more Chicano professors on campuses, including him, and for the increase in both undergraduate and graduate students. The Chicano Movement assumes an even larger role in Duarte's novel, set in part during the period of the movement and the Vietnam War. Teresa, the protagonist of the story, attends the historic National Chicano Moratorium of August 29, 1970, when some twenty-thousand people, mostly Chicanos, marched and protested against the war in East Los Angeles. Teresa marches and is beaten with a billy club by the county sheriff when police forces unjustly attack the demonstrators at Laguna Park (now Ruben Salazar Park), killing three Chicanos, including Ruben Salazar, which in a way links the Chicano Movement to Salazar's novel, discussed in this text.[27]

Religion is still another theme. In Duarte's novel, the mother character, Alicia, is deeply religious as a faithful Catholic along with the other women in the barrio of El Cielito. She believes in the power of prayer and blesses her son, Jesse, before he leaves for the war in Vietnam. It is her faith that sees her through her grief after Jesse is killed. In fact, she is in church when she receives the fateful news of her son's death. Many years later, she believes that God has sent Jesse's spirit to see her and to suggest a pilgrimage to the Vietnam Memorial in Washington, DC, as a way to bring closure to the family's grief. As a result, Alicia organizes what will be a caravan of family members and family friends to do a *peregrinación*, or pilgrimage, to the memorial, where they can touch Jesse's name and reconcile their grief. Religion permeates the novel.[28]

Sexuality, specifically homosexuality, is referenced in part in the autobiographies of Richard Rodriguez and John Rechy. As noted, I analyze these two texts by expanding Du Bois's concept of "double consciousness" to a "triple consciousness," which includes not only race and nationality, as Du Bois did to deal with the dialectic of African American identity, but also sexuality as part of Rodriguez's and Rechy's confrontations with identity. Both writers in their coming-of-age autobiographies provide hints, it seems to me, of their initial struggles with their sexuality.

Finally, the concept of citizenship is another implied theme in the narratives I engage with, but citizenship here is at different levels. First, there is political citizenship, in that most of the writers of these narratives are U.S. citizens, including Ruben Salazar, who became a naturalized citizen as a young immigrant boy. With this U.S. citizenship is an implied sense of entitlement to one's constitutional and legal rights. For example, Morales writes about the rights of Mexican American workers, and Ruiz writes about the civil rights of Chicanos. But as U.S. citizens, these writers are promoting a form of cultural citizenship as well. That is, they believe in one way or another that Mexican Americans and other Latinos have a right to be themselves. They believe in cultural diversity and cultural pluralism. Ponce honors the bilingualism and biculturalism of her family and friends, and Salazar seems to be struggling for a kind of cultural third space between Mexican immigrant culture and assimilation, just to mention two examples of cultural citizenship, or the right to be a U.S. citizen and still have your ethnic culture respected.[29] Finally, there is what I would call "economic citizenship." By this I mean that Mexican immigrant workers—such as Morales's brick workers and the undocumented Central American refugees in Cortez-Davis and López's autobiographies—through their hard work and economic contributions to the nation's wealth deserve to be accepted as citizens and deserve respect and protection for their work. Immigrant labor needs to be recognized as a form of citizenship.

III

All these themes are embedded in the chapters of my text. Although I address many of these themes directly, I am also suggesting here that knowing about them before reading further can better put the chapters into a broader historical context. Literary narratives are historical texts, and I, as a historian, am interpreting them as such, giving readers here a guideline to how these narratives are linked to Chicano/Latino history.

PART I

AUTOBIOGRAPHY
AND TESTIMONIO

1

THE HISTORIAN AS AUTOBIOGRAPHER

Ramón Eduardo Ruiz Urueta's
Memories of a Hyphenated Man

In my last year at Smith, I had lectured at the University of Texas at El Paso,
where at a luncheon the history department had brought a young student to my
attention. I was told that he wanted to be a history professor. All through the
lunch, he just sat and stared at me. He was Mario García.
—RAMÓN EDUARDO RUIZ URUETA,
MEMORIES OF A HYPHENATED MAN

THIS CHAPTER'S EPIGRAPH is a passage from Ramón Eduardo Ruiz
Urueta's autobiography.[1] Although I have told Professor Ruiz that I do
not recall just staring at him during that lunch in spring 1969 (and perhaps this is the politics of memory), the fact is that, as the saying goes, the rest is
history. Because of my meeting Professor Ruiz, I would within one year join him
at the University of California, San Diego (UCSD), after he left Smith College.
At UCSD, he became my mentor, and I became his PhD student and would go
on to become a historian of the Chicano experience.[2] I do not believe that this
would have happened without Professor Ruiz's intervention and support. None
of my all-white professors at the University of Texas at El Paso (UTEP) ever
encouraged me to go on for a PhD in history, even though I was a good student.
It took a person of my Mexican American background to take it on himself and
move me in his direction. For this I am deeply grateful.

All of this is what I think is called "truth in packaging." When asked to consider
writing an essay on academic autobiography, I immediately thought of Ramón
Ruiz's story. But my life has been very touched by his, and so I want to be clear to
my audience that this chapter contains an autobiography within an autobiography.

I

Ramón Eduardo Ruiz Urueta was a distinguished historian of Mexican history. Born in the San Diego area in 1921, Ruiz grew up in Southern California, the son of Mexican immigrants. He attended local public schools and later San Diego State College. After the U.S. entry into World War II, Ruiz joined the U.S. Army Air Forces as a junior officer and learned to fly combat planes, although he did not see direct military action. As a veteran, Ruiz joined thousands of others who took advantage of the GI Bill of Rights and returned to school. After receiving his BA in history from San Diego State, he obtained an MA in Latin American studies from the Claremont Graduate School and from there advanced to UC Berkeley, where in 1953 he gained his doctorate in Latin American history. After a few temporary positions, he landed a tenure-track appointment at Smith College in Massachusetts, where he spent the first significant years of his career. Reaching full professor there, he was recruited in 1969 back to San Diego as professor of history at the recently established University of California, San Diego. He remained at UCSD for the rest of his highly productive years as a historian and department chair. As a historian of Mexico, Ruiz researched and wrote several significant books and edited volumes on the land of his parents' birth and a country he came to know intimately over the years. His most notable books are *The Great Rebellion: Mexico, 1905–1924*; *Triumphs and Tragedy: A History of the Mexican People*; *On the Rim of Mexico: Encounters of the Rich and Poor*; and *The People of Sonora and Yankee Capitalists*. In 1968, Ruiz also wrote a well-received analysis of the Cuban Revolution entitled *Cuba: The Making of a Revolution*. Recognized in both the United States and Mexico for his work as a historian of Mexico, Ruiz had the distinct honor in 1998 of receiving the prestigious National Medal of the Humanities conferred on him by President Bill Clinton. He died in 2010.

II

In 2003, Ruiz published his autobiography, *Memories of a Hyphenated Man*, one of the first academic autobiographies by a Mexican American scholar. Professor Kevin R. Johnson's autobiography, *How Did You Get to Be Mexican? A White/Brown Man's Search for Identity*, is another, although it deals with a later period than Ruiz's. In my analysis of *Memories of a Hyphenated Man*, I want to employ certain insights on autobiographies by historians provided by Jeremy D. Popkin in his 2005 book *History, Historians, and Autobiography*.[3] In his analysis of the growing number of autobiographies by historians not only in the United States but also in Europe and elsewhere, Popkin suggests the close linkage between history and autobiography, including when historians become autobiographers. "In my view," he writes, "when historians turn to the genre of autobiography, their projects raise important questions about the nature of history and the potentialities of autobiography itself."[4] Popkin notes that at one point, history and autobiography were almost one and the same; by the nineteenth century, however, as history developed into a more singular profession, historians distanced themselves from autobiography, believing that the latter marred their objectivity. This separation would remain until the 1960s, when historians began to focus more on history from the bottom up and, in doing so, to appreciate subjective personal accounts as providing sensibility and human agency to the making of history.

Combining the modern, or perhaps postmodern, historian's interest in objectivity/subjectivity, Popkin further suggests that autobiographies written by historians represent a new and creative way to understand history. Here he joins hands with noted scholars Paul Eakin and Mark Freeman, who advance two basic notions about how historian-autobiographers can break new ground in advancing historical understanding. The first is that, as they put it, "a historically trained autobiographer might be able to connect the story of individual experience highlighted in most autobiographies with the larger flow of collective experience in which it is embedded, and thus overcome autobiography's tendency to attribute to its subjects an excessive degree of personal autonomy."[5] Hence, the first challenge or opportunity for the historian-autobiographer is to link individual history with collective history. The second has to do with how the historian-autobiographer can go beyond simply reporting events and use his or her historical training to analyze why certain events surrounding an individual's life happened and how they are linked to larger issues that are not accidents of history, but are the result of human actions. The historian-autobiographer should be able to use his or her skills to go beyond recording individual life changes and to suggest how and why societies evolve and change.[6]

III

Using the Popkin/Eakin/Freeman model, I believe that Ruiz, in his own way, successfully links his personal experience with a more collective one. Ruiz was a child of Mexican immigrants. His father, born in Mazatlán along Mexico's

Pacific coast, and his mother, born near Parral in the northern Mexican state of Chihuahua, both on their own crossed the U.S.-Mexico border in the early twentieth century. Meeting in San Diego, they married and raised their family, including their eldest and first son, Ramón Eduardo. Both parents came from proud backgrounds, and his father had been a member of the Mexican navy during the era of the dictator Porfirio Díaz. The Ruizes settled in Pacific Beach, just north of San Diego, where the father operated a greenhouse nursery business for many years and where they in time built their own home. Not as severely affected by the racism against Mexicans, Ruiz's parents worked hard to raise their children with moral standards, high expectations for themselves, and appreciation and honor for their mexicano heritage, including speaking Spanish at home and with their relatives. Although the Ruiz family did not live in a Mexican barrio, their home reflected a mexicano lifestyle and culture.[7]

In his autobiography, Ruiz narrates these different aspects of his early family life, and insofar as it goes, it is an interesting family story. Yet, Ruiz as a historian goes beyond just the family saga. He understands that this narrative possesses a collective connection. As a result, he correctly positions his family story within the larger context of the beginning of mass Mexican immigration to the United States. Between 1900 and 1930, perhaps as many as (or more than) a million Mexican immigrants entered the United States, about one-tenth of Mexico's population. They represent what in my own work I call the immigrant generation in Chicano history. Of course, there have been several generations of Mexican immigrants. I distinguish the early twentieth-century immigrant generation by noting that no subsequent cohort of Mexican immigrants so totally dominated Mexican life in the United States: demographically, economically, politically, and culturally. Later immigrant generations by contrast would have to coexist with new generations of U.S.-born Mexican Americans.[8]

Of this great migration, Ruiz writes, "Papá was one of 220,000 Mexicans in the United States, although scholars assure us that many others entered illegally.... A decade later there were more or less 500,000 Mexicans in the United States."[9] Of this great migration, he added,

> Almost always Mexicans were hired to do the dirty, back-breaking labor, chiefly in agriculture and for paltry pay. In the Imperial Valley, just over the mountains from San Diego, Mexicans picked tons of raisins, tons of walnuts, countless boxes of lemons, and even more boxes of oranges. They tended vineyards and melon fields elsewhere in California, picked cotton in Arizona and Texas, and dug sugar

beets out of the soil in Colorado, Wyoming, and Montana. In the hot day sun, Mexicans wielded picks and shovels for city streets and for ditches for water pipes; mixed sand, gravel, and cement for bridges; and in San Diego poured concrete for the Coronado Hotel across the bay.[10]

Mexican immigrants in the early twentieth century, as part of what were called the "New Immigrants" entering the United States as a whole, especially from eastern and southern Europe, left their homeland for both internal and external reasons, the so-called push and pull theory. Economic dislocation, especially in the rural areas as a result of Díaz's land policies in league with American imperialism, transformed Mexican agriculture into agribusiness and forced millions of peasants off their lands, and in time they migrated to El Norte. In addition, the outbreak of the long-lasting Mexican Revolution of 1910 pushed many other Mexicans out of their country, and they sought refuge in the United States. My maternal family came at this time as political refugees. The pull forces from the other side of the border were American employers—railroads, mining companies, agribusinesses, and others—pulling in Mexican immigrant workers as new and needed sources of cheap and manageable labor. The result was the arrival of thousands of Mexican immigrants and political refugees, who would significantly augment the smaller number of Mexican Americans already living in the Southwest region and California, including the descendants of the earlier Spanish and Mexican residents of what at first was the northern frontier of New Spain and later El Norte of the independent Mexican republic.[11]

Ramón Ruiz's family was part of this immigrant generation, even though it was slightly better off and lived in a more integrated setting. The same was not true of most other Mexican immigrants, as Ruiz acknowledges. For most Mexican immigrants, life remained difficult. The American dream eluded them, as did their concept of a Mexican dream, the idea that they would work hard, save money, and return after the Revolution to a better life in la patria. Even Ruiz's father harbored the Mexican dream, although he and most others never realized it, at least not to the extent of their dreams. In fact, most Mexican immigrants were positioned as pools of cheap labor in what were literally called "Mexican jobs" and paid "Mexican wages," the dirtiest jobs ("dirty Mexican") and the lowest pay. They lived in hardcore urban barrios or rural colonias with few if any facilities. To add insult to injury, their children were forced to attend segregated and inferior public schools called "Mexican schools." This "Mexicanization" of the immigrants in turn constituted the racialization of the Mexican in the

United States, that is, the inference that Mexicans were not only a different race but also an inferior race not capable of doing more than menial physical labor.[12] Of this racialization, Ruiz recalls,

> The title "American" . . . was very seldom used for us; we were condemned to remain Mexican generation after generation. Some Anglos, to pour salt into the wound, used *Mexican* as a pejorative, an insult. In the sixth grade, for instance, James Harvey and I got into a fight; when I got the better of it, he called me a "dirty Mexican." He was much too young to arrive at that conclusion on his own, so he must have heard that snide remark from his parents, neighbors, or classmates. Nor will I forget how I felt specifically targeted when Miss Drury, the fifth-grade teacher, labeled as cowardly and cruel the Mexicans who killed the defenders of the Alamo during the Texas rebellion against Mexico.[13]

As a way of resisting discrimination, Mexican immigrants, like Ruiz's parents, asserted their culture and identity as mexicanos; they invented a new version of mexicanidad, or Mexican cultural nationalism, on the U.S. side of the border. This, of course, was (and is) not unusual; all immigrants to some degree do the same as a way of creating a new immigrant community. This immigrant nationalism was reinforced by the zeitgeist of the Mexican Revolution, which promoted a new national identity for Mexico. As a result, Ruiz grew up in a very mexicano family culture, which he acknowledges in his story. "Anglo neighbors aside," he stresses,

> our family was very Mexican. Its head, at least in theory, was our father. . . . Our home was a Mexican home . . . a Spanish-language haven. We spoke only Spanish to our parents . . . and they spoke only Spanish to us. I do not remember when this rule was broken; never did I utter a word of English to either of our parents. . . . We were told to speak only Spanish among ourselves. . . . All of this has to do with the daily battle to conserve our identity, to keep ourselves from being forced into a suffocating conformity, where we supposedly would be like all other Americans. . . . In the California of our day, the inescapable fact was that whiteness of skin conferred social acceptance. Loyalty to one's Mexican "racial" ancestry, therefore[,] was not merely an act of pride, *orgullo* in Papá's words, but also of courage.[14]

It is within this context that Ruiz, the historian-autobiographer, locates his family history. He fulfills the notion of Popkin and others that the historian can rise above the personal narrative to provide the more collective context of his or her story, not just in passing but in a conscious effort to put his or her story in a broader historical setting.

IV

A second link with a collective self in Ruiz's autobiography has to do with his generational experience. Ruiz belongs to what I call the Mexican American generation in Chicano history. This is the generation, both biological and political, that succeeds the immigrant generation. Made up mostly of the children of the immigrants, the Mexican American generation came of age in the 1930s and 1940s, as Ruiz did. It is historically sandwiched between the Great Depression, World War II, and the Cold War. It is also a generation that is neither Mexican nor American but Mexican American. The term itself comes out of this period. The children of Mexican immigrants, as in other ethnic cases, are a product of dual or even multiple cultures, but they are neither one nor the other: they are a composite; they are hybrids; they are a new version of cultural mestizos. They are bilingual and bicultural or multicultural. They, like Ruiz, have loyalties and strong ties to their mother mexicano culture, and yet they also recognize that they are U.S. citizens and that for them, there is no mythical Mexican dream, only their version of the American dream or a Mexican American dream. Members of this generation experienced continued discrimination and racialization, and yet they were more cognizant of their rights as U.S. citizens as a result of their acculturation through schools and mass media. As Ruiz writes, "By birth, I am an American, but by culture, thanks to my parents and to the upbringing they gave me, I am also Mexican."[15]

The Mexican American generation experienced the effects of the "Mexican schools," which were segregated and inferior, with teachers who had low expectations of the students. Ruiz did not attend one of these schools, yet even though he did well as a student, he still experienced some forms of racial discrimination. He recalls in particular being made to feel ashamed when he entered school speaking only Spanish and had to repeat a semester because of this. As he progressed in his mostly white schools, Ruiz also experienced a good deal of social marginalization because of his Mexican American background. Still, he escaped the worst aspects of public education for Mexican Americans. By contrast, for many if not most Mexican Americans of the period, schooling meant perhaps no more than an eighth-grade education; high dropout rates; and movement into the blue-collar working class. To contextualize the Mexican American school experience, Ruiz, for example, mentions the Lemon Grove School, just east of San Diego, where in 1931, the local school board attempted to remove Mexican American students from the lone school into a dilapidated barn the board called the "Mexican school." Ruiz was spared such an experience, but as a historian he acknowledges that his was not the typical Mexican American experience in the schools.[16]

The 1930s, as Ruiz entered his teenage years and young adulthood, was a trying decade for Mexicans in the United States. Because of the Depression, thousands lost their "Mexican jobs" as unemployed whites clamored for them. Moreover, in one of the great historical tragedies in U.S. history, Mexicans were accused not only of taking jobs away from "real Americans," but also of posing a social and health hazard. This resulted in the largest deportation and repatriation in U.S. history, when around half a million Mexicans were forced out of the country, including many U.S.-born Mexican Americans, specifically U.S.-born children of immigrants. Ruiz's family was not affected by this crisis, but he recalls it and, as a historian, integrates this sad affair into his story. "I remember this shameful episode," he notes, "because I accompanied Papá on his visit to a Mexican coastal freighter . . . that docked in the harbor of San Diego to carry Mexicans back home. It weighed anchor with 800 on board. A consulate official never forgot the screams of a woman passenger as the ship left its birth [sic]: 'Let us off. . . . I am just going to die. [I have] no money, no one knows me in that town in Mexico.'"[17]

If the Great Depression marked a historical generational experience for the Mexican American generation, so too did World War II. Indeed, the war provided an opportunity for Mexican Americans, especially men, to prove their loyalty and patriotism to the United States. From the barrios and the fields, thousands joined or were drafted into the military, mostly in combat units. It is estimated that 350,000 to 500,000 Latinos, mostly Mexican Americans, served in the military during the war, an exceptionally high figure given the still relatively modest Mexican population in the United States at that time. Many died or were wounded. At home, Mexican American men and women worked to support the war effort through their jobs, including some in military industries. The war was a defining historical moment for Mexican Americans, and it furthered their acculturation within American society.[18]

Ruiz attests to this larger collective history through his personal experience. After being rejected by the navy on what he considered to be racist grounds, he joined the army air forces and learned how to fly bombers and other planes. His extensive training took many months, however, and the war ended before he could serve in combat. Ruiz saw his military service as something unavoidable that he would make the best of with his training and status as a junior officer, one of the few Mexican Americans in this capacity. War, of course, by its very nature is a collective experience, and in his autobiography, Ruiz notes this and places his personal wartime story within the larger picture. "More than 400,000 men of Mexican ancestry," he writes, "in bonds of brotherhood, helped fight the 'Good War,' as today's pundits refer to it. . . . On the battlefields of Europe, Africa, and the Pacific, on land and the high seas, Mexican soldiers, marines, and sailors fought gallantly and died. . . . All told, Mexicans earned more Medals of Honor than any other ethnic group—although most were given posthumously."[19]

V

After the point in his story when Ruiz has become a professional historian, he continues to link in his autobiography his personal experience with larger historical events. This is evident in his chapter on his years at Smith College, a small New England school for women, from the late 1950s to the late 1960s. With the still lingering effects of McCarthyism and the anticommunist witch hunts of the 1950s, Ruiz locates himself upon arrival in 1958 as one of the few "radical" professors at Smith. Ruiz had come to his left-of-center politics through his experiences with racism in California as well as his study of Latin American history, through which he came to understand the role of U.S. imperialism in maintaining the underdevelopment of Latin America and to appreciate and sympathize with anti-imperialist and nationalist movements in the region, including the Mexican Revolution of 1910, which would become his main area of expertise. In describing this experience of being a more radical or progressive faculty member among conservative or less critical professors as well as students, Ruiz writes about his Smithie students:

> What troubled me was that these students tended to think alike. Once in a while I ran into a hard-core conservative but seldom a radical. Even the tiny handful of African Americans, though bitter on the subject of race, rarely dissented, though occasionally a bright Jewish student from New York City might surprise

me. These were the passive 1950s, when Republicans managed affairs in Washington and spineless Democrats ran to keep up with them. Rarely did a student want to be labeled a conservative, even though thinking like one and voting for Ike [Eisenhower] and Dick [Nixon]. They claimed to be "liberal Republicans" and read avidly David Riesman's *The Lonely Crowd*, a critique of the American tendency to conform, which claimed that when a society became "other directed," people sought peer approval by accepting group dictates. Smithies worshiped the book, unable to see that Riesman, perhaps unintentionally, had careers in business—which many of their parents had—in his gunsight.[20]

Ruiz as a Smith professor of Latin American history also reflects in his autobiography on the issue of race in the 1960s. He observed the limited number of black students on the campus into the period of the black civil rights movement. Smith was and remained a mostly white campus, including its faculty. "A large majority of professors were Anglo-Americans," he recalls, "though Jews had begun to join their ranks. I was the only professor of Mexican ancestry, but a woman from Spain and a man from Argentina taught in the Spanish department."[21] Despite the paucity of blacks and their still limited number at the time of his departure in 1969, Ruiz notes that as far as Smith was concerned, and indeed throughout the Ivy League, the discussion of race concerned only blacks and not other minorities. Being from California, Ruiz understood that race was more than a binary between whites and blacks. Yet, the exclusion of Mexicans and other Latinos in the dialogue on race created for Ruiz an interesting and ambivalent situation. As a Mexican American, he knew full well that American racism targeted not only blacks but also Mexicans and that the discourse and analysis of race and racism had to be broadened to include Mexicans and Latinos as well as other minorities. And yet, Ruiz came to understand that unlike California and the Southwest, where racism against Mexicans was clearer and more manifest, the limited number of Mexicans in New England in a sense "deracialized" and "de-Mexicanized" individuals of Mexican ancestry like him. Rather than being seen in racial terms, Ruiz, at least at Smith, was seen as an almost exotic, nonracial, or even "white," Latin American. "To my colleagues, especially the older ones," he notes, "I was a Latin American, and students often saw me that way, too."[22] While Ruiz undoubtedly understood the irony in this situation, he also recognized the advantage it gave him compared to being a Mexican American professor in California or the Southwest, where racism against Mexicans was pronounced and where universities, at least until the late

1960s, largely excluded Mexican American professors, especially in the teaching of Latin American history. The state of affairs was different at Smith because of the lack of a history of prejudice against Mexican Americans, and because Ruiz was not thought of in Mexican terms. Ruiz benefited from this ambivalence about his "racial" profile. "Easterners were just as bigoted," he observes, "but not necessarily against Mexicans, whom they rarely saw. . . . In New England, so far as I can tell, I personally never encountered racial hostility."[23]

As a professor of Latin American history at Smith in the 1960s, Ruiz was also able to take advantage of the growing interest in Latin America, which stemmed largely from interest in the Cuban Revolution of 1959 and the subsequent attempt to overthrow the nationalist and anti-imperialist revolution led by Fidel Castro and Che Guevara. The perceived threat posed by Cuba in fomenting anti-American revolutions in Latin America, magnified by the Cuban Missile Crisis of 1962, proved to be a boon to Latin American studies, which experienced significant growth in U.S. universities. As the lone historian of Latin American history at Smith, Ruiz was in a position to benefit from this renewed interest in Latin America. "At Smith," he writes, "I was free to interpret Spanish American life and culture to my heart's content."[24]

Besides teaching and expanding the curriculum in Latin American history, which became quite popular not only among Smith students but also with nearby students at Amherst College and the University of Massachusetts at Amherst, who could enroll in his classes, Ruiz began to write essays and book reviews on Latin American issues in such venues as the *New Republic*. More significantly, Ruiz began to research and write on the Cuban Revolution and to integrate this material into his classes. In his autobiography, Ruiz adds his critical understanding of history and his sensibility as an intellectual of Latin American background when he notes that his book on Cuba was revisionist history in tune with the growing revisionist American historiography of the 1960s, which challenged dominant and standard but conservative interpretations. Rather than writing still another history of Cuba that would justify or ignore the U.S. imperialist role in Cuban history, an issue at the heart of the Cuban Revolution, which sought to liberate Cuba from this relationship, Ruiz set out to place the revolution within its proper context as he saw it, a perspective shared by many among the Latin American Left as well as revolution supporters in the United States: "I was familiar with the Cuban struggle for independence, their efforts to throw off the American yoke, and sympathized with them. Cubans had every right to be free of the United States and to manage their own affairs. . . . So I decided to write my own interpretation, underlining that Cuban aspirations could not be separated from U.S. imperialism."[25] The result was his 1968 book *Cuba: The Making of a Revolution*, which was favorably reviewed and made Ruiz a much sought-after speaker on Cuba at various campuses. "How many times I spoke on Cuba," he recalls, "I don't remember, generally before college audiences." Ruiz also opposed the U.S. war in Vietnam, which only adds to his image as an oppositional historian influenced by his times, who in his autobiography uses his personal experiences—in this case, of his years at Smith—to reflect on some of the key issues of the period.

VI

Ruiz further links his professional career as a historian, especially being able to move from Smith College to the ambitious new campus of UCSD in the late 1960s, to the Chicano Movement of that period. He places his mobility, which he labels "Exile's Return," in relation to the protest politics of the era and the demographic changes on California campuses involving minority students. Indeed, the civil rights and ethnic pride movements had prompted Ruiz to consider returning home in the first place. He recalls giving a lecture on the U.S.-Mexico War around 1968 at California State University, Los Angeles, and being challenged by a Chicano student about why he lived in New England, if he was a historian of a conflict so crucial to Chicano history as well as being Mexican American. Why wasn't he in California helping Chicanos? "The retort annoyed me, but, when I look back," Ruiz reflects, "it made sense. What was I doing at Smith when Chicanos badly needed teachers who spoke their language?"[26] This sense of guilt but also of opportunity convinced Ruiz to return to California and accept the UCSD offer. "I returned," he writes, "largely to work in a university setting and to teach students of my flesh and blood, an imperative that I had belatedly come to acknowledge. I had outgrown Smith, not that I ever aspired to being a Mr. Chips. I was irrelevant to its students. They were neither poor nor underprivileged nor exploited. They would go on whether I taught them or not."[27]

Not that Ruiz believed he was only an affirmative action appointment for UCSD, since his reputation as a historian of Mexico was his main appeal to the History Department at that campus. Still, Ruiz was politically astute enough to realize that the ethnic tensions and civil rights movements of the 1960s formed the backdrop to his new career move, in addition to specific minority tensions at UCSD that, prior to his arrival, had undoubtedly influenced the decision to offer a position to a Mexican American professor. The Chicano Movement of the late 1960s and early 1970s was helping change the political landscape in California and the Southwest, the area of the United States where the majority of Mexican Americans lived. A new generation of Latinos was coming of age in the sixties, and encouraged by the black civil rights movement as well as by the later black power movement, this generation conceived of a new, more militant and radical struggle led by Mexican Americans who chose to call themselves Chicanos, a term linked with barrio life and culture. Chicanos elevated that term to higher political levels. To be a Chicano now was to identify and participate in the movement—a movement for civil rights, for a new ethnic awareness, and for a commitment to empowering the Chicano community. The Chicano Movement was the largest and most widespread political movement by Mexican Americans in U.S. history. Its use of direct action, politics in the streets, and confrontational mass protests forced the system to open up and provide access to more Chicanos.[28]

This access as a result of the collective movement's militant and radical pressures intersects with Ruiz's story. The movement pressured institutions of higher education, such as the UC system, to institute affirmative action and diversity programs for both students and faculty. Out of this came not only an important increase of Chicano undergraduate and graduate students in California and southwestern universities, but also the effort to recruit Chicano or Mexican American faculty. Ruiz was a recipient of these changes even though he did not see himself as a Chicano, which he defined as an assimilated Mexican American, something he denied being. Here, perhaps, he might have been influenced by the notable Mexican poet and intellectual Octavio Paz, who in his classic *The Labyrinth of Solitude* criticized Mexican Americans, especially the pachucos, or street dudes, as being totally un-Mexican. Ruiz, as a self-identified radical or radical liberal, did not subscribe to Paz's more conservative political views, but he did seem to share some of Paz's negative views about Americanized Mexicans. Even though he might not fully acknowledge the movement's importance to his career mobility, the fact is that without the movement, he might not have been recruited at UCSD. Of course, as noted, Ruiz had the credentials for such an appointment, but the movement created the political climate for it.

"These were the years of the battle for civil rights, and the heady days of the Chicano movement," he observes, "a crusade led by university students,

Mexican Americans who referred to themselves as Chicanos. The Southwest—or Aztlán as they baptized it, from where their pre-Columbian ancestors supposedly came—was the ancestral home. Offspring of the militant 1960s, the Chicano movement marked the first time that people of Mexican background as a national group claimed a place for themselves."[29]

Although not calling himself a Chicano, Ruiz nevertheless plunged into a politically charged environment at UCSD, where he was often sandwiched between the demands of Chicano students for him to be more Chicano and his personal inclination to stay above the movement and contribute from his more academic position. This middle ground was not always easy. Still, to his credit, Ruiz adhered to his principles of equal opportunity and representation at the university level for Chicanos. As an insider, both as a professor and later as chair of the History Department in the early to mid-1970s, he battled to recruit Chicano faculty as well as graduate students. In doing so, he encountered resistance disguised in the form of white faculty upholding "standards."

"No matter how strong the Chicano hunger for professors of their own," he recalls with some bitterness,

> not many could be found, especially when Anglo academics raised the red flag of standards. Chicanos were not "qualified" was the hue and cry of these hypocrites, many of whom had scarcely published themselves; these naysayers scoffed at Chicano studies and believed that Chicanos were not bright enough to write books, nor did they have a history worth writing about. I remember a remark by a colleague at San Diego who voted against hiring a Chicano to teach Latin American colonial history but voted for him to teach Chicano history; the candidate was "not talented enough" to teach colonial history, "a reputable discipline," but was good enough to teach "Chicano history." The young man went on to win a MacArthur grant—on my recommendation.[30]

Ruiz's struggles to diversify UCSD—efforts mostly unknown to militant Chicano students—proved to be quite successful in increasing Chicano and minority faculty and graduate students in history (here is where my story intersects with Ruiz's, as does that of other students, such as Alex Saragoza and Miguel Tinker Salas). Still, Chicano student leaders in MEChA (Movimiento Estudiantil Chicano de Aztlán) and even Chicano graduate students challenged him to do more. "Campus life was a rough and rolling sea," he notes,

Student unrest brought turbulence and unpredictable behavior. There were demands for ethnic history, for minority professors, and for ethnic bureaucrats. Chicanos, graduates in particular, were not forbearing with their mentors. I remember a Chicana in my seminar on the Mexican Revolution who drove an English sports car but berated me for asking her to read memoirs of blue bloods of the Old Regime, and a Chicana teaching assistant, usually quiescent, giving me the Bronx cheer because in a class lecture I had extolled the help I received from my parents. "You did not get ahead on your own," was her retort! I can call up memories of angry Chicanos, blacks, and Asians, among them one of my graduate students, stomping into my office to tell me that I must hire minority historians. When I tried to explain that I wanted to but that it would take time, they walked out in a huff.[31]

Despite these ups and downs, Ruiz succeeds in relating the political temper of the Chicano Movement on campuses and, in so doing, linking his role as autobiographer to his role as a historian. Throughout these conflictive years, Ruiz remained a highly popular professor, with large enrollments in his Latin American and Mexican history classes. Later generations of Chicano students seemed to value him even more when in 1992, MEChA, which had criticized him for not being Chicano enough, presented him with its annual award for distinguished service for Chicanos at UCSD.

VII

The second notion, as observed in section II, of how historians can use their autobiographies to advance historical understanding has to do with how societies change and who or what causes these changes. I find a mixed picture by Ruiz on this issue. As noted above, he seems to have an understanding that the changes in his life in the late 1960s and early 1970s are somehow linked to the Chicano Movement. American society changed not from the top down but from the bottom up. New historical subjects emerged, such as Chicanos, to change the contours of American history. The civil rights and ethnic empowerment movements of that era forced a new political agenda on the country and significantly challenged the status quo. Though Ruiz did not identify as a Chicano, he was impressed, as a self-proclaimed man of the Left, with the movement's willingness to militantly confront the system and to assert a counter identity as Chicanos. Where Ruiz has more difficulty seeing the relationship between his own life and social change has to do with his generational experience as part of the Mexican American generation. Here, perhaps, Ruiz is too close to his coming-of-age era, which possibly signals a difficulty for some historians to be able to judge and evaluate their own key times. This certainly seems to be the case with Ruiz. He could have used his experiences from the 1930s to the 1950s to shed more light on the initial Mexican American civil rights movement, prior to the Chicano Movement. That period was characterized by important and new civil rights struggles led by Ruiz's generation of Mexican Americans, in organizations such as the League of United Latin American Citizens (LULAC), the American GI Forum, the Spanish-Speaking People's Congress, the Community Service Organization (CSO), the Asociación Nacional México-Americana (ANMA), and others. This political generation took on school segregation, job and wage discrimination, exclusion from public facilities, jury discrimination, and lack of effective political representation, among other issues, displaying historical agency by confronting institutions that denied Mexican Americans basic rights. Prior to the Chicano Movement, the Mexican American generation began the process of struggling to empower the Mexican American community.[32]

Yet, this is precisely what Ruiz fails to acknowledge. That he did not engage in these movements nor study them might explain his silence. That history does exist, including my book *Mexican Americans: Leadership, Ideology & Identity, 1930–1960*, and I know that he read the book because I personally gave him a copy after its publication in 1989; in fact, he mentions it in his autobiography. No, a lack of knowledge is not the explanation; to be blunt, it is his unwillingness to agree that the Mexican American generation, or at least the generation's civil rights leadership, actually accomplished some good. Ruiz's problem here is a perceived cultural and identity issue. Ruiz sees himself as remaining more "authentically" mexicano culturally than his generational peers, whom he sees as too acculturated, too Americanized, too *pocho* (a pejorative term used in Mexico against Mexican Americans), and consequently a lost generation, culturally speaking. "Many Mexicans of my generation," he proposes, "were accommodationists, seeking acceptance on the terms of the Anglo establishment."[33] Seeing them as "brown Americans" and as "an apolitical generation," he does not acknowledge their civil rights contributions. Ruiz prides himself on his ability to speak Spanish, his retention of various Mexican cultural traditions, and, as a historian of Mexico, his familiarity and comfort in Mexican society south of the border. What Ruiz fails to recognize, however, is that he is not that different from many of the Mexican American generation. He is Mexican American, and his bilingual and bicultural status mirrors to one degree or another that of many of his peers. The main difference is that Ruiz sees the hyphen often used in Mexican-American as representing a chasm or divide, while most of the Mexican American Generation, in my opinion, saw it as a unifier, creatively bringing together the Mexican and the American into a new and innovative Mexican American culture that is as "authentic" as Ruiz's insistence on his "mexicanidad." There is no such thing as an "authentic" culture since all cultures are hybrids to some extent. Ruiz's obsession with his perceived ability to remain more "mexicano" than his peers blinds him to the fact that he is closer to many of them than he realizes and that shunning them furthers his unwillingness to acknowledge their historical subjectivity.

VIII

While there has not been enough space to explore all the implications of Ramón Ruiz's fascinating personal and intellectual autobiography, I hope I have given a sense of the relationship of the historian's autobiography to history and the possibilities that exist for the historian to employ the genre of autobiography not just to reflect on an individual life but to shed more light on history and the making of history by using the tools and thought processes of a historian. Being a historian does not guarantee being always able to do this (witness Ruiz's problems with his own historical generation), yet the possibilities are there, and the historian as autobiographer should take advantage of them.

2

IDENTITY AND GENDER IN THE MEXICAN AMERICAN TESTIMONIO

The Life and Narrative of Frances Esquibel Tywoniak

We tell ourselves stories of our past, make fictions or stories of it, and these narrations become the past, the only part of our lives that is not submerged.
— CAROLYN G. HEILBRUN, *WRITING A WOMAN'S LIFE*

I

RECENT CHICANA AND LATINA TEXTS rewrite the traditional Latina narrative by focusing on women as subjects, as historical agents, and by imagining a new future for women. Their subjects in different ways challenge the traditional Latino model for women's proper sphere. Rather than accepting what Shari Benstock terms the private self as representing the world of women, the new Latina writers project themselves and their subjects into the public world as well.[1] While the private may not always be political, it is certainly not divorced from women's public roles and public aspirations. In effect, as Carolyn Heilbrun suggests about other transgressive writers, who dare to cross previously closed borders concerning identity and self-representation, these Latina writers reject "womanhood," at least as defined in traditional patriarchal terms, and instead rewrite the definition of being a woman—a more liberated womanhood. They dare, to use Heilbrun's term, to be "ambiguous women."[2]

The conflict between the private and the public in a Mexican American context, and the attempt to merge the two, is one of the dominant themes that emerges from an oral history project I conducted in the early 1990s. In 1990 after completing another oral history project, concerning Bert Corona, a longtime Mexican American activist in Los Angeles, I embarked on a second testimonio.[3] Testimonio is a Latin American genre of autobiographical texts that are the result of oral history projects, usually involving collaboration between a scholar or journalist and a grassroots activist. While the testimonio has been recently recognized as a new and more populist genre in Latin American literature, its roots actually lie deeper in the oral tradition of Latin American culture. Moreover, testimonios are not just literary texts. They are above all parts of political struggles. Perhaps the best-known testimonio is *I, Rigoberta Menchú: An Indian Woman in Guatemala*, cowritten by anthropologist Elisabeth Burgos-Debray and the indigenous activist and Nobel Peace Prize winner Rigoberta Menchú.[4]

My testimonio project involved the aunt of a former student at the University of California, Santa Barbara. Unlike the Corona text, which is similar to the Latin American testimonio in that it is overtly political and centered on Corona's participation and leadership in the Mexican American community's struggle against injustice and discrimination, Frances Esquibel Tywoniak's narrative is not. Her life, unlike Corona's, is not a political one, at least not in the traditional sense. Her testimonio is an attempt to redefine and rewrite Latina lives in order to assert what Mary G. Mason refers to as "the other voice."[5] In this effort, gender and ethnicity are linked together, along with race and class, although in a state of tension, to re-create not only a new woman but a new Latina. Yet this rewriting, or self-inscription, is not an attempt to create an essentialist notion of a Latina woman.

What I conclude, for example, in examining Corona's life is that his sense of ethnic, racial, class, and gender identity is multiple. Corona's ethnic self is the result not of some inherent essence of being Mexican, but of various historical, ethnic, cultural, class, ideological, and personal influences on his life. His sense of ethnicity is determined not by just one of these influences at one particular juncture of his life, but by multiple influences throughout his life. Corona's ethnic self is a good example of the argument put forth by Werner Sollors and others that ethnicity is a constantly changing variable.[6] It is not something fixed in time. Instead, it is invented and reinvented. One finds in Corona's narrative multiple or polyphonic voices negotiating a particular concept of ethnic identity. The same can be said of the narrative of Frances Esquibel Tywoniak, or Fran, as I refer to her in this chapter.[7]

I believe that for Mexican Americans, ethnic identity has been not a singular experience, but a multifaceted one. As for other American ethnic groups, identity represents a dialogic relationship. That is, the experience involves a historical and ethnic dialogue on at least three levels: one, a dialogue with the dominant culture framed by what we refer to as Anglo-American society; two, a dialogue with other marginalized ethnic/racialized minorities; and three, a dialogue within the Mexican American community itself.

The intersections of these dialogic relationships have resulted in a Mexican American *heteroglossia*, to adopt a term from the Russian literary critic Mikhail Bakhtin. There is not one Mexican American world but many. Heteroglossia implies the presence of a multiplicity of voices in a literary text. I use the concept here to suggest that in the actual social relationships of Mexican Americans exists a multiplicity of voices and subjects rather than one voice and one unified subject. From this perspective, identity—both individual and social—is multiple rather than singular. For example, in response to the unified masculine subject proposed by some in the Chicano Movement of the late 1960s and early 1970s, new Chicana writers of the 1980s, such as Gloria Anzaldúa, Cherríe Moraga, and Sandra Cisneros, proposed a complex, multifaceted subject constructed at the intersection of ethnicity, race, gender, class, and sexuality.

Moreover, experiences like the Mexican American one suggest that the process of "imagining community," to use Benedict Anderson's term, in a multiethnic society such as the United States has not been limited to only white ethnic groups.[8] In contrast, a critical multicultural approach interprets issues of national identity both dialectically and dialogically to propose not only a synthesis of national expression, but the persistence and validation of ethnic and cultural difference.

From this perspective, I analyze in this chapter the multiple influences on the gender and ethnic identity of the young Fran Esquibel.

II

Born in 1931, Fran Esquibel's early childhood to age six was set in southeastern New Mexico. In 1938 her parents and their three children joined the Dust Bowl migration to California to seek a better life during the Great Depression. Fran's testimonio is largely her memories of growing up in the rural and semirural environment of California's San Joaquin Valley. There Fran confronted who she was and what she wanted to be. Developing as an excellent student in her high school years, Fran was one of the few Mexican American women in the late

1940s who was able to attend college. In 1949 she received a scholarship to the University of California, Berkeley, and graduated in 1953 with a degree in languages. She doesn't recall ever encountering another Mexican American, male or female, at Berkeley during her undergraduate years. After graduation, and after marrying and having her first child, Fran went on to become a successful teacher and school administrator in the Bay Area. She retired in 1992 after serving almost forty years in the San Francisco school district.[9]

Although raised largely in the San Joaquin Valley of California, the context of Fran's earlier life in New Mexico was extremely important. Her New Mexico experience unconsciously fixed in her mind a sense of ethnic community based on the extended family, or what Albert Stone terms the "immediate community."[10] This community was centered around her maternal grandparents, whose roots in New Mexico went back several generations. As shepherds, the Flores family struggled to retain their lands and their way of life despite the dislocations of the Great Depression. Fran recalls a closely knit extended family, where aunts, uncles, and cousins lived close, and all interacted as one family. Later in California, when she struggled with her self-identity as a Mexican American female, Fran carried with her and came to appreciate her New Mexican background. Returning years later to New Mexico as a mature adult, she was moved by the warmth and familiarity with which her relatives, particularly her aunts, welcomed her back. "When I returned to New Mexico for a visit for the first time in almost forty years," she notes, "my aunts greeted me as if I had never been away. 'Our own daughter,' they declared, is 'one of ours' [*una de las nuestras*]."[11]

Like most other Mexican Americans, and indeed most other ethnic Americans, Fran grew up with ambivalence about her ethnic identity. She experienced what W. E. B. Du Bois observed of African Americans: the sense of a dual consciousness—of being part of an ethnic/racial minority and of being American.[12] Not that this duality is always conscious, but anyone who has grown up in a racialized environment can attest, I believe, to this sense of duality. Fran experienced these tensions. She aspired to become "American" but at the same time sensed that she was really not "American." Part of her struggle consisted of wanting to be seen as her own singular self and not just reflecting a self-representation shaped from the outside by Anglo-Americans who stereotyped Mexicans.

Yet she was also part of a family and part of other cultural constructs she recognized even though she was somewhat alienated from them. As she in time confronted these tensions and attempted, consciously and unconsciously, to negotiate ethnic, gender, class, and cultural border crossings between competing forces, Fran reclaimed and reinvented her New Mexican identity. These historical memories provided her with what Doris Sommer and other critics refer to as the "plural self" or the "collective self."[13] The New Mexican memories reawakened in her the strength of family and of community. The New Mexican collective self helped to balance the alienated sense of individuality that gnawed at her during her coming-of-age years.

Carolyn Heilbrun notes that most women, unlike men, have only been able to write about themselves in relationship to other individuals. Heilbrun suggests that this represents an expression of women's sense of inferiority and dependence in comparison to men.[14] I disagree and suggest that Heilbrun's contention is culturally biased. In a different cultural context, women writing about their relationship to others, especially regarding family, may be more of an expression of what is referred to as the collective self, or "collective identity."

Hence, in Fran's narrative, her memories of her early New Mexican childhood, for example, create a historical context to the personal struggle she later engaged in. That is, her attempt to participate in the debate over the proper role for women and the issue of private versus public is not divorced from a Mexican American context. Her individual struggle and quest is also an ethnic one. Her attempt to resolve the gender and ethnic ambivalences she felt are not separated from her sense of ethnic loyalty and ethnic community. For Fran, rewriting a woman's life is also rewriting the meaning of being Mexican American or Latina.

III

Within her extended family, Fran recalls a strong sense of what she calls a "quiet love." Family members were not particularly affectionate. Yet she remembers a pervasive sense of solidarity that permeated family relationships. Since her maternal grandfather, the patriarch of the family, died one year after Fran was born, the extended family revolved around her grandmother as the matriarch. Fran's sense of gender identity within a Mexican American context was partly shaped by the memories of her grandmother:

> My grandmother I remember very well. She was a very tiny, tiny lady with very dark wavy hair and very green eyes. She had a very positive presence. I've always wondered how she could have had all those children beginning at age fifteen, when she married my grandfather, and at the same time worked tirelessly on the

ranch. I have a memory of her as a partner to her husband. This memory or what I was told about her has influenced my own thinking. As I see today the concern over the role of working women, I recall that in my grandmother's days women also worked. Perhaps not for an outside wage, but as working partners with their husbands in the home and, as in the case of my grandmother, on the ranch.

This sense of a woman's role being that of a partner rather than a subordinate wife, whether really true for her grandmother or not, influenced Fran's interpretation of the concepts of womanhood and marriage. Her grandmother's image as partner became one of Fran's models.

Of course, her relationship with her mother helped frame part of Fran's New Mexican collective self as well as part of her gender and ethnic identity. What she drew from the memories of her mother in New Mexico is an appreciation of the importance of obtaining an education. Her mother struggled for what little formal education she acquired. Fran recalls her mother telling her that she had attended a segregated school of Hispanos (Mexican Americans in New Mexico) and that this school provided only a third-grade education. Despite her limited schooling, Fran's mother always supported and encouraged education for her children. While her mother was not prepared to break with traditional Hispano gender roles, which largely relegated women to being wives, mothers, and secondary breadwinners, she aspired to more for her daughters. In her own way, Fran's mother surreptitiously aided Fran's rejection of this structured gender role.

Fran also discerns from these particular New Mexican memories the beginning of bilingual influences within her family, partly initiated by her mother. Even though Fran lived in a largely Spanish-speaking world in New Mexico, some English was incorporated into daily life. Her mother had learned English at school, and Fran recalls her mother reading to her in English from a Sears Roebuck or Montgomery Ward catalog while looking for items to order.

But Fran's early identification with her family was not limited to her mother's side. She was also deeply influenced by her relationship with her father. Her father represented a sense of family and ethnic community, but he was also a symbol of what she later sought to reject—the patriarchal culture. Fran negotiated this tension over time, not outside her family cultural environment but within it. In New Mexico her father represented an outsider. He was the "Mexican" of the family. He had been born in northern Mexico and had first migrated to work in Texas. He had then worked as a laborer in southeastern

New Mexico, where he met his future wife and eventually became integrated into the New Mexican extended family.

Additionally, Fran's father represented another ethnic and cultural influence. His Mexican and southwestern cultural baggage merged with his wife's southeastern New Mexican influences. In particular, Fran recalls the strong Mexican Catholicism centered on the cult of the Virgen de Guadalupe, which her father had introduced into the family. Her father was more religious and devout than her mother:

> He was devoted to the Virgen de Guadalupe. He did the novena in early December around the feast day of the Virgen. He introduced the devotion to the Virgen to my mother's family, and we did the novena. I can remember kneeling what seemed to me an eternity. My family set up an elaborate altar to the Virgen, and many people joined us for the nine days of the novena. To me religion in New Mexico was my father's dramatic devotion to the Virgen and to Christ. Not so much God. It was Jesus Christ and the Virgen. I learned a lot from my father about the Virgen and about humility. That was an important message.

Fran's father was part of a wider Mexican and southwestern cultural tradition growing within the region of southeastern New Mexico. Migrant workers from Texas found employment on the land owned or leased by Fran's family. She particularly recalls these workers in the evening sitting around their automobiles and listening to a Spanish-language radio station that played Mexican and border ranchero music, especially the songs of the legendary Lydia Mendoza. Fran's father, like some other mexicanos, would bring out a guitar and sing rancheras. This was a man's cultural world, but Fran recalls being allowed some access to it as a child.

What Fran's early childhood in New Mexico provided, even after her family migrated to California, was a sense of roots, of a physical space that she knew she belonged to in some way. For Fran, going back, going home, would not be to Mexico or to some other southwestern location, but would be to the rural plains of southeastern New Mexico. This sense of place and of identifying with others from New Mexico provided Fran with a certain distance from other Mexican Americans in the San Joaquin Valley and underscored the great regional diversity among Mexican Americans. Fran recalls that in California, her mother would often recognize other people or neighbors. "Es de Nuevo México," her mother would say: "There was that identification with people from New Mexico. I guess patterning myself after that, I still do that to myself. I feel affinity with people from New Mexico. So this identification has been meaningful. It has been an integral part of me."

If Fran's New Mexican experience has meant anything, it has reinforced, perhaps unconsciously during her coming-of-age years, a sense of collective selfhood, despite whatever competing acculturating tensions were associated with her relationship to family, particularly to her parents. Family provided Fran with support, which helped her to negotiate her self-identity: "My early childhood in New Mexico had a profound influence on me that I didn't know for some time and didn't appreciate until much later. I think the influence was that there was 100 percent family support. It was a given. In retrospect, I was one of many, yet I was also made to feel that I was important."

IV

Fran's gender and ethnic self was further shaped by class forces, which dislocated her family during the Great Depression, from small ranches and farms in New Mexico to California in the late 1930s, to begin life anew as migrant agricultural workers. Instead of helping to manage the Flores ranch in New Mexico, Fran's father now reverted to being strictly a laborer in the California fields. In California Fran underwent important changes regarding gender and ethnic identity during her coming-of-age years in Visalia. This section focuses on Fran's experiences between the ages of ten and fourteen—her age of puberty and of youthful adolescence.

During this period, she began to recognize the "double consciousness" referred to by Du Bois. Fran sensed being "other" but did not want to be seen as "other." She also experienced the dilemma, shared by many other ethnic subjects, over which personal strategy of self-identity to pursue. Fran's dual consciousness, or what she now refers to as "parallelism"—the growing divide between home and school environments, between Mexican American and Anglo-American worlds—manifested in different ways during these years.

Fran recalls that around age ten, she began to feel tensions over what seemed to her to be an abyss between her Spanish at home and her English at school. Like most other Mexican Americans, and indeed other ethnic Americans, Fran's English-language experiences in school meant that she was becoming more proficient and functional among her peers in English. She began to undergo what Richard Rodriguez suggests is the sense that Spanish in a Mexican American cultural context represents a "private language," whereas English symbolizes the "public language."[15] Rodriguez's assertion can be and has been criticized with some justification, for it is too rigidly polarized. In an increasingly Spanish-speaking environment like California, Spanish and English can be both private and public.

Nevertheless, for a young adolescent girl, this was not as clear. Hence, Fran's sense of language separation was as real then as it was for Rodriguez. Her increasing alienation from Spanish interacted with her growing struggle against family control, especially the control of her strict father. Speaking English outside the home, but—more importantly—attempting surreptitiously to integrate it at home, was for Fran, as she later acknowledged, part of her adolescent rebellion: "Spanish became increasingly burdensome as a responsibility because of what I believe was my natural orientation to oppose parental authority. Language was tied to parental authority because my father was adamant about the use of Spanish in my early years."

As the division of language was framed in youthful rebellion against parental authority, it also reflected Fran's growing recognition that Spanish (a metaphor for family and culture) represented the "other." Previously, Spanish had stood for security and familiarity; now it became an embarrassing symbol for parental culture, which was perceived by the Anglo-American world as foreign. This damaging experience is too often repeated in ethnic America: "I started dealing with the fact that my parents were perceived as foreign and didn't function fully in English. I became very conscious of the fact that the world of school was a separate world within which my parents didn't function."

Yet while Fran perceived school and family to be completely separate cultural spheres, she also experienced alienation from her English-speaking school environment. While at one level she may have sought assimilation, at another she struggled against it, or at least for a bridge between two cultures. She recalls, for example, that the stories she read in school seemed totally unreal and foreign to her:

> My life was not in the books. My experiences were not in the books. I was not in the books. I remember *Heidi of the Mountain* and detesting that story vehemently. It was a book read to our class over a period of weeks when I was in grade three or four. Even though I had grown up with animals, I couldn't identify with Heidi. We had no goats when we were growing up, and worse, I couldn't imagine any

little girl being so interested in goats and climbing up hills in Switzerland or wherever it was, a land that seemed so alien to my experiences. I had no clue what the story was about and I could have cared less. I remember deliberately not listening and instead occupying my mind in observing the teacher's behavior and the behavior of other pupils. The teacher was oblivious to my existence as a person. I hated Heidi and didn't want to hear about Heidi, and I hated this teacher droning on and on about Heidi.

Finding alienation both at home and at school, Fran attempted to create a separate consciousness for herself: something that was neither home nor school, but in reality some of both. This constituted what Gloria Anzaldúa refers to as a border area, or *la frontera*—a space, territorial but also symbolic and cultural, where Chicanos (Mexican Americans) invent something uniquely their own.[16] "We're talking about those early years," Fran explains, "and my guess is that about this time, I started what ultimately would become somewhat more pronounced later, which is a realization that I was dealing with separate worlds in my life. My world at home, my world at school, and my world in my head."

Fran's struggle to create a more autonomous self-identity, or what Heilbrun terms a "quest plot," is related to both gender and ethnicity and is influenced by class position and race structure.[17] Fran's efforts to understand herself as a young woman and as a Mexican American were affected by the distinct social structure in the San Joaquin Valley, in which Mexican Americans were relegated to menial positions as farm laborers and segregated in a Mexican American cultural world. Fran's attempts at self-representation, for example, through physical appearance, specifically forms of dress, reveal the intersections of gender, ethnicity, race, and class.

Fran perceived at first that there seemed to be only two basic models of appearance: an Anglo-American and Mexican American. Initially, she believed that she really had little choice. The Anglo-American model was inaccessible. Fran was not an Anglo-American and didn't deceive herself into thinking that she was. Even if she believed she could transform herself through appearance into an Anglo-American, she could not. If not her clothes, then her bronze skin and dark hair signified her Mexican ancestry. While issues of both racial and ethnic differences were ambivalent factors in Fran's early life, she was still subject to the racialized system that Anglo-Americans have imposed on Mexicans since the U.S. seizure of Mexico's northern frontier, including California, in the mid-nineteenth century.

More basically as a member of a poor family, Fran could not afford to purchase the type of clothes worn by her Anglo-American peers. Hence, for better or for worse, there was only one model that she could relate to or transform, the Mexican American model:

> I was aware that Mexicans were different in appearance from Anglos and my models in terms of physical appearance were from the Mexican community. These were the only models I knew. There was no reason for me to look elsewhere for models. As soon as I became aware of the outside world, I could see that relative to the Anglo community, I was different in appearance, and that was a source of extreme discomfort and anguish because I couldn't match that model, that hairdo, and that type of clothing.

While at one level, Fran lamented that she could not become an Anglo-American through appearance, there was also a sense of rejecting this appearance and of choosing one that reflected more of herself. She rejected the Anglo-American model because she perceived it as too babyish and immature. Fran recalls that she was already physically developed as a young woman, even before becoming a teenager, and that she opted for the more mature style of the *pachuca* look of the 1940s. This decision was also influenced by her recollection that, unlike the Anglo-American community, in the Mexican American one there seemed to be no real childhood or adolescent stage: "It was babyhood and then adult-type behavior, including self-adornment through hairdo, earrings, facial make-up, and clothes. The Anglo kids maintained a more youthful look, a look that was more in the direction of children's clothing that barrio kids considered to be wimpy, in contrast to their effort to appear more adult-like."

Rejecting the Anglo-American look, Fran instead adopted a modified barrio style, consisting of a scaled-down bouffant hairdo accompanied by a tight skirt and a sweater that, according to Fran, "revealed the emerging young girl versus the baby—the Anglo kid with a loose-fitting dress and straight hair with little barrettes, the smockey child look." Fran doesn't recall wearing much lipstick but notes that many Mexican American girls her age did, and some wore a great deal of it.

Yet Fran's ethnic and gender look was really an ambiguous one. By her junior high school years, the ambivalence about herself and her relationship to both the Anglo and the Mexican American worlds led her to adopt a more "mainstream," less barrio look. In this period, Fran appears to have consciously decided that, if she were to have a future outside the traditional and prescribed role for Mexican American women like her mother, it had to be separate and apart from the barrio. There was no future for her there. This decision was accompanied by a change in her appearance. It was not so much that Fran opted to become an "Anglo," but that she attempted to design a strategy that would empower her as both a young woman and a person of Mexican descent.

Yet this change brought her into direct confrontation with some of her Mexican American peers—specifically the pachucas of this era. Pachucos and pachucas (male and female) were Mexican Americans who, not unlike Fran, expressed ambivalences about both Anglo-American and Mexican American cultures, and in response, they rebelled against both in the hope of creating their own cultural and stylistic space. Yet for them, unlike for Fran, this space was to be within the barrio, not outside of it. Fran did not essentially reject the barrio. She was partly a product of it, but she believed that to remain there would doom her to a fate not unlike that of her mother and of other women in her family outside the barrio.

What was at work here was, I believe, an integrationist strategy, not of an "Uncle Tom" or "Tío Taco" variety, but one with oppositional connotations. Fran's personal strategy was similar to the political strategy of integration pursued by what I have labeled the Mexican American generation. Groups such as the League of United Latin American Citizens (LULAC) and the American GI Forum, as well as more radical ones like the Spanish-Speaking People's Congress advocated integration—not assimilation—as a viable way to break down discriminatory barriers erected against Mexican Americans. While Fran's strategy was not political per se, it nevertheless possessed the same basic understanding that one viable option for Mexican Americans to achieve equal opportunities lay in an integrationist philosophy.[18]

This strategy was also a gender-based one. For Fran, liberation from the traditional role for Mexican American women could only come by altering gender expectations and moving in the direction of new cultural fronts: education and professional careers.

To achieve her integrationist goal, Fran modeled her appearance to reflect a more "mainstream look." "I began to choose clothing that I thought made me look good even if the clothes were different from the clothes worn in the barrio." Skirts and blouses along with Spaulding white bucks—the Anglo bobby-sox look—made up Fran's junior high school and high school wardrobe. Yet, as Fran explains it, this was not a totally mainstream look, since she retained and modified a stacked hairdo and never was able to afford the cashmere sweaters favored by the Anglo girls. Opposed to this was the pachuca look, adopted by other Mexican American girls. It consisted of a short and tight black skirt, a baggy sweater, high-top shoes, and black bobby-socks. The pachucas wore their hair in exaggerated bouffant styles. Lipstick and cosmetics added to the statement.

Dressed differently from the pachucas, Fran recalls tense encounters with them, especially after school and on the way home. She remembers being taunted and engaging in what was called "mad dogging," the exchange of hostile looks. According to Fran, pachucas in Visalia had a reputation for violence, but she never engaged in physical conflict with them. Fran believes that a dual form of assertiveness was involved here, with each form possessing different objectives. The pachucas of Fran's era authored their lives in one particular way, a defiant way, but it was not Fran's way. For Fran, the pachucas embodied the worst aspects of the barrio, those that Fran believed promoted conformity and an inward-looking perspective, one that frowned on those who desired mobility out of the barrio.

Fran explains how she could not accept this. She says she saw this mode of thinking as reinforcing—at least for her—the traditional expectations of Mexican American women. For Fran, the struggle against dominant female gender roles required an integrationist strategy and perspective that was not accommodationist but oppositional—oppositional to the limitations imposed on women within Mexican American culture, and oppositional to the discriminatory attitudes and practices of Anglo society against Mexican Americans, both men and women.

Fran did not see herself as wanting to become an Anglo. But she recognized that to achieve success in school and career mobility, she would have to make personal and cultural choices. These choices likewise involved differentiating herself from other Mexican American students who—for whatever reasons—did not share her aspirations. Fran concentrated first on stylistic choices, but she was also making a statement regarding social class. Fran's aspirations to make something of herself beyond the farmworker/barrio experiences of her parents and her Mexican American peers contained a desire to escape her working-class position and to achieve middle-class status. She recalls that these were not easy choices. They were the result of ambivalences, insecurities, and tensions of her youth, which followed her into her high school years:

I was a successful student in high school, but during those years, I was having a difficult time defining myself. Every success in school increasingly separated me from other Hispanic students and, I felt, from Hispanic culture. Being an academically successful student meant that I had to accept being "different." My school friends increasingly became other academically successful girls.

I knew that there were many places in town where Mexicans were not welcome, and I knew that in town, job opportunities for Mexicans were almost nonexistent. But I also knew I had tenacity and the ability to succeed.

To Fran, the barrio represented not a romanticized haven, but a closed environment with limited opportunities. Unlike New Mexico, which to Fran was defined by a sense of community, the Visalia barrio remained an uncertain place. For young Mexican American women, even for those with some education and some hopes of a better life, the opportunities for mobility in the barrio were limited by racial, ethnic, and gender discrimination. The best one could aspire to was a job as a store clerk or a bank cashier; even this depended, as Fran recalls, on the shade of your skin:

I think that at that early age, I began to understand that Visalia was a dead-end place in terms of opportunities for a person like me. I did not see myself in any sense tied to Visalia. I definitely knew that I would be going on in some fashion. Life was going on elsewhere for me. I think that as I was going through these years, comparing myself to others, I was acquiring a definite sense of "I can do more—I can do better." There is more, and I can reach out for more because there is more.

Perhaps the experience that most tellingly and sensitively illustrates Fran's attempt to remake her life as a Mexican American woman was her break with her barrio boyfriend, Peter Nava. Fran met Peter when she was in junior high school and he in high school. They dated for about a year and a half. Fran recalls Peter as a sensitive and caring individual—the antithesis of the traditional macho type. Peter never put any pressure, either social or sexual, on Fran. Yet Fran began to recognize that there was little if any point to their relationship. She wanted an education and some kind of career. Peter would not go to school beyond high school and seemed preordained to remain part of the Visalia barrio. Fran knew that if she stayed in Visalia, her only future with Peter would be marriage and children. Fran believed that other Mexican American girls would be content with this:

> The girls I was surrounded by did not seem to be future oriented. There was not much discussion of the future. I don't remember any discussion among the girls as to what tomorrow holds. I think that they accepted being in the barrio and that was it, and the expectation was that they would marry. I certainly don't remember talking about getting married or having babies or that sort of thing, or saying to Peter, "Let's get married, let's have babies." I think it was just kind of an accepted way of life: women as marriage partners or sex objects.

Fran ended her relationship with Peter as she entered high school. As she recalls, she loved Peter, but she knew that the relationship had no future:

> It was clear to me that going to school meant changing my associations. I think I perceived that having a boyfriend meant getting married, and I knew that was not it for me at that time. I wasn't pro-marriage or against marriage. My family didn't talk about it, but it became crystal clear to me that marriage was not for me at the time. Peter and I couldn't continue seeing each other, caring for each other as much as we did, and not consider marriage. We both understood this without talking about it publicly. I was young, and I had my schooling to attend to. We were physically attracted to each other, but that was all it could be.

V

Frances Esquibel Tywoniak's testimonio is much more involved and complex than I can portray in this short space. The multiple influences on her coming-of-age identity were to be compounded in young adulthood, especially after her marriage to Ed Tywoniak, a man of Polish Jewish background whom she met as a student at the University of California at Berkeley. What I do want to conclude, based on the segments of her text that I have analyzed here, is that Fran's narrative, what Bernice Johnson Reagon calls a "cultural autobiography," and that of other Latina postcolonial ethnic women represent a new form of authorship.[19] This is an authorship that seeks to rewrite the very nature of both gender and ethnicity. To paraphrase, modify, and expand on Heilbrun: "I believe that [ethnic] women have long searched, and continue to search, for an identity 'other' than their own. Caught in the conventions of their sex, they have sought an escape from [both] gender [and ethnicity]."[20] While these narratives are not nor should be whole or closed texts, they do reveal challenging efforts to engage in a dialogic relationship concerning gender and ethnicity. By constructing through oral narrative what amounts to an "exemplary life," Fran challenges us to dismantle the past and to reimagine the future based on the invention of an alternative, autonomous, and powerful self.

3

TRANSCULTURATION, MEMORY, AND HISTORY

Mary Helen Ponce's *Hoyt Street—An Autobiography*

The memory is a mysterious—and powerful—thing. It forgets what we want most to remember, and retains what we often wish to forget. We take from it what we need.

—MARY HELEN PONCE, "NOTE FROM
THE AUTHOR," IN *HOYT STREET*

[A]utoethnography . . . refer[s] to instances in which colonized subjects undertake to represent themselves in ways that engage with the colonizer's own terms.

—MARY LOUISE PRATT, *IMPERIAL EYES:
TRAVEL WRITING AND TRANSCULTURATION*

I

MEXICAN AMERICANS, OR CHICANOS, are no strangers to American history. As a largely mestizo population (that is, a mixed ethnic group of Indian and Spanish backgrounds), Chicanos can trace their particular history as far back as the indigenous civilizations of Mexico and what would become the U.S. Southwest, as well as to the Spanish conquest of the Aztec empire and of other native communities beginning in 1521. The mixing of genes and culture in what the great Cuban anthropologist Fernando Ortiz termed "transculturation," or what Mexicans refer to as *mestizaje*, took place over three hundred years of colonial rule. Chicano history also includes Mexico's independence struggle, beginning in 1810 and concluding in 1821. Independent Mexico stretched from present-day Central America to the current California-Oregon border. Not being able to defend its northern frontier—El Norte—against the expansionist United States, with its religious sense of Manifest Destiny, Mexico in the U.S.-Mexico War (1846–48) lost close to half its territory, stretching from Texas to California. It was with the conclusion of this war and the annexation of El Norte that the first official Mexican Americans appeared as a new American ethnic group, even though they and their ancestors had been in this area for centuries. The conquered generation in Chicano history (1848–1900) felt the full brunt of conquest, and although the members of this generation were admitted as citizens and technically enumerated as "whites," most succumbed (although not without resistance) into a subaltern second-class citizenship. Only the commencement of mass Mexican immigration at the turn of the twentieth century would, at least numerically, rescue Mexican Americans from historical obscurity. From 1900 to 1930 more than a million Mexican immigrants crossed the border, and with the exception of the Great Depression years of the 1930s, they continued and are still arriving. Over these one hundred-plus years, the Mexican American, or Chicano, experience has been characterized not only by this continuous migration, but also by generational changes through the children, grandchildren, and great-grandchildren of immigrants. In this historical context, I situate my discussion of Mary Helen Ponce's autobiography.[1] But first a word about terminology. The term Chicano, as far as can be determined, was first introduced by working-class Mexican immigrants in the early twentieth century. Most believe it is an indigenous-influenced pronunciation of mexicano. By the 1940s, as part of an interesting example of transculturation, U.S.-born Mexican Americans had reappropriated the term, especially in the urban barrios. In the 1960s, with the militant Chicano Movement, the term Chicano was overtly politicized to refer to activists in the movement. The term Mexican American refers to U.S.-born Mexican Americans, and its genealogy is found in the 1930s and 1940s among the children of Mexican immigrants. Later terms, such as Hispanic and Latino, are umbrella labels to categorize all people of Latin American descent in the United States. In this chapter, I interchangeably use both Chicano and Mexican American to refer to U.S.-born Mexicans.

Scholars under the rubric of assimilation and acculturation have traditionally studied ethnic groups in the United States with the thesis that immigrants initially face what historian Oscar Handlin calls cultural shock, but in time they begin their linear journey toward Americanization.[2] This process is further accelerated among their (hyphenated or not) compound children, as occurred among German Americans, Italian Americans, Russian Americans, Jewish

Americans, and Irish Americans. Although these European groups retained some symbolic ethnicity (e.g., celebrating Columbus Day or St. Patrick's Day) as part of their Americanization, for the most part, they became full-blown assimilated and acculturated Americans within a generation. This one-way process has been challenged by later scholars from a more postmodernist perspective, who stress multiculturalism and fragmentation of identity, but the assimilation/acculturation model still has strong support among some in the academy and, perhaps more importantly, among many white Americans who cannot accept the idea that for other immigrant groups, especially those of color and their descendants, such as Chicanos, this process has been more complicated. Many Americans today believe that Mexican Americans, unlike people of European descent, refuse to acculturate, that is, to Americanize themselves. This belief—a mistaken one at that—has led to tensions, as evident in Arizona's passage of SB 1070 in 2010, mandating that police officers check the legal status of anyone they stop or detain, which in practice is primarily aimed at the Chicano community; the further passage by Arizona of a law prohibiting the teaching of Chicano studies and other ethnic studies in public schools; and recent hostilities against Chicanos for transforming their celebration of Cinco de Mayo, which marks the Mexican army's defeat of an invading French army in 1862, into a feast day of cultural pride and ethnic identity. As Ponce notes in the introduction to her autobiography, written in 1992 in Santa Barbara, where she was a dissertation fellow in Chicano studies, "Mexican-Americans need to tell their side of the story in order to put to rest negative stereotypes."[3] The fact is that Mexican Americans, including immigrants, do change and do acculturate, but the process is perhaps more involved than for other immigrant groups. This complexity has to be understood as the result of three major geohistorical factors: (1) Mexico is right next door, with a common border of almost two thousand miles, so there will always be some evident Mexican ethnic and cultural influence in the United States; (2) unlike European and Asian immigration to the United States, Mexican immigration, influenced by the proximity of Mexico as well as the economic imbalance between both countries, has been mostly continuous since 1900, again ensuring a noticeable Mexican ethnic and cultural presence north of the border; and (3) the racialization of Mexicans in the United States—that is, the perception that people of Mexican descent are racially inferior—has ensured for many Chicanos their continuing marginalization within the United States and even second-class citizenship, a racialization that also affected some European immigrants but only through the initial immigrant generation. These three factors have kept most Chicanos and other Latinos at arm's length from other Americans, not because Mexican Americans have not wanted to integrate and become part of the American whole, but because other Americans have not welcomed them. These conditions, then, have resulted not in a traditional assimilation/acculturation pattern, where one is transformed from one culture and identity into another in the way that some traditional anthropologists suggest, but in what Ortiz in his classic study of Cuba calls transculturation. By this he means that when cultures meet, sometimes by force, instead of one culture fully absorbing the other, they mix in a syncretism or dialectic of cultures, as in the mestizaje of colonial Mexico. Culture contact, or what literary scholar Mary Louise Pratt calls "contact zones," as in the history of Cuba (especially after the Spanish conquest), with its varied ethnic and cultural groups, including African slaves, does not result in acculturation so much as transculturation.[4] This process does not mean that all cultures are regarded as equal, since transculturation is the result, as Ortiz notes, of European and other forms of imperialism. In a process of transculturation, cultures mix in a state of tension. Moreover, the transculturated subalterns are not simply victims of this process; they creatively adjust, create, and invent a new culture for themselves. Transculturation is not a passive process but a dynamic one.[5] Ortiz explains why transculturation is a more accurate term for what happens:

> I am of the opinion that the word *transculturation* better expresses the different phases of the process of transition from one culture to another because this does not consist merely in acquiring another culture, which is what the English word *acculturation* really implies, but the process also necessarily involves the loss or uprooting of a previous culture, which could be defined as a deculturation. In addition it carries the idea of the consequent creation of new cultural phenomena, which could be called neoculturation. In the end ... the result of every union of cultures is similar to that of the reproductive process between individuals: the offspring always has something of both parents but is always different from each of them.[6]

II

It is under the theme of transculturation that I analyze Mary Helen Ponce's *Hoyt Street—An Autobiography*. In her 1993 coming-of-age autobiography, similar to a bildungsroman or what Pratt refers to as "contact literature," Ponce provides one of the richest accounts available of Mexican immigrant and Mexican American culture covering the period of the 1940s. A student of anthropology herself, Ponce provides what Clifford Geertz calls a "thick description" of culture.[7] Of this influence, she has said, "I see myself more and more as an anthropologist who writes fiction, because I am always interested in the way cultures interact."[8] Her story is set in the San Fernando Valley of the Los Angeles basin, in the small town of Pacoima, or Paco, as the Chicanos call it. She and her family lived on Hoyt Street, where she situates much of her account of growing up Mexican American. She later received her BA and MA from nearby California State University, Northridge, and her PhD from the University of New Mexico, where her dissertation was on the early twentieth-century writer Fabiola Cabeza de Baca. Ponce's fictional work includes *The Wedding* (1980) and *Taking Control* (1987). The context of her *Hoyt Street* concerns the children of the immigrant generation in Chicano history. This is that generation of Mexican immigrants who arrived in the United States in the early twentieth century to find work on the railroads, in agriculture, in mining, and doing sundry other forms of unskilled labor throughout the Southwest. As I note earlier, I use the term immigrant generation even though there were subsequent generations of immigrants because at no other later time would immigrants so totally dominate the Mexican experience in the United States: economically, politically, and culturally. There are some exceptions to this domination, such as northern New Mexico, which was bypassed by the immigrant trail, but most other places were transformed from nineteenth-century Mexican American communities—the conquered generation—into Mexican immigrant ones, such as Los Angeles. By contrast, later immigrants, after the Great Depression, had to coexist with expansive generations of U.S.-born Mexican Americans. The first of such generations, the one I call the Mexican American generation in Chicano history, is Ponce's generation in part. Ponce's ethnographic autobiography, or what Pratt terms "autoethnography," examines the transculturation of the Mexican American generation through her early life up to age fourteen and that of her siblings and friends. She calls her story a communal one and a social history of her hometown, what one of her friends called Mary Helen's Macondo, in reference to Gabriel García Márquez's mythical town in *One Hundred Years of Solitude*. This generation is characterized by being bilingual and bicultural because at one level, they are affected by Americanization through school programs and mass culture, but at another level, they are able to assert their Mexican cultural roots in the creation of a syncretic and inventive hyphenated, or transcultural, position. As historical subjects, they undergo a form of cultural reconciliation as a group and as individuals.[9] In this chapter I examine how Mary Helen Ponce and the Mexican American generation of Pacoima, specifically on Hoyt Street, demonstrate these changes.

But before I do this, I want to note that the immigrant generation—the parents of the Mexican American generation—also undergoes change, or "cultural learning," but not as dramatically as their children do.[10] Just being immigrants in and of itself is already a major change. Living in Spanish-speaking immigrant communities, these immigrants were able to relocate not only themselves—their bodies—but also their culture. Through their family traditions and community building with other immigrant families, the immigrant generation was able to ameliorate Handlin's Americanizing cultural shock by living in more culturally sheltered immigrant enclaves. This was also true of other immigrants and is, in fact, an immigrant characteristic throughout the world. Despite this tendency toward cultural shelter, however, the immigrant generation did undergo some level of transculturation. Some picked up a modicum of English, perhaps at their workplaces or in contact with English-speaking Americans, for example, by working as domestics in American households. Certainly, they changed by adapting to new consumer products, such as canned foods and household goods. In their predominantly Catholic churches, members of the immigrant generation often had to deal with non-Mexican priests and nuns, since not many clergy accompanied Mexican immigrants, unlike European Catholic clergy. As part of their transculturation, some Mexican immigrants, such as Ponce's parents, were able to buy their own homes and possess a greater stake in American society. A few, like Mary Helen's father, even took the step to become U.S. citizens, while most Mexican immigrants did not, many believing that they would return someday to Mexico—not an unreasonable belief given Mexico's proximity and a land rather than a water crossing. While immigrants retained much of their mexicano way of life, they were not immune to Americanizing forces as they, historian George J. Sánchez suggests, began the process of becoming Mexican Americans.[11] This process of "becoming" involves transculturation, where dual or multiple cultures meet and are transformed into something new. Members of the immigrant generation commence this process, although they still lean more toward the mexicano side; their children would advance the process even more, to the extent that it would become quite noticeable. Adult immigrants of whatever ethnic background will always be culturally distinct in their immigrant culture, accents, and even appearance. But this changes with their U.S.-born children, who learn English in the schools as well as the history and cultural traditions of the country. They speak English with little or no accent. Their socialization is likewise influenced by American mass culture, such as movies, music, and dance. This new, more Americanized generation, the Mexican American generation, dominated the period between the 1930s and the early 1960s, prior to the Chicano Movement. By 1940, U.S.-born Mexican Americans made up the majority of people of Mexican descent in the United States. The term "Mexican-American" was coined in this era and is symbolic of the transculturation makeup of this generation. That is, this generation bridges its mexicano parental culture with the English-speaking American culture of the schools and larger society. The hyphen can be considered a syncretic symbol of the new generation and new Mexican American culture. Ponce's text reveals these transculturating influences at the grassroots level.

Before deconstructing how she does this, however, I want to note that the Mexican American generation is also important from a political perspective, as I have addressed in my research on this generation. Besides a biological Mexican American generation, which Ponce represents, there was also a political generation, which forged the first significant civil rights movement by Mexican Americans in the United States. Led by new political leaders and new organizations, such as LULAC and the American GI Forum, to name just two of the more prominent ones, this political generation stressed integrating Mexican Americans into U.S. society by breaking down the barriers of racism and discrimination that kept Mexican Americans locked out of the mainstream. This generation's political leaders focused especially on struggles to desegregate the infamous segregated and inferior "Mexican schools" of the Southwest. They further attacked discrimination in jobs, wages, public facilities, representation in juries, political representation, and stereotyping in the mass media. Although often criticized by later Chicano studies scholars as being assimilationist, this leadership supported cultural pluralism and a diverse American society.[12] This culturally pluralist perspective through the process of transculturation, or the sharing of cultures, is also evident at the community level, as we can see in Ponce's narrative.

III

Transculturation begins at home. Mexican Americans such as Ponce are primarily influenced by their mexicano home and community culture, where they first learn to speak Spanish and are socialized to a mexicano identity and culture that is representative of immigrant communities. They are part of the working-class culture of their parents. Mary Helen's father first worked in the fields and then as a self-employed hauler of wood. The mexicano influence on her was furthered by the chain migration of other relatives, arriving from Mexico to live temporarily with the Ponce family.[13] Yet, as Mexican American children grew up, generational tensions became evident. Parents were not in favor of changes they believed were diluting mexicano cultural influences. Americanization seemed to lead to their children having less respect for their parents and other elders. As children began to learn English, parents became concerned that their offspring were losing their ability to speak correct Spanish. Ponce's mother, for example, emphasized to Mary Helen and her siblings the importance of speaking Spanish correctly. Food tastes among their U.S.-born children also changed as kids developed preferences for new foods. Ponce notes the changes in dress as well, especially among her older sisters, who worked outside the home, which provided them more gender freedom and the ability to purchase stylish American outfits compared to the more modest dresses their mother wore. Still, despite these developing cultural tensions within families, the home remained a transculturating experience for Mexican Americans that nourished the Mexican side of the equation. Increasingly, however, the other side manifested itself, so that Ponce and other Mexican Americans grew up aware that, as she puts it, they lived in two worlds.[14]

IV

Schools are unquestionably the main Americanizing agents for children of immigrants of whatever background. This is certainly the case with Mexican Americans, as Ponce's story reveals. Most immigrant children first learn English in school, although some with older siblings already in school enter already knowing some English, as Mary Helen did. She notes that before entering kindergarten, she knew English, including her ABCs and numbers to one hundred.[15] But most other Mexican Americans apparently knew much less if any English. Hence, the public schools in the barrios, called "Mexican schools," from the very beginning had English-only policies. "At school," Ponce recalls, "we were constantly told: 'Speak English, English only. You're not in Mexico now.'"[16] The exclusively Anglo-American teachers in Mary Helen's school were also role models, especially if they were young, slim, and pretty, such as eighth-grade teacher Mrs. Blynders. Ponce and many other Mexican American girls wanted to look like their teacher, whom Mary Helen considered to be a "fairy-tale princess."[17] Although called "Mexican schools," these institutions aimed to deculturize and Americanize the Mexican American students. Ironically, certain aspects of the Mexican schools, at least for Ponce, actually helped preserve some aspects of Mexicanization, which ended up producing hybrid Mexican American students. For example, despite the English-only emphasis of the schools, most Mexican American students did not lose their facility with Spanish since it was replenished at home. Most if not all spoke Spanish with their parents but used English with their siblings and friends, although Ponce notes that with her friends, sometimes she spoke in Spanish.[18] Indeed, in one part of her text, she expresses pride that she was bilingual. During her family's annual late summer migration to work in the fields of Southern California, Ponce attended a special school for the children of migrant workers as well as those of the growers. Although the migrant children were made to feel their difference from the white students, when it came to reading, Mary Helen proudly displayed her bilingual reading skills. She writes, "It was only when we read aloud that I felt I was as smart as the regular students. I *was* bilingual, able to pronounce with ease the names of such early Spanish conquistadores as Cabeza de Baca, Hernán Cortés, and Ponce de León (who I inferred was a relative) . . . If nothing else, I could read with the best of them."[19] Ponce further notes that in her Pacoima elementary school, the songs that students learned were mostly in English, but some were in Spanish. For example, at Christmas time, the students sang Spanish songs such as "Noche de Paz." Other songs such as "The White Dove" were sung in both English and Spanish. And, in Mary Helen's eighth-grade class, Mrs. Blynders ordered a music book that included songs about Mexican life that were, as Ponce stresses, "in a language we were otherwise told not to use when in school."[20] Such Mexican cultural apertures in the school only reinforced a bilingual and bicultural identity for Mexican American students such as Mary Helen and represented part of the transcultural process experienced by these students, rather than a strictly linear Americanization.

Another interesting example of the Americanization of Mexican American students such as Mary Helen and of the Mexican American generation as a whole was the tendency to anglicize their first names to avoid being perceived as "the other" or as "the stranger." Either kids changed their names among themselves or teachers did it for them because they could not pronounce the Spanish names. On this, Ponce writes, "[W]e liked our names in English best, never questioning teachers who, rather than struggle with our 'foreign' names, quickly deduced their American counterparts and entered them on our school records. In time we identified with our names in English and even forgot how to spell our Spanish names."[21] Name changes also signified a generational break with parents, who had named and baptized their children with Spanish first names. Their children rebelled against this and, at least at school and among their friends, changed their names. María Elena Ponce became Mary Helen Ponce. Her siblings did the same. They became Nora, Elizabet, Berney, Joey, Ronnie, and Norbert. Her friends also changed their names. Santos became Sandy. "My good friend Teresa López went from 'Theresa' to 'Tere' to 'Terry' in one week," Ponce observes. She notes that the name Terry was "the current rage."[22] At the same time, not all her friends changed their names. The sister of her friend Sandy insisted that she be called Ana Teresa. Moreover, not all teachers changed Spanish names to English ones, and her principal at school, Mrs. Goodsome, attempted to pronounce Spanish names correctly.[23] In addition, even though students such as Mary Helen changed their first names or liked having them changed, many in turn invented Spanish or bilingual nicknames for each other. Nita became "la mocosa" because she refused to wipe her nose; Virgie became "la mioña" because she once had peed in her pants; and Nancy was "la volada" because she liked to flirt with the boys. Another friend was nicknamed "El Bugs Bunny" because of his buckteeth.[24] These examples of reversions to the use of Spanish reflect the more nuanced process of cultural change linking the Mexican to the American to produce something uniquely Mexican American.

V

Still another example of a transcultural experience was and still is the practice by bilingual sons and daughters to translate for their parents. The Mexican American generation became a translating and interpreting generation, bridging themselves between their Spanish-speaking parents and the larger English-speaking world. In the Ponce family, the children, both older and younger, served as translators for their parents. Elizabet translated English-language mail for her mother; Mary Helen translated the English newspaper to her symbolic grandmother, Doña Luisa. At Sunday evening English-language movies shown in the church hall, Ponce provided a running commentary to Doña

Luisa and her Spanish-speaking friends. Sometimes, however, Mary Helen could not think of the correct Spanish word and ended up improvising, which often confused more than enlightened Doña Luisa and her friends.[25] And, in a sense, Ponce in her autobiography further serves as a translator for us.

VI

Mass cultural influences along with the schools were a major force for cultural changes and innovations. The movies were perhaps the most significant influence. Young Mexican Americans loved Hollywood films and attempted to look and act like their favorite film stars. By comparison, they saw their parents as old-fashioned. Mary Helen's older sisters, for example, took to wearing the tight skirts that female stars wore.[26] Mexican American females, in particular, associated slim bodies with American culture, and some, like Mary Helen, who were chubby probably associated that with being Mexican. As Ponce puts it, "In the movies the slender girl always got her man."[27] Starlets who were especially idolized by her and her friends included Hedy Lamarr and "la Rita Hayworth." The mention of Rita Hayworth is of particular interest since she was actually Mexican, having been born in Tijuana as Rita Cansino. It is doubtful that Mexican Americans were aware of this, however, since Hayworth seems to have kept this a secret in order to pass as white. A particular favorite of Ponce's older sisters was Joan Crawford. Trina, for example, attempted to arch her eyebrows just like Crawford. Besides going to see movies, Mexican American youth avidly read movie magazines.[28] While Hollywood films helped Americanize Mexican Americans, other circumstances associated with moviegoing complicated this process and led to a more transcultural one. For one, Mexican Americans saw English-language films in segregated theaters, which only brought attention to their Mexicanness. According to Ponce, theaters that catered to European Americans did not officially deny entrance to Mexican Americans, but it was common knowledge that they were not welcomed there. Moreover, the only theater in nearby San Fernando that catered to Mexican Americans also showed Mexican movies. Mary Helen notes that she also liked these films, especially with stars of Mexico's golden age of filmmaking, such as María Félix and Jorge Negrete. After World War II, other theaters openly allowed entrance to Mexican Americans.[29] Of this desegregation, Ponce observes, "Not until after World War II did Mexican-Americans become socially acceptable at local movie houses and restaurants. Men from the barrio, it became known, were also wounded and killed while fighting for their country, the good old USA. It was unpatriotic to turn away nonwhites in uniform, especially those with medals and Purple Hearts pinned to their chests."[30] This cultural duality associated with moviegoing and movie influences, however, only added to the bicultural nature of the Mexican American generation.

VII

In addition to English-language films, Mexican Americans were also influenced by American music and dance. Young Mexican American women such as Mary Helen's older sisters joined their white counterparts in swooning over Frank Sinatra. Some also liked black singers, such as the young Fats Domino. Ponce's younger brother, Joey, learned to play jazz on the saxophone.[31] Their sister Trina and her friends loved to dance to American music. "They experimented with 'slow dancing,' a style popular in the Los Angeles dancehalls," Ponce writes, "which allowed couples to hold each other close and to slide back and forth in time to the sultry music. Now and then the girls jitterbugged, twirling away for hours, until they fell to the floor from exhaustion. Once they had rested, back they went to dancing the very latest and most 'hip' steps."[32] Clearly influenced by black music, Ponce's sisters used slang such as "cool it" and "chick." They referred to guys who dressed sharp as "cool cats" and to others as "squares."[33] At the same time, Mexican Americans were not completely turned off to Mexican music played on Spanish-language radio stations and heard at home. Some even liked it, including singers such as Jorge Negrete.[34] In fact, as Anthony Macías documents in his insightful book *Mexican American Mojo*, Mexican American musicians before and after the war experimented with synthesizing Mexican and Latino musical forms with American ones, such as jazz and swing.[35] Musical and dance tastes along with musical production only added to Mexican Americans' transcultural reaction to mass culture.

VIII

Finally, World War II proved to be a major Americanizing experience for the Mexican American generation. Estimates range from 350,000 to 500,000

Latinos, mostly Mexican Americans, who saw military duty during the war. These men are part of the greatest generation. For most, it was the first time they had left their hometowns. They now scattered throughout the states for their military training, in contact for the first time with many other ethnic Americans. Many, of course, saw action in Europe and in the Pacific. Many never returned, and those who did came back either physically or emotionally wounded or both. Despite lingering stereotypes that somehow Chicanos and Latinos do not really want to be part of the United States, the fact is that Mexican Americans and other Latinos have spilled blood in all of America's wars, including in Iraq and Afghanistan. There is no greater proof of loyalty to one's country than putting your life on the line for it.

In her autobiography, Ponce notes the impact of World War II on Pacoima, on Hoyt Street, and on her family. Many of the young Mexican American men in the community either volunteered or were drafted into the military. Those who enlisted on their own preferred the Marines because of the attractive dress uniform as well as for its reputation of machismo. Brother Berney wanted to join his friends in the service but was declared 4-F, or ineligible, due to a hearing problem. He felt shame for not being in the war and embarrassed that his friends might think he did not have the courage to fight. Many friends, including boyfriends of Mary Helen's older sisters, went to war. Mary Helen recalls that she and her preadolescent girlfriends were attracted to the military uniforms worn by Mexican Americans except for the army one, which they disliked. They wished that they were old enough to date the guys in uniform. She writes of the great outpouring of community sentiment to the burial of Daniel Torres, who received the Congressional Medal of Honor for his valor. Torres was one of many other Mexican Americans who won this highest honor during the war. But the war did not just affect the young men; some Mexican American women also served in the military, although not in combat duty, and many more, like her older sisters, went to work in the new defense industries in Southern California—these women can all be considered part of the greatest generation.[36] While the war proved to be a major socialization tool of patriotism and Americanization, it also possessed a transcultural side, in that the immigrant parents and, indeed, the entire Mexican community of Pacoima, both U.S. born and immigrant, participated in supporting the war and in celebrating the U.S. victory, as Ponce writes: "Many families on our street were affected by the war. Those who could afford to, bought war bonds; others stuck gold and silver stars on the front door, anxious for neighbors to know that someone in their family was fighting or had died for his country. Young girls with boyfriends in the army and navy sold war bonds as part of the war effort."[37] In this way, all Mexicans were affected by the war and, in turn, contributed to the war effort. Moreover, when Mexican Americans *veteranos* returned from the war, many discovered that while they had been fighting to preserve democratic freedoms, they were still denied many of these freedoms at home through continued segregation and discrimination. As such, Mexican American veterans forged an accelerated civil rights movement in the postwar period, influenced by their socialization in the war, but also by their commitment to having their ethnicity and culture respected.

IX

Mary Helen Ponce's *Hoyt Street*, in my opinion, is one of the best autobiographical texts written by a Chicano/Chicana writer. While it lacks the fascinating introspectiveness of Richard Rodriguez's classic *Hunger of Memory*, it compensates for this by its rich ethnographic depiction of Mexican immigrant and Mexican American family and community life. Furthermore, as an example of transcultural generational changes between immigrants and especially U.S.-born Mexican Americans, *Hoyt Street* is a valuable contribution from a historical and an anthropological perspective. As such, Ponce's text not only debunks many stereotypes about Mexicans in the United States, but also reveals the more intricate, nuanced, and creative nature of Chicano identity and culture. As a historian who works on such issues, I take much from this text about Mexican everyday life in the United States.

4

AMERICANIZATION, ETHNICITY, AND SEXUALITY

The Triple Consciousness of
Richard Rodriguez and John Rechy

I

A T THE BEGINNING of the twentieth century, the great African American civil rights leader and intellectual W. E. B. Du Bois addressed what he referred to as the double consciousness of African Americans in the United States. He ascribed to them a dilemma of having to reconcile their national identity as U.S.-born Americans with their racial and ethnic identity as Negroes, the term prevalent in Du Bois's times. This dialectic was rooted in their historic racialized subjugation, first as slaves and then after emancipation as second-class citizens considered racially inferior to whites. They were Americans but black Americans, and the interstitial space between the two created what Karl Gunnar Myrdal later called "An American (Black) Dilemma." They were never allowed to see themselves as whole, experiencing only a divided self. Of this identity crisis, Du Bois wrote in *The Souls of Black Folk* (1903), "It is a peculiar sensation, this double-consciousness, this sense of always looking at one's self through the eyes of others, of measuring one's soul by the tape of a world that looks on in amused contempt and pity. One ever feels his two-ness,—an American, a Negro, two souls, two thoughts, two unreconciled strivings; two warring ideals in one dark body; whose dogged strength alone keeps it from being torn asunder."[1]

Mexican Americans along with other Latinos in the United States have also had to face such a duality, as have other discriminated-against American ethnic groups, until the point where they are assimilated as full white Americans.

This latter distinction has on the whole not pertained to Mexicans because of their permanent racialization by white America. Conquered as a people in what became the American Southwest in the U.S.-Mexico War (1846–48), dispossessed of their lands, contracted and exploited as immigrant workers into the twentieth century, Mexicans and their Mexican American children were likewise treated as an inferior race ("dirty Mexicans") and excluded from the American dream. They were Americans or became Americans but were never treated as such. The term "Mexican American" in part suggested their version of Du Bois's double consciousness.

But while this duality is related to race and class discrimination, it also stems from the second-generation experience of many Mexican Americans. They are the products of Mexican immigrant parents as well as of their own acculturation or transculturation as they come of age in the United States. Although they retain certain aspects of their parents' immigrant culture—*lo mexicano*—by a process referred to as "selective acculturation," they also become Americanized through their education and the influence of American mass culture. They become Mexican Americans, or hyphenated Americans. They experience their own version of mestizaje, the bridging of cultures or the invention of a new syncretic culture. They are who they are. Still, despite this inventiveness, they experience seeming contradictions. Are they Americans? Are they Mexicans? Who are they? These tensions emanate from both inside and outside their cultural position. Inside, they are made to feel inadequate because they do not speak Spanish as well their parents and do not adhere to all their family traditions. They are "pochos," or Americanized Mexicans. On the outside, they are still seen by white Americans as Mexicans, strangers, immigrants, "illegal aliens," and un-American. This is their dilemma.[2]

My field of Chicano studies has grappled with such issues of identity, or double identity, affecting Chicanos (a barrio term for Mexican Americans). Born out of the cultural nationalism of the Chicano Movement of the late 1960s and 1970s, Chicano studies on the whole has projected an ethnic/cultural nationalist or modernist view of identity based on the "authentic Chicano." This is a Chicano identity rooted in an "authentic culture," with linkages to *indigenismo*, the Mexican Revolution of 1910, *pachuquismo* (or the cult of the pachuco), hard-core barrio life, and a rejection of Americanization. I am generalizing here because obviously there have been cleavages in this essentialist notion of identity, or what Emma Pérez calls third-space opposition, especially from internationalist, socialist, gender, and sexual interventions.[3] Nevertheless, Chicano studies still bears the legacy of the Chicano Movement's nationalist agenda, or what is determined to be that essentialist legacy. In this agenda, issues such as assimilation and acculturation are anathema since they convey a betrayal of the home culture and identity. Change is arrested in order to assert a changeless Chicano identity—*órale!* Yet the contradiction here is that the Chicano Movement and Chicano studies themselves were and are expressions of acculturation or transculturation in that they reflect a hybrid experience, as U.S.-born Mexican Americans become "Chicanos."[4]

Nevertheless, such a totalizing assertion of culture and identity has affected how Chicano studies has reacted to writers who, for example, seem to be out of step with the imagined world of the field. I maintain that this has been the case with both Richard Rodriguez and John Rechy. There is no question that Rodriguez was made into the epitome of the Tío Taco or brown Uncle Tom when his classic autobiography, *Hunger of Memory*, was published in 1982. He was excoriated for what appeared to be his rejection of his parents' Mexican immigrant culture and his full embrace of the American dream. For all practical purposes, *Hunger of Memory* was blacklisted from Chicano studies. By contrast, the reaction to Rechy has been more muted, and as Beth Hernández-Jason notes in her work on Rechy, some Chicano studies critics have included him as a Chicano writer.[5] Despite this, reluctance to fully embrace him as a Chicano writer remains, because of what is perceived as his non-Chicano writing and Americanized identity, a perception that may stem in part from his surname. He is also incorrectly seen as only a "gay writer" and not a "Chicano writer." Of course, Rechy like Rodriguez should be regarded as simply a great American writer. What I am suggesting, however, is that many Chicano studies scholars are not integrating his writings into their curriculum because they incorrectly believe that his work is not relevant to Chicano studies.

This chapter is an attempt to challenge these perceptions of Rodriguez and Rechy by examining their complex and hybrid identities through the lens of Du Bois's double consciousness, expanded to an even more involved triple consciousness, which includes Rodriguez's and Rechy's negotiations of their American identities, their Mexican American or Chicano identities, and their sexual identities as gay men. I analyze their autobiographical texts—Rodriguez's *Hunger of Memory* (1982) and Rechy's *About My Life and the Kept Woman* (2008)— from my vantage as a historian and not as a literary critic.[6] My appreciation of both writers' negotiations of their identities is based on my own historical studies of the evolving identities of Chicanos in the United States as they move from generations of Mexican immigrants to second-generation U.S.-born Mexican Americans or Chicanos. Confrontation with a double consciousness has been and still is quite a challenge, much less having to also confront one's nonheteronormative sexual identity, as Rodriguez and Rechy do. Being a U.S.-born American of Mexican or other Latino descent as well as being gay is not easy in a nativist, racist, and homophobic society. Moreover, I approach these life stories as historical documents that inform us not only about the past, but also about our present evolving confrontation over the meaning of being an American.

II

Let me first deal with the American identity of Rodriguez and Rechy. Like all second-generation ethnics or children of immigrants, both are not immigrants but U.S.-born Mexicans. Their birthplace already determines their sense of being American, whether others accept this or not. But even more central to this process is their education in English-language schools. The schools have historically been the main transmitters of acculturation, or Americanization. Rodriguez's attendance at Catholic schools in Sacramento accelerated this journey. Indeed, public schools as well as Catholic schools in the United States during the early part of the twentieth century included what were literally referred to as Americanization programs, aimed at the children of European immigrants—the so-called New Immigrants, composed of such groups as Italians, Poles, and Russians. In the Southwest, including California, Americanization programs in the schools were primarily focused on Mexican American children. These programs were intended to instill American historical and cultural traditions, centered on learning English and discarding the immigrant or foreign cultural baggage of the students. These programs were intended to produce a "new American" who would be loyal to his or her country and not in any way challenge the prevailing system.[7]

Rodriguez notes that his Americanization was affected by the fact that most of his schoolmates were white middle-class children, as were the teaching nuns. Learning English and Anglo-American culture began to transform the young Richard. In these schools he became a "scholarship boy." He began to feel the pull of the new culture and identity as well as his growing separation from his mostly Spanish-speaking parents. "It is education that has altered my life," he writes.[8] In time, he began to believe that he could not reconcile his new American identity, acquired at school, with the Mexican identity of his home. Thus commences the double consciousness. "The scholarship boy does not straddle, cannot reconcile, the two great opposing cultures of his life," he concludes.[9]

English acquired at school without doubt is the most visible marker of acculturation that affects second-generation ethnics. It is the entryway into their new American life and culture. Many do not completely lose their parents' language, such as Spanish, so they transition as bilingual and bicultural ethnics, although not without tension between the two poles. Some, such as Rodriguez, begin to lose most of their facility with Spanish. Language changes in first names are one of the first signs of this acculturation. For example, María becomes Mary, or "la Mary." José become Joe or Joey. In Rodriguez's case, not only did the nuns change his name from Ricardo to Richard, but they also attempted to Americanize his surname. Rodriguez remembers the first time he experienced this transformation: "The nun said, in a friendly but oddly impersonal voice, 'Boys and girls, this is Richard Rodriguez.' (I heard her sound out: Rich-heard Road-ree—guess.) It was the first time I had heard anyone name me in English."[10] Richard would pronounce it the same afterward. In one of the most controversial aspects of his autobiography, Rodriguez maintains that he came to learn in school that English was a public language and the entryway into American society, as opposed to his or his parents' private home language, Spanish. I say controversial since Spanish has now become the unofficial second language in the United States, and one can argue that it has attained the status of a public language along with English. Nevertheless, for Rodriguez growing up, his sense was that only English could occupy that linguistic space. English to him was not only a language of educational mobility but also a part of his birthright as a U.S. citizen. It wasn't a privilege but a right by birth. "What I needed to learn in school," he asserts, "was that I had the right—and the obligation—to speak the public language of los gringos."[11] Yet, he soon came to recognize that becoming English dominant also began to separate him from his parents' world. But Richard perceived this as inevitable, not a choice. He observes, "After English became my primary language, I no longer knew what words to use in addressing my parents."[12] English gave the young Richard a level of authority over his parents in that he now corrected their mistakes in English.

Despite a growing estrangement between Richard and his parents over language, his parents agreed to speak only English—their limited English—at home after one of the nuns requested they do so to facilitate Richard's mastery of the language. No doubt painful for them, his parents agreed because of their interpretation of immigrant success. Immigrant parents often envision success not by their own limited mobility but by that of their children. This means supporting education for their offspring and making cultural compromises at home. This is not always the case, however, because Mexican immigrant fathers often authoritatively insist: "Dentro de mi casa es México, afuera es los estados unidos." Rodriguez's father did not espouse this view, or at least not in all instances. "For their children," Rodriguez writes, "my parents wanted chances they never had—an easier way. It saddened my mother to learn that some relatives forced their children to start working right after high school. To 'her' children she would say, 'Get all the education you can.' In schooling she recognized the key to job advancement."[13]

Through the schools and by learning English, Rodriguez, like other children of immigrants, empowered himself. The Chicano Movement and Chicano studies perceive that acculturation as a loss, but it leads to empowerment. That is, by learning English and American ways, second-generation Chicanos/Latinos have been better able to understand their rights and to articulate their interests and concerns, including demanding their rights. They can speak directly to the system—a system they understand through their education. The second generation, for example, can go to school boards and address the problems of the schools for their children. Immigrant parents cannot do this or certainly cannot do it as well. It is no accident of history that second-generation American ethnics, not immigrants, are the ones who lead civil rights struggles. This has certainly been true in Chicano history—beginning in the 1930s, the Mexican American generation forged the first significant civil rights movement by Mexicans in the United States. The succeeding political generation, the Chicano generation—also composed of predominantly second- and even third-generation Mexican Americans—militantly expanded not only a civil rights agenda, but also a community empowerment struggle (self-determination).[14]

Through his own acculturation, Rodriguez learned to appreciate this empowerment. Acculturation in his terms meant becoming a "public man." As a public man he could function in an English-speaking environment. At the same time, he acknowledges that acculturation also represented a loss of what he refers to as the "private self," meaning his Spanish-speaking parental culture. But there is no other way, he believes, to achieve mobility in American society as well as empower one's self. This is why, in one of the other more controversial parts of his story, he challenges the Chicano argument for bilingual education. For Rodriguez, you can't have it both ways. You can't have a private self (Spanish speaking) and a public self (English speaking). While his views on the efficacy of bilingual education can certainly be challenged, the fact is that all second-generation ethnics attain whatever empowerment and even mobility they achieve as a result of their acculturation, and that has meant mastery of English and American ways. On this, Rodriguez concludes, "Only when I was able to think of myself as an American, no longer an alien in gringo society, could I seek the rights and opportunities necessary for full public individuality. The social and political advantages I enjoy as a man result from the day that I came to believe that my name, indeed, is Rich-heard Road-ree-guess."[15]

Rodriguez comes to eventually see himself as a middle-class American. This is the core of his identity. He knows that he has changed, and that this change means some loss of his parental culture, but in the exchange he is better off as an American. Yet Rodriguez also correctly understands that there never really was a choice anyway. The children of Mexican and Latino immigrants go to English-speaking schools and live in an English-speaking mass cultural world, so acculturation is inevitable. You can affect or perhaps even control the degree and extent of acculturation, but you can't prevent it. You look ahead, not behind. That is why he challenged, at least in his mind and writing, Chicano Movement activists and intellectuals who asserted that they could be U.S. born and still retain their indigenous, mestizo, mexicano identity as Chicanos. "Aztec ruins hold no interest for me," Rodriguez critically pronounces.[16] These Chicanos believed, Rodriguez comments, that there was no separation between them and their immigrant parents. The truth is, of course, as Rodriguez correctly observes in his own life, that there is a separation, and that it is a predictable one. This does not mean, I would add to Richard, that no connections exist; this is where selective acculturation and transculturation come into play, but second-generation Mexican Americans are not immigrants, and they are not their parents. This recognition lends itself to the invention of a new identity appropriate to being a U.S.-born ethnic. It represents a third space, where a creative amalgamation of cultures takes place. Rodriguez does not recognize this space, believing that one has to choose between being Mexican and being American, even though he cannot fully escape the pull of this duality. His effort to go from one to the other leads Rodriguez to conclude about his autobiography, "This is my story. An American story."[17]

III

John Rechy's American identity also commenced with his education, but in El Paso, in an earlier period, during the late 1930s and the 1940s. Born of a

Mexican immigrant mother and a Scottish Spanish father who was raised in Mexico, Rechy first identified as Mexican. Like Rodriguez, however, his education moved him into double consciousness by inventing his American identity, which became his dominant one. This process began in elementary school, a mixed school of Anglos and Mexican Americans since Rechy lived in a transition area between predominantly Mexican El Paso and Anglo El Paso. As such, he was spared having to attend one of the notorious "Mexican schools" of South El Paso, or El Segundo Barrio. The legacy of the segregated and inferior Mexican schools, however, still affected those Mexican Americans who attended "integrated" schools, where they faced being segregated in their classrooms, ostensibly because of language difference, although the main factor was racism. In these schools, the equally notorious tracking system often placed Mexican American students in vocational classes, where the emphasis was to teach them to work with their hands, not their heads, based on the racist notions that they were not as mentally advanced as the Anglo students.[18]

If Rechy's family had remained in their neighborhood, which was becoming mostly Mexican, he would have had to attend Bowie High School, the Mexican high school. But when the Rechy family moved just north of the tracks, into central El Paso, after Rechy graduated from elementary school, he could now attend the "Anglo" El Paso High School. Although some more mobile Mexican Americans also attended this school, they were a minority. They and Rechy were exposed to better education at El Paso High, but Rechy added to his American identity by "passing" as white due to his biracial background, which gave him his light complexion and light-colored hair. He didn't necessarily desire to be accepted as white, but it proved to be the line of least resistance.

The issue of "whiteness" for Mexican Americans has always proved to be a dilemma. Although most people of Mexican descent were and are mestizos, the product of biological mixing after the Spanish conquest of the indigenous people of Mexico, they were incorporated as "white" Americans after the U.S.-Mexico War (1846–48), when the United States conquered and annexed Mexico's El Norte—everything from Texas to California. Yet, the new Mexican Americans—whom I refer to as the conquered generation in Chicano history—were never treated as white and very quickly became a racialized subaltern group, looked down on as an inferior race of people. The same pertained to the thousands of Mexican immigrants who crossed the border in the early twentieth century, escaping poverty and land dispossession as well as fleeing the ravages of the Mexican Revolution of 1910. These immigrant workers and their families were subjected to "Mexican jobs," "Mexican wages," "Mexican schools," and "Mexican barrios."[19] Within this racial setting, the issue of whiteness created complex dilemmas for Mexicans, since they spanned the phenotype spectrum from very dark to very light. As a result, some could pass for "white" at least biologically if not culturally. This was part of Rechy's own personal double consciousness.

Rechy recalls this consciousness in his autobiography when he writes about his acculturation in high school and yet still retaining his awareness of his "racial" background:

> My "Anglo" coloring contributed to allowing me to become a "popular student" at El Paso High School, a position I sought aggressively, becoming, eventually, president of several clubs, a student council representative, and . . . editor of the school paper, *The Tattler*. Still, my ambiguous identity as a *guerro* exiled me doubly. Other Mexican students were cool. Among "rich Anglos" who did not know I was Mexican, I felt like a trespasser.[20]

Nevertheless, Rechy thrived in this Americanized environment. Already proficient in English from his early schooling, he plunged into his studies, especially his growing love of literature. He read widely and beyond his assigned reading. This included authors such as Hawthorne, Poe, Melville, Emily Brontë, Dos Passos, James Farrell, and even books banned by his own Catholic Church, such as Kathleen Winsor's *Forever Amber*. His success as his own version of Rodriguez's "scholarship boy" was marked by graduating in the top ten of his senior class of several hundred. At his graduation ceremony, his teachers assigned him to read a patriotic speech: "I am democracy in action. I am the United States."[21]

Rechy's sense of his American identity led him to go on to college. Not only was he encouraged to do so as a "white" student, but he also had the example of his older brother Yvan, who after being in the military in World War II used the GI Bill to attend college. In college, Rechy furthered his attraction to literature by majoring in English, adding to his reading repertory books by Milton, Pope, Dryden, Donne, Swift, James Joyce, and Gertrude Stein among many others. He also became the controversial editor of *El Burro*, the campus literary magazine, which Rechy tried to turn into a more experimental and avant-garde publication, only to be forced to resign because of this.

As with Rodriguez, Rechy's Americanization had a lot to do with his mastery of English. The language also became his entry into education and social mobility. It defined him as an American, and in the perception of Anglos, he was a "white" American. If Ricardo Rodriguez became Rich-heard Road-ree-guess, then Juan Rechy became John or Johnny Rechy. The name change in Rechy's case began in kindergarten, when his Anglo teacher told him: "I'm going to call you Johnny.... You look much more like a Johnny than a Juan."[22]

Rechy's acculturation had much to do with his "looking American." He did not have to confront the issue of race daily, as did most other, darker-skinned Mexican Americans. He and other lighter-skinned Mexican Americans could avoid this by allowing themselves to be considered whites. For example, a Mexican American girl that he liked in high school had falsified her name from Alicia Gonzales to Isabel Franklin in order to pass for white. She also lied about living in South El Paso to be able to attend El Paso High. On their one and only date, Rechy, who was aware of this subterfuge from his older sister, pretended to go along with it, since he was also permitting himself to pass for white, or at least not overtly asserting his Mexican background. But this passing gave Rechy concern. "I became sure—as I was sure she was sure—that we, Isabel Franklin and I, were aware of each other as vague conspirators in exile, looking as if we 'belonged' but not belonging, or perhaps really even wanting to belong."[23] Moreover, Rechy's initial experience in heterosexual sex probably was the result of his looking white. In an erotic passage in his autobiography, Rechy describes how he was seduced by his young female high school teacher in her apartment. Given the racialized sexual boundaries even in a more liberal border city like El Paso, it is doubtful that his teacher would have engaged in what may have amounted to illegal sex with a minor if Rechy had appeared Mexican.

Appearing American even affected his family relations and exposed how some Mexicans on both sides of the border prioritized whiteness. When his uncle's wife organized a *quinceañera* for her daughter in Juárez, across the border from El Paso, she asked Rechy's mother if her son could be her daughter's escort. Rechy demurred, exposing his reluctance to participate in a Mexican ceremony marking the coming-of-age (fifteenth) birthday for Mexican girls. "'I don't understand why they want me to be the escort,' I told my mother," Rechy recalls. "As if it were merely to be taken for granted—nothing exceptional—my mother said 'Because you look like an American.'"[24]

Rechy's American identity was also the result of growing up during World War II, when as many as half a million Latinos, mostly Mexican Americans, joined the military to fight the "Good War." This included his two older brothers. Many other young Mexican American men also joined or were drafted.

The war proved to be a major opportunity for Mexican Americans to prove their loyalty and patriotism toward the United States. It further represented a significant socializing experiment for Mexican Americans in that they accepted the ideology of fighting for the preservation of American democracy and made this part of their identity. But most of all, putting your life on the line for your country said it all for these Americans of Mexican descent. In El Paso, the young Rechy was very much aware of this Americanizing influence of the war. In addition to his family, he noticed how many other families had sons in the military. Almost every home, according to Rechy, displayed a cross signaling that a family member, perhaps more than one, was in the military. If the cross was replaced with a gold one, it meant that someone from that family had died in battle. There were many crosses and many gold ones in the Mexican American neighborhoods.

This linkage of military service with one's Americanization affected Rechy himself in time. After he graduated from Texas Western College in El Paso, he decided to join the army during the Korean War (1950–52). While he was not sent to the war, Rechy, like his brothers, was prepared to sacrifice his life for his country. Like the character of Richard Rubio in José Villarreal's 1959 novel *Pocho*, who joins the military to find his American identity, Rechy added to his view of himself as an American by going into the army.[25] This was not easy for him, but he felt the need to do so. He would especially miss his mother and recalls thinking, "Leaving my mother—especially leaving her still in the projects—was one of the most mournful moments in my life."[26]

IV

Despite Rodriguez's and Rechy's acculturation as Americans and their invention of an American identity for themselves, neither could ignore or shed the other side of Du Bois's dialectic, their consciousness of being of Mexican descent—their Mexican identity. In their autobiographies both consciously reveal this double identity, perhaps as a way of compensating for not favoring this part of their lives. In their memories they can at least try to make amends as they, in Rodriguez's words, feel the "hunger of memory," their Mexican memories. This Mexicanness was to a degree inescapable since it began at home and with their mostly if not exclusively Spanish-speaking parents. Rodriguez, for example, was the child of working-class Mexican immigrants. Within the family, he came to distinguish between what he calls a "private" family culture as opposed to a "public" outside society. One is Spanish speaking and Mexican, and the other is English speaking and Anglo-American. As Rodriguez went through school, he came more and more to distinguish these two environments. He was aware of the Mexican, and it affected his view of himself, but he came to be embarrassed by it and attempted to separate himself from his parents, a trope for being Mexican. "I was not proud of my mother and father," he writes. "I was embarrassed by their lack of education. It was not that I ever thought they were stupid, though stupidly I took for granted their enormous native intelligence. Simply, what mattered to me was that they were not like my teacher."[27]

Language above all reminded Richard of his Mexicanness, or at least of his family. Spanish was the language of home, of his parents. "*Español*: my family's language that seemed to me a private language."[28] Although conceding that their children, including Richard, were becoming more facile in English, his parents still attempted to preserve as much Spanish as possible and by extension Mexican culture as part of their children's heritage. At dinner, for example, they played word games in which the parents and the kids invented new words using English verbs, but giving them Spanish endings. Despite these efforts, Richard grew less and less comfortable with Spanish and with the efforts through language to maintain in him his Mexican heritage. "My parents would say something to me and I would feel embarrassed by the sound of their words," Rodriguez with guilt admits. "These sounds said: *I am speaking with ease in Spanish. I am addressing you in words I never use with los gringos. I recognize you as someone special, close, like no one outside. You belong with us. In the family. (Ricardo).*"[29] Part of Rodriguez's Mexican identity, whether he willed it or not, resulted from the role he had to play growing up as a translator and interpreter for his parents. This is a role that all second-generation ethnics also assume. Being bilingual or still knowing enough Spanish, for example, the children of immigrants translate and interpret for their non-English-speaking parents. The second generation is a translating generation. They are the go-betweens for their parents' immigrant culture and the rest of American society. Rodriguez recalls doing this for his mother and for his grandmother at the local supermarket.

But the second generation, or at least some, like Rodriguez, find it hard to be translators as they lose more and more of their parents' language. The young Richard was reminded of this, and as such of his Mexicanness, when Spanish-speaking relatives visited his home and made him feel ashamed of his loss while scolding his parents for allowing it. These relatives called him a "pocho," or the diminutive "pochito," derogatory terms used by Mexicanos for those they consider to be Americanized Mexicans. Rodriguez recounts one incident when one of his uncles attempted to shame him and his parents. "After listening to me, he looked away and said what a disgrace it was that I couldn't speak Spanish, 'su propio idioma.'"[30]

Even in adulthood, despite his American mobility and American identity, Rodriguez was reminded of his Mexicanness by others, who assumed that because of his surname and his strong Indian, or mestizo, features that he was still very mexicano. This is not an unusual situation for second-generation Mexican Americans and other Latinos, and some can rise to the occasion because they have remained bilingual and bicultural; however, others such as Rodriguez are put in a very difficult situation that they often have to explain unsatisfactorily to their confronters. Richard got this reaction from both the Right and the Left. The latter saw the Americanized Richard, with his public reservations about bilingual education and affirmative action, as a brown Uncle Tom, a Tío Taco. And on the Right, after courting him because of his controversial views, he is still reminded of his Mexicanness, even here at one of the many lunches and dinners to which he was invited to speak: "A dainty white lady at the women's club luncheon," Rodriguez recalls one of these incidents, "approaches the podium after my speech to say, after all, wasn't it a shame that I wasn't able to 'use' my Spanish in school. What a shame."[31]

Rodriguez resented such reactions to him, but these and his family situations continued to remind him of his Mexican side, which he could not escape, especially since his very body and surname called out to him in Spanish. This was his double consciousness.

V

John Rechy, like Rodriguez, also could not avoid or escape his Mexican identity, which shaped part of who he was. This identity likewise began at home with his Spanish-speaking parents. His mother spoke only Spanish. His father knew English but preferred Spanish at home, including with his children. Rechy recalls that his mother never learned English because she believed that this would be a betrayal of her culture and mother country. As a result of first speaking Spanish at home, Rechy did not know English when he started kindergarten. He notes that his awareness of being Mexican was brought to bear his first day in school, when the teacher was separating the Mexican children from the Anglo ones, assuming that the Mexican children spoke only Spanish. Because Rechy looked "American," she first separated him with the Anglos. When one of the Anglo students spoke to him in English, however, Rechy responded in Spanish, to the consternation of his teacher. "Overhearing me," he remembers still with some disturbance, "the teacher—a deadly frown crinkling her white-powdered forehead—yanked me back, mumbling something, while leading me back to rejoin those still in the classroom."[32] And later in college, when he and his girlfriend, Barbara, decided to do an English translation of Lorca's *Bodas de Sangre* (Blood Wedding), she inadvertently prompted Rechy to admit his Mexican background. "'Wait now,' Barbara said, 'Do you know Spanish?' 'My mother is Mexican,' I said."[33]

In addition to Spanish, Mexican home culture also connected Rechy to his ethnic roots. His family celebrated his mother's birthday not on her actual birth date, but on the feast day of Our Lady of Guadalupe since that was his mother's name. His father, a professional musician, arranged for other musicians to serenade his wife in the early morning with the traditional Mexican birthday song "Las Mañanitas." Growing up, Rechy's mother would take him and his siblings to the Colón Theater, the only Mexican Spanish–language movie house in El Paso. When his sister got married, it was a Mexican wedding in the main Mexican Catholic Church in South El Paso.

Rechy's sense of being Mexican was further augmented when later, by the time he attended the local college, his parents had to move into public housing, the projects in the barrio, because of worsening family economic conditions. There the Rechys lived among predominantly Mexican families with the sound of Spanish in every building. "Now I lived in the Second Ward," Rechy notes, "the section of the city identified as the 'poor Mexican section.'"[34] He lamented this not so much because it made him feel Mexican, but because it brought attention to their poor circumstances. This feeling was compounded by the fact that other Mexicans there, especially the notorious pachucos—countercultural street dudes—rejected him as a real Chicano. They thought he was an Anglo. These uncomfortable feelings, reflecting both ethnic and class sentiments, made Rechy hope that, especially for his mother's sake, the family might be able to leave the barrio, particularly the projects, which, as he writes, "branded us as poor Mexicans."[35]

But more than anything, what made Rechy aware of his mexicanidad was the racism against Mexicans that he observed and personally experienced in

El Paso. "I had witnessed many manifestations of discrimination in El Paso against Mexicans—there were very few 'Negroes' then in the city. Anglo waitresses at the Newberry lunch counter pointedly hesitated to wait on Mexicans, so that, often, a family so disdained would walk away."[36] Rechy asserts that while he never denied that he was Mexican, he did not publicly confront or oppose such racism.

Racism did affect him personally on some occasions. One involved inviting an Anglo girl to his high school senior prom. Most other Mexican American boys dated only Mexican American girls. The girl, Virginia Taylor, accepted Rechy's invitation and agreed for him to pick her up to go to the dance. Yet, when Rechy called her home on the day of the prom to get her address, Virginia's mother refused to let him speak to her daughter. "I know who you are, boy," Rechy with anger still recalls her words, "Over my dead body will my daughter go out with a Mexican." She then spat into the telephone and hung up. Rechy notes that after his anger calmed down, he thought, *"How the hell did that bitch know that I'm Mexican?"*[37]

The racism in other parts of West Texas, even more overt than in El Paso, was brought to Rechy's attention when in college he accepted an invitation from two Anglo friends, Scott and Ross, to visit Ross's aunt at her ranch. Before they had dinner with her, Rechy and his friends decided to attend the only movie theater in the small town and one of the few places with air conditioning to escape the intense heat of the summer.

Rechy's friends had no idea that he was Mexican. When they bought their tickets, the cashier told them, "Now you city boys be sure to sit on the left side, ya heah? Right side's for spics, Saturday afternoon's spic day."[38] This racist statement created an almost existential crisis for Rechy, who paused in the entryway and questioned which side he should sit in. He began to move to the right side only to encounter surprised looks from the Mexicans that an "Anglo" was standing there. He recalls the drama of it all: "I took a step in, moving toward the right side. I waited, now the object of stares from both sides of the aisle. I took another step, another, faster, to the right side of the hall, where the Mexican kid had been yanked in by his own parents. 'Hey!' the old man who had sold us the tickets stood glowering at me. 'What the hell ya think you're doin', boy? I told ya—'"[39]

Rechy obeyed and joined his friends on the Anglo side. After the movie, as they walked back to their car, Rechy noticed a sign outside a restaurant that read: "We do not serve niggers, spics, or dogs."[40]

But his encounter with the racism of this town did not stop there. Later that evening, at dinner with his friend's aunt, she told them that she couldn't eat when a new Mexican girl servant was working for her. She explained that she had this phobia about eating around Mexicans, but that they should go ahead and eat. No doubt affected by his earlier experience that day, Rechy responded, "Then I shouldn't be here. . . . If you can't eat when Mexicans are in the room with you, ma'am, then I don't want to be here to ruin your dinner." "What ya mean by that, handsome?" the aunt asked. "That my mother is Mexican, Miz Crawford."[41]

These direct encounters with racism brought to Rechy's attention that despite his Americanization, he could not escape, at least in his mind, his Mexican identity, even by passing. In his own way, Rechy stood up for his Mexican identity and even on occasion asserted it. He notes that he was never ashamed of being Mexican.

VI

If an American national identity and a Mexican American ethnic identity characterize the double consciousness of both Rodriguez and Rechy, sexual identity, specifically gay identity, constitutes a third consciousness. This identity, however, is dealt with quite differently in each text. Since Rechy's life story extends into his more mature years, when he openly asserts his gayness, this theme is more explicit in the second part of the autobiography. In Rodriguez's text, which is much more a coming-of-age narrative, this identity is very subtle and some might even contend nonexistent, although I do not agree with that. In any event, here I focus only on their youthful tales, where they do not yet acknowledge this sexual identity, and examine the clues to this last of the multiple identities that mark both writers.

Rodriguez's sexual identity is hinted at on four levels: (1) his focus on his male body as he grows up; (2) his relations with the opposite sex; (3) his linking of literature and sexuality; and (4) his self-identity as Mr. Secrets. Rodriguez recalls his fixation with his body, including his dark skin color. He suggests that his darkness and indigenous features made him feel sexually inferior, less manly, which seems to have affected his relations with girls in school. He denies his maleness because of the shame he feels about his brown and underdeveloped body. He is attracted to the strong and brown bodies of the Mexican braceros, or immigrant workers, that he saw on the streets of Sacramento. "I was unwilling to admit the attraction of their lives," he writes. "But what was denied became strongly desired."[42] This feeling of physical insecurity began to dissipate later, as his body matured, when he was attending Stanford and doing physical labor during the summer. He became more in tune with his brown body. Physical labor in the sun, working with his shirt off, became sensual. "I would take off my shirt to the sun," he describes, "and at last grasp desired sensation. . . . I was no longer ashamed of my body. No longer would I deny myself the pleasing sensations of my maleness."[43] While these passages alone do not explicitly suggest a homoerotic desire at these stages of his life, one can still see them as clues to that end. It should be noted that at the time *Hunger of Memory* was published, Rodriguez had not yet come out. Hence, one can only imagine that in the text, he is leaving evidence of how he grappled with his sexual identity.

A second clue is in his reflections on his lack of success with girls. There is no mention of girlfriends, for example, in his story. Indeed, he notes that this absence was perhaps due to his physical and sexual insecurities: "Fifteen, sixteen. I was a teenager shy in the presence of girls. Never dated. Barely could talk to a girl without stammering. In high school I went to several dances, but I never managed to ask a girl to dance. So I stopped going. I cannot remember high school years now with the parade of typical images: bright drive-ins or gliding blue shadows of a Junior Prom."[44] Later he observes that at Stanford, he now had "something like a conventional sexual life," but then somewhat contradicts himself by stating, "I don't think, however, that I really believed that the women I knew found me physically appealing."[45]

The lack of success with women, or perhaps his lack of sexual interest in women, may be another bit of evidence of his wrestling with his sexual identity. Perhaps still another clue is contained in passages where he recalls his father seeming to hint that Richard's attention to reading and schooling were not typically masculine activities and did not constitute real man's work. He told his son that he would never know "real work" because his "hands were so soft." "At such times," Rodriguez recalls thinking that "education was making me effeminate."[46] He felt that he was betraying the Mexican male sense of being *formal* or masculine because of his interest in reading and education, especially his love of literature. "And it seemed to me that there was something unmanly about my attachment to literature. Even today when so much about the myth of the 'macho' no longer concerns me, I cannot altogether evade such notions. Writing these pages, admitting my embarrassment or my guilt, admitting my sexual anxieties and my physical insecurity, I have not been able to forget that I am not being *formal*."[47]

Most critics now seem to believe that the ultimate clue Rodriguez inserts in his autobiography is his last chapter, entitled "Mr. Secrets." While ostensibly this chapter concerns the fact that Richard, at family gatherings as an adult, rarely speaks of his work in San Francisco, hence the nickname Mr. Secrets, the chapter title more than likely refers to his ultimate secret—that of being a gay man, a secret that he felt hesitant to disclose to his family. Yet he seems to hint in the chapter that in his "public life," he has already revealed this secret outside his family. He feels more secure in doing this. As he writes, "There are things so deeply personal that they can be revealed only to strangers."[48] After *Hunger of Memory* was published but before Richard came out, his critics attacked him largely based on his seeming inability to reconcile his double consciousness of being both an American and a Mexican, but ironically, this vicious criticism has now been tempered by his acknowledgment of his sexual identity. That is, his gay identity has now provided a shield against his critics, who in a politically correct manner seem to be concerned about being labeled homophobic if they further critique Rodriguez.

VII

Rechy, in recounting his youth in El Paso, provides his own clues about his later sexual identity. He recalls, for example, as a young boy going with his father to see his older brother Robert play basketball in the city league. After Robert's team had won the game, Rechy followed him to the dressing room to congratulate him. As he stepped into the room, he was struck by seeing the naked players preparing to shower. He became fixated on their bodies: "I stared at the naked flesh about me, the patches of hair between the legs matted with water or sweat."[49] This is not to say that the young Rechy already had homosexual tendencies, but only to comment on how Rechy recreates an almost homoerotic scene as a very early preface to his later expression of a gay identity.

Much more suggestive of this later identity is when Rechy, in telling about his trip with Scott and Ross to visit Ross's aunt, recollects two scenes that can more definitely be interpreted as homoerotic. In one scene, the young men decided to break into the public swimming pool for a midnight swim. Inside, Scott and Ross took off all their clothes and went skinny dipping. They called out to a reluctant Rechy to do the same. After some effort, they finally forced him to disrobe, although he still did not enter the pool. What happened next is not fully explained by Rechy, who is perhaps leaving it to the imagination of his readers: "They approached me there, movements exaggerated in grabbing me. I did not move."[50] Later that evening, after they returned to the ranch, they went to their bedroom, which had only one bed. After trying to decide on the sleeping arrangements, they started to horseplay:

> Scott grabbed Ross's legs; I grabbed his shoulders. Ross pushed away, power-fully. Pulling and tumbling, we all fell back onto the floor, sweat soaking through our shorts, outlining our groins, gluing limbs to limbs in shifting positions, two bodies on top, one on the bottom, two on the bottom, one on top, rolling side-ways, sliding against hot moist flesh, hands grabbing, pushing away, bodies inter-twined in sweaty friction, as we gasped breathless with increasing heat—our bod-ies', the room's, the overwhelming night's—laughing, falling back on the floor exhausted."[51]

In still another part of Rechy's story that prefigures his expression of sexual identity, he writes about his relationship with Wilford Leach, the playwright, who was stationed in the U.S. Army at the local base in El Paso. Rechy and Leach met because of their frequent visits to the public library and struck up a friendship, although Leach was somewhat older, and Rechy was still in his late teens and a young college student. Although Leach was aware that Rechy ostensibly had a girlfriend, he nevertheless seems to have become physically attracted to him. This attraction was hinted at, but not until Leach informed Rechy that he was being reassigned out of El Paso did the older man take this attraction, possibly reciprocated by Rechy, to another level, or at least attempted to do so. On the night before Leach was scheduled to depart, Rechy borrowed his brother's car and drove Leach around until they stopped at a park. Rechy recalls what happened next, which suggests a potential sexual encounter:

> Wilford touched my shoulder. His hand remained there.
>
>   I forced myself not to pull away from the unexpected gesture. I sat tensely, feeling the weight of his hand increasing, the weight of his touch, knowing that the gesture was about to become an embrace.
>
>   "John, I want to say that I—"

I pulled away, stopping words I inferred, words I had naively dismissed from any place in our friendship. Now, even though not spoken, they had resonated in my mind as if, all along, they had been shouted but left unheard.

"I'll miss you a lot, too, Wilford," was all I could say. I started the car. I drove back to the bus stop where I had met him—he wanted to be dropped off there—and where he would leave for Fort Bliss, his last time in El Paso.[52]

Although those inferred words are not spoken, they are left to our imagination. They will be spoken later in Rechy's life as he no longer struggles with his sexual identity but instead embraces it.

VIII

From the point of view of a historian, I want to share how the triple consciousness in these two autobiographies inform us about the Chicano experience in the United States. To me, Rodriguez's and Rechy's negotiations over and struggles with identity have much to say about the social position of Chicanos and other Latinos. Through the ideology of Americanization, whether the melting pot theory or liberal pluralism, Chicanos have been socialized to assume an essentialist American identity, yet the understructure of this ideology has worked against this outcome. Mexicans, whether immigrants or U.S. born, have largely been prized as sources of cheap labor in addition to their land dispossession after the U.S. conquest of the Southwest region in the mid-nineteenth century. Subjected to what George Mariscal terms "class racism," Mexicans have largely and historically been a subaltern group, with limited opportunities for educational and economic mobility in addition to being politically disempowered.[53] What gains they have accomplished have been less the result of the American capitalist system than the hard-won outcome of their own struggles to reform or change the system. These contradictions of being told that they are Americans and yet not being treated as first-class citizens have helped create an ambivalence of identity. Chicanos are told to be Americans and yet are treated as inferior, and the result has been identity confusion and even crisis for some. This is Du Bois's double consciousness Chicano style. These ambivalences can be seen in both Rodriguez's and Rechy's life stories, particularly their coming-of-age accounts. Both writers are the products of Americanization, and yet there are interstitial gaps within this process that reveal to them their lingering Mexican backgrounds, which they cannot escape, avoid, or refuse to acknowledge. This has been the experience not only of these two writers, but also of many other Mexicans in the United States and, I suspect, of many other minorities throughout the world.

Individually, Rodriguez and Rechy reflect their own historical periods, especially in their youth, when they first have to encounter these identity issues. Rechy, who is a generation older than Rodriguez, grew up in the 1940s and 1950s, when the Mexican American generation led a limited civil rights movement, yet there was still no concerted or larger political effort by Mexican Americans to assert their ethnic identity, even though as second-generation ethnics they were clearly already negotiating this identity, even being inventive and creative in doing so by attempting to bridge both cultures. But such an effort was not so visible that it affected Rechy, and hence his struggle over his double identity was largely a private one. This was equally true about his sexual identity or whatever early gay inclinations he may have already had while couched in homophobic American and Mexican cultures, which both discouraged or censored any expression of gay culture and identity. Consequently, Rechy had to relate to and forge his triple consciousness largely on his own until later in his life when, thanks to both the Chicano Movement and the early gay rights movements, he could more openly express his multiple identities.

Rodriguez's identity navigation is just as complicated at an individual level, but his historical and generational location is different. Reaching maturity during the black civil rights movement and the Chicano Movement, Rodriguez is more cognizant of the role of race and ethnicity in American culture. While he embraces his Americanization through his "public self," he cannot avoid ethnic identity, in his case, Mexican identity, because of the ethnic revivals of the 1960s and 1970s. His own confrontation with his Mexican identity as revealed in his autobiography has much to do with his reaction to these ethnic movements and in particular to the Chicano Movement. While he is critical of what he regards as the "false consciousness" of the movement about Chicano identity, he is nevertheless reacting to it. His attempt to reconcile his dual identity by recapturing his historical memories and his lament for not being more sensitive to the Mexican side of those memories illuminate the meaning of his book title, the "hunger of memory" implying that through the loss of those moments, he is deprived of or hungry of memory. Rodriguez's text, while interpreted by some as an anti–Chicano Movement text or a postmovement text, in my opinion is a movement text in that it is a dialogue about Chicano identity framed by the movement, not outside of it. Curiously, Rodriguez does not engage in a similar dialogue with his sexual identity, even though he, unlike Rechy, was writing in an unprecedented period when gay rights and gay identity were being increasingly asserted. Instead, Rodriguez remains Mr. Secrets. He does so, I believe, because while the American side of his identity is moving in this direction, and at the time of publication, he appears to have already come out to non-Mexicans in San Francisco, he still feels constrained to do so in a Mexican American context that remains much more opposed to gay culture. It would take another decade or more for Rodriguez to publicly confront his sexual identity as a gay Latino and, like Rechy, now confront all sides of his triple consciousness.

In the end, both autobiographies reveal much not only about two major American writers of Mexican descent who happen to be gay, but also about the historical struggle by Chicanos and other Latinos to find their place, identity, and voice in a society that attempted to deny them those opportunities. But no longer. As one Chicano cultural leader often says, "Our time has come!" This means that with the "browning of America," the very meaning of what is an American is being not only challenged but transformed.

5

BEYOND CHICANISMO

Gendered Transitions and Central American
Women's Autobiographies

I

N THE 1980S, thousands of Central American refugees and other immigrants began arriving in the United States as a result of the civil wars and repressive governments in that region. All told, about a million Central Americans arrived in that decade, laying the foundation for increasing heterogeneity among Latinos in the United States, particularly in California, where many Central Americans, such as Salvadorans, relocated. Prior to the 1980s, and certainly in California, the overwhelming majority of Latinos were of Mexican descent. Mexicans still dominate the Latino demography in California, but in the last three decades, they have had to share that space with Central Americans. What connects Mexicans and Central Americans historically, in addition to ethnicity and culture, are that most of them descend from the immigrant experience. Mexican immigrants, as both political and economic refugees, began to cross the U.S.-Mexico border in large numbers beginning in the early twentieth century, and with the exception of the 1930s, they have continued to leave Mexico for the United States in successive generational waves. Central Americans traversed the border as political refugees in the 1980s, as had many Mexicans fleeing the Mexican Revolution of 1910. In this diaspora, the role of gender has played a significant part in the decision to emigrate and in the process of resettlement in the United States. In this chapter, I focus on this dual process by analyzing two immigrant women's autobiographical texts: *Undocumented in L.A.: An Immigrant's Story* (1997), a testimonio authored by Dianne

Walta Hart in collaboration with Yamileth López, and *December Sky: Beyond My Undocumented Life*, written by Evelyn Cortez-Davis and self-published in 2005.[1] Both narratives deal with Central American migration, which has been less studied than the Mexican and in that sense takes us beyond Chicanismo. It also brings into discussion Chicano history and Latino history. Chicano history is the study of Mexicans in the United States, whether as immigrants or U.S. born. Latino history is the study of the varied Latin American groups in the country, such as people of Mexican descent, Puerto Ricans, Central Americans, Cuban Americans, people from the Caribbean, and those from South America. At the same time, the term Latino can be interchanged with the term Chicano, for example, when one is attempting to support a larger connection of this history with those of other Latino communities.

II

In my analysis of the role of gender in these immigrant stories, I am using the important study of gender and Mexican immigration by Pierrette Hondagneu-Sotelo entitled *Gendered Transitions: Mexican Experiences of Immigration*, published in 1994.[2] Hondagneu-Sotelo, a sociologist at the University of Southern California, considers gender not only an understudied part of the immigration experience but perhaps one of the most significant aspects. "I came to see that gender is a fundamental category of analysis for developing theories of immigration and settlement," she writes, "and that in turn, immigration and resettlement experiences are vital to our understanding of how new immigrants reconstruct gender relations."[3] For Hondagneu-Sotelo, migration is gendered.[4] I would not go so far as to propose such a totalizing perspective because, in my opinion, immigration possesses multiple causes; nevertheless, I do agree that gender is an important area of immigration to study, as this chapter demonstrates. Hondagneu-Sotelo divides the relationship of gender and immigration at two levels: immigration and resettlement. She notes the following gendered features of immigration, which I use in my analysis of Hart's and Cortez-Davis's texts:

- The role of gender has to be seen within a specific social context in the sending community.
- Gender relations in families and social networks shape diverse patterns for women and men that influence immigration.

- The emergence of a postindustrial economy in the United States, beginning in the 1970s, created a demand for domestic labor and related jobs that female immigrants have filled.

There are several types of gendered migrations, including, as I explore in this chapter, independent migration and family stage migration.

- Women negotiate the decision to migrate at different levels with husbands.
- Women often take advantage of opportunities to migrate.
- Single mothers with children often instigate migration.
- Women working in their home countries often gives them leverage in the decision to migrate.

Family patriarchy does not always pose an insurmountable obstacle to female migration but can be malleable. Hondagneu-Sotelo proposes the following gendered characteristics of the resettlement process:

- Resettlement leads to weaker family patriarchy.
- New gender relations in resettlement motivate women to prolong settlement in the United States.
- Women play perhaps the most important part in solidifying resettlement.
- Economic pressures in the United States lead to women working, helping relax patriarchal ideology, which maintains that women should not work outside the home.
- The presence of women and entire families in resettlement is the key to successful settlement.
- Reconstructed gender relations emerge out of the resettlement experience.

Using Hondagneu-Sotelo's characterizations of what she refers to as gendered transitions, based on her study of Mexican immigration, I explore how these characteristics can be translated to the Central American experience. Let me first, however, provide a synopsis of the two texts.

III

Undocumented in L.A. is a testimonio, or oral history, written by Dianne Walta Hart, a professor of Spanish at Oregon State University, based on her interviews with Yamileth López, a Nicaraguan woman. In the early 1980s, Hart had interviewed Yamileth and her family in Nicaragua for another oral history project, which was published in 1990 as *Thanks to God and the Revolution: The Oral History of a Nicaraguan Family*.[5] When Yamileth went to the United States in her late thirties, at the end of the 1980s, she reconnected with Hart, who decided to do a follow-up oral history focused on Yamileth and her decision to leave Nicaragua and resettle in the United States. Yamileth was born around 1955 (her exact birth year is unclear) to a poor campesino family in a rural area of Nicaragua. Her father abandoned his family before Yamileth was born, so she was raised by her mother. Yamileth received only a sixth-grade education. What changed her life was the Sandinista revolution, beginning in the 1970s, against the dictatorship of Anastasio Somoza Debayle. She and her sister, Leticia, and her younger brother, Omar, joined the revolution. Yamileth specifically worked with the female wing of the Sandinistas, which included learning to bear arms and teaching other women how to defend themselves against the U.S.-sponsored contras, or counter-revolutionaries, after the overthrow of Somoza in 1979 and the coming to power of the Sandinistas. Throughout the next decade, the Ronald Reagan administration in the United States waged a proxy war against the Nicaraguan government by arming and supplying the contras as well as imposing sanctions on Nicaragua. In 1988 Yamileth's sister, Leticia, left the country to join her husband in the United States, and they eventually resettled in Los Angeles. Leticia left her four daughters in Yamileth's care. In a few months, Leticia arranged for Yamileth and Yamileth's son, Miguel, whose father had been killed in the revolution, to escort her daughters to the United States with no documents. Although Yamileth believed that she would soon return, she found herself doing domestic work in Los Angeles and in Oregon, where she reconnected with Hart. After a short stay in Oregon, she returned to LA to live with her sister and worked again as a domestic as well as cleaning offices and selling cosmetics to other Latinas. One year later, because she feared that the gang violence in South Central LA and in the Pico-Union area where they lived might bring harm to her son, she and Miguel returned to Nicaragua. Yet unable to find work and pregnant by her boyfriend, David, Yamileth decided to return to LA with a temporary visa in 1990, after the electoral defeat of the Sandinistas, to work and raise her children, although she still kept alive the dream of returning to her home country—her Nicaraguan dream. She did return once more to Nicaragua, but only to renew her visa. This time she would return to live in Los Angeles permanently. Despite an unsuccessful effort to operate her own bakery, Yamileth resorted to working as a domestic, working in a factory, and assisting Leticia in her beauty shop. In LA she began to learn English and how to negotiate her undocumented life once she overstayed her visa. At the end of her story, she married a U.S.-born Latino in 1996, not so much out of love but as a way of securing permanent residency. Her greatest fear, as with many other Latino immigrants, was of being deported. Her story, with all its ups and downs, is an example of Hondagneu-Sotelo's gendered transitions, as I analyze further in this chapter.

The story in *December Sky* focuses on Evelyn Cortez-Davis and her family, especially her mother, Rosario, from El Salvador. In my analysis of gender and immigration, I pay particular attention to Rosario. The Cortez family lived in the suburbs of San Salvador, and both parents came from poor backgrounds with limited education. They had four daughters, including Evelyn, who was born in 1969. After the birth of their children, and because of economic hard times, the parents decided that one of them should go to the United States to find work to help sustain the family. They concluded that Rosario should go because a friend of hers was already working in Washington, DC, and had informed Rosario that she could help her get a domestic job. Rosario left in 1973 in what would be the first of three separate trips to the United States without her family, and that would take her from El Salvador to Washington, DC, and then to Los Angeles. With a few return trips to see her family, Rosario lived and worked in the United States for eight years on her own, although she lived with relatives in Los Angeles. She labored mostly in domestic jobs as a live-in maid and nanny, but she also cleaned buildings and worked in factories. Because of her remittances to her family and her husband's job, they were able to send their children to private nonreligious schools, where they felt their daughters could receive a better education and be in a safer environment, especially after the commencement of El Salvador's bloody civil war in 1979. Unfortunately, the conflict at times spilled over into Evelyn's school, as guerrilleros of the Farabundo Martí National Liberation Front waged battles against the repressive military in support of the autocratic rule of the elite ruling families. Battles, killings, and curfews all interrupted Evelyn's education. One of her uncles was arrested, accused of supporting the rebels, and tortured. The civil war severely damaged the Salvadoran economy as well as threatening the lives of civilians.

In 1981, Rosario again returned to El Salvador but this time to bring her entire family to Los Angeles, where they would be safe and more secure economically. Without documents, Rosario and her daughters crossed into Mexico from Guatemala in early December of that year, hence the title of Evelyn's autobiography. They crossed into the United States from the Tijuana area. Evelyn's father stayed in El Salvador temporarily to arrange to get his pension before crossing into the United States, also without documents, and joining the family in Los Angeles. They settled with other relatives in the San Fernando Valley, north of downtown Los Angeles. There both parents secured low-end jobs and enrolled their children in public schools. Evelyn was twelve years old when the family moved to the United States. The rest of the story concerns Evelyn's struggle to learn English, ultimately becoming an excellent student through high school. Encouraged by one of her teachers, she applied and was admitted to the University of California, Los Angeles (UCLA), in 1987, where she majored in civil engineering. She did very well in her classes, but—like many other Latino students today—she had to always worry about her undocumented status. Fortunately, the 1986 Immigration and Control Act allowed Evelyn, her parents, and her sisters to receive amnesty and permanent resident status in 1989. Evelyn has gone on to a successful career as a civil engineer for the city of Los Angeles. She became a U.S. citizen in 1995. Like the story of Yamileth, Evelyn's story and especially that of her mother, Rosario, reveal the gender implications of the immigrant experience.[6]

IV

Hondagneu-Sotelo notes that the study of immigration too often focuses on macro forces to explain why people leave their home countries and migrate to another. National and international economic changes and, particularly today, the implications of the global economy are often referred to as the key causes for immigration, along with, at times, national political upheavals such as civil wars or revolutions in the home country. No one denies this; however, what this macro force analysis fails to take into account is that immigration is also the result of family and personal decisions, and therefore is part of a specific social context. "Immigrants respond to opportunities created by macro-level forces," Hondagneu-Sotelo observes, "but they do so in a social context."[7] It is within this context, largely related to family and personal social networks, that some decide to emigrate and some do not. If macro forces explained everything about the causes for immigration, then most everyone in countries such as Mexico or in Central America would be in the United States, but that clearly is not the case. Moreover, placing immigration within the context of family and personal social networks humanizes the immigration process; in the end, regardless of macro forces, leaving one's home country is a decision made by the individual and family, and gender plays a significant role in this decision. "Conspicuously absent from the macrostructural perspective is any sense of human agency or subjectivity," Hondagneu-Sotelo correctly concludes.[8]

This is very much the case in the story of Yamileth and that of Rosario. Yamileth's decision to leave Nicaragua and go to the United States has to be seen within the context of the civil war in her country and her particular circumstances within that context. She supported the Sandinista revolution and became empowered as a woman by her participation as a member of that movement. In the end, however, the revolution failed to fulfill its promises to women such as Yamileth. Yamileth left Nicaragua in part because the prospects of a better life for women, including new job opportunities, did not materialize. Of course, a significant factor in this failure was the U.S.-sponsored contra war. But it is fair to say that these unfulfilled promises also resulted from the shortcomings of the Sandinista revolution itself. In any event, although Yamileth still considered herself a Sandinista and never saw herself as a political refugee, she found it very difficult as a single mother to provide for herself and her son, so given the opportunity, she left for the United States with Miguel. But the decision was hers and hers alone, and she made this decision primarily as a mother, although within the context of the Nicaraguan condition.[9]

In *December Sky*, Rosario's decision to leave El Salvador for the United States is likewise within the context of poverty and lack of economic opportunities in her country in the 1970s, and then augmented by the civil war later in that decade and into the 1980s. Her personal decision, however, was directly related to a more equitable relationship with her husband, Miguel, who agreed that Rosario needed to be the pioneer immigrant because of her already established social network in the United States, centered on her friend Bertha, who was working in Washington, DC, and who encouraged Rosario to join her with the promise of a readily available domestic job. While the violence of the civil war in El Salvador certainly motivated the entire Cortez family to leave the country, the decision was also within the specific context of Rosario's previous three experiences working in the United States as well as having a network of other relatives already living in Los Angeles. Those personal and family connections to the United States were central to the decision to emigrate, and here gender plays a decisive part given Rosario's lead role in this process.[10]

V

The decision by Yamileth and Rosario to emigrate is further explained by their particular gender relations within their families. In many cases it appears that the male head of household makes the decision with little if any negotiation with his spouse or family. Hondagneu-Sotelo notes that this is the common pattern in Mexican immigration because of the prevalence of a traditional patriarchal family culture. But this pattern is not always uniform, as revealed in these two texts. Yamileth's household, for example, has no patriarchal presence because her father abandoned the family, and her mother became the head of household, providing an example of an independent single mother—an example later emulated by Yamileth. She commented on growing up without a father figure when she spoke to one of Hart's classes at Oregon State. She observed that many other Nicaraguan women had experienced this because of similar family abandonments by fathers. Yamileth pointed out, however, that this absence had not mattered much to her in her life or in that of her children. "She added," Hart observes, "that it would have been nice to have had one [a father] as a role model, but she had done all right anyway."[11] In her own married life, Yamileth did not have to confront a patriarchal relationship when she decided to leave Nicaragua because her husband had been killed in the revolution against Somoza. Her lover, David, a Sandinista soldier, was a married man and exercised no control over Yamileth's life, nor did she allow such control anyway, as a strong and empowered woman as a result of her participation in the revolution. Moreover, while she admits that she might have remained in the country as long as her mother lived, the death of her mother provided her and her sister, Leticia, the additional freedom to make their own decisions to emigrate. Patriarchy is often further manifested by older brothers, who in Latino culture serve as surrogate father figures. But Yamileth had no older brothers, and her younger brother, Omar, possessed no such authority over his older sisters.[12] As a result, Yamileth's decision to go to the United States and ultimately remain there was made with no patriarchal influences.

Although Rosario, unlike Yamileth, was a married woman, she fortunately had a fairly equitable relationship with her husband, which enabled her to negotiate a joint decision for her to be the *sola*, or pioneer, immigrant to the United States. Affecting this more egalitarian marriage relationship were several factors: one was that Rosario had grown up influenced by her own strong mother figure, who had owned and operated a seamstress business; a second was that her father had died when she was only twenty, and thus she had escaped her father's patriarchal influence on her as a young woman; third, as the oldest of her siblings, Rosario had taken on a leadership role with her brothers and sisters; and fourth, Rosario at an early age had asserted her strong, independent personality and character as well as an entrepreneurial drive. Of this, Cortez-Davis writes,

> By her early teens, Mami was buying, selling, trading, sharing, marketing, manufacturing, and investing, all to help her parents support her six younger brothers and sisters. The tiny town of Chilanga had never seen a more promising young entrepreneur. She set up vending booths for fruit punch, cookies, coconut candy, and cigarettes. Town fairs and Sunday soccer games gave way to her shaved ice empire: her concession stands complete with homemade strawberry and pineapple syrups were a hit. She helped my grandmother, Mama Lola, buy and sell all kinds of fruits, cheese, sardines, lemons, and dried shrimp at the marketplace in the nearest town, over three kilometers away.[13]

Moreover, Rosario was a working woman in the same factory where she had met her husband, and she continued to work even after her marriage, which gave her financial leverage with him. Her economic contributions in addition to her own strong streak of independence enabled her to successfully negotiate becoming the initial immigrant in her family.

VI

The changing global economy makes it possible for women such as Yamileth and Rosario to emigrate to the United States, as Hondagneu-Sotelo stresses. By the 1970s, industrial nations like the United States were entering a new, postindustrial era, with traditional industrial enterprises being outsourced to third world nations, chiefly to take advantage of cheap nonunion labor. In the place of these runaway manufacturing industries, the U.S. economy became more characterized by high-tech computer-driven enterprises, best exemplified by Silicon Valley and by expanded financial and service industries, complementing the growing concentration of wealth among American elites and the increased demand for domestic labor. This economic shift provided the opportunity for immigrant women such as Yamileth and Rosario to go to the United States, where they could find easily available secondary-sector jobs such as domestic work and related employment.[14] Hence, Yamileth first went to the United States because Leticia, already in Los Angeles, told her that she would have no problem securing a domestic job. Yamileth first worked as a domestic in LA and in Oregon. Later, she also worked cleaning offices. The same was true for Rosario, who initially found domestic jobs in Washington, DC, including a short stint as the household assistant to the Brazilian ambassador's wife. When she later moved to LA, Rosario found similar domestic jobs. For both Yamileth and Rosario, domestic work included childcare.[15]

VII

The type of migration strategies pursued by Yamileth and Rosario were likewise affected by gender considerations. Yamileth as a single mother engaged in what Hondagneu-Sotelo calls an independent migration, when people (male or female) migrate on their own to the United States in the hope of securing work and then bringing other family members.[16] Yamileth was given what Hondagneu-Sotelo calls a "social opportunity" to go to the United States when her sister asked her to escort her nieces (Leticia's daughters), and Yamileth readily agreed. While this can be seen, at one level, as what Hondagneu-Sotelo refers to as family stage migration, I would argue that it really wasn't since Yamileth's nieces were not part of her immediate family, which consisted of only herself and her son, Miguel.[17] Moreover, even though she escorted her nieces to the United States, Yamileth's decision to leave was hers and hers alone. She independently made up her own mind; no family decision was involved because Yamileth was a single mother, what Hart refers to as a "non-tied" immigrant woman.[18] In fact, Yamileth's accompanying her nieces represents a gendered relationship since her sister believed that Yamileth as a woman and an aunt could care for Leticia's children on the potentially dangerous trip. And Yamileth's position as a single mother would in the end determine her decision to remain permanently in the United States. As earlier noted, one of Hondagneu-Sotelo's characteristics of gendered transitions in the immigration process is that single mothers with children often instigate migration.

In Rosario's case, even though she makes three trips to the United States on her own, and this represents a form of independent migration, all her migrations, including the final one with her children, are the result of family decisions and represent family stage migration. Unlike Yamileth, who leaves no immediate family behind since she takes her son with her, Rosario initially leaves her children and husband behind, until 1981, when she and her husband make the decision to leave El Salvador as a family. The first family stage migration, then, is represented by Rosario's first three exploratory trips, which lead to the second stage, when she migrates with her children, and then the third stage, when her husband travels on his own to Los Angeles and is reunited with his family. In each of these stages, gender is a significant consideration, largely because of Rosario's established experience, after the first trip, as a female migrant. She knew more about how to get to the United States and therefore was in a better position than her husband to negotiate the trip with her children. Cortez-Davis, who was twelve years old when she and her siblings accompanied Rosario on the final part of their potentially dangerous journey to the United States, recalls that her mother was totally in control when she had to deal with corrupt Mexican immigration officials and give them *mordidas*, or bribes, and with the coyotes, who smuggled them into the United States for a fee.[19] Moreover, Rosario used her experiences from her earlier undocumented trips to the United States to prepare her family for the final migration. Of Rosario's migration strategy, Cortez-Davis writes,

> Mami was careful to pick shampoo and soap and other toiletries she had brought with her from the United States one month earlier so we would appear more like tourists on our way through Mexico. We removed clothing labels, luggage markings, and brand names from everything we packed. We even burnt off the well-known Bracos name from the soles and the sides of our new tennis shoes. Mami thought of everything—there was no room for mistakes.[20]

VIII

Finally, these two texts clearly show that, as Hondagneu-Sotelo observes, family patriarchy does not, despite prevalent stereotypes, pose an insurmountable obstacle to female migration but is instead a malleable one. This is true for both Yamileth and Rosario. For Yamileth, patriarchy is not even an issue since she is a single mother with no husband, father, older brother, or dominating boyfriend to contend with. Yamileth makes her own decision to migrate and resettle in the United States. In fact, Hart observes that Yamileth as a strong single mother was not necessarily an anomaly in Nicaragua: "I heard that Nicaragua had always been a country of strong women without men, the years of violence and the irresponsibility of machismo had taken their toll. Nicaraguan women . . . carried not only the responsibility of parenting and domestic work but also most of the economic maintenance of the family, to a greater extent than women in other Central American countries. It has been that way for years."[21] Rosario also is not restricted by patriarchy, given her equitable relationship with her husband, based on her strong personality, sense of independence, and history of entrepreneurship in economic matters. Her ability to work outside the home, including her work in the United States, further provided her leverage with her husband in family matters, including the decisions on migration. In many respects, as Cortez-Davis observes, her mother was the dominant figure in the family rather than her father. "Mami had a distinctly better disposition toward change, she always had," Cortez-Davis concludes.[22]

IX

If gender played a major role in the immigration experiences of Yamileth and Rosario, it likewise did so in the resettlement process in the United States. Both women were significant actors in the permanent settlement of their families, specifically in the Los Angeles area. One of the initial characteristics linked to this gendered process is the weakening of family patriarchy, but for Yamileth, this family patriarchy was nonexistent to begin with, and for Rosario, this weakening was not a new manifestation but a continuation and augmentation of an already fluid family patriarchy.

Yamileth's independence as a single mother continued in the United States, where she remained free of strong male influence. If anything, her independence was further encouraged by her sister's separation from her husband and emergence as a female entrepreneur when she opened up her beauty shop. Inspired by Leticia, Yamileth also operated her own business, a bakery, for a short while. She refused to accept or acquiesce to a traditional female role, subordinate to men, which was further evident after Leticia acquired a boyfriend, Roberto. Yamileth was very critical of him for being a freeloader. She tells Hart, "The boyfriend's Salvadoran. He says he's a *guerrillero*, but that's a lie. He's a man without shame and an opportunist. In the time I've known him, he hasn't had a job. He lives at the expense of Leticia, and that's why the money doesn't last."[23] By contrast, Yamileth says of herself: "I didn't leave my country to come here and be a parasite, to let someone support me and do nothing. I'm not used to seeing men kept by women. It's not that way in our country. Men and women both work so that they can live together and share the needs of the house. That's what I'm used to, not to things like that."[24] When the coyote, Mundo, and Leticia's husband, Sergio, tried to coerce Yamileth into giving them more money for helping her enter the United States, she refused to succumb to this male pressure because she knew that she did not owe them such money and that they were trying to swindle her.[25] Even when Yamileth decided to get married in LA, it was on her own terms, and she did so less for love than for the use of her new husband's U.S.-born status to obtain a green card for her and her son.

For Rosario, resettlement in the United States was a continuation of her equitable relationship with her husband, which was further strengthened because of her greater familiarity with life in the United States, including her ability to speak English and, unlike her husband, to find readily available work. All this gave her even greater leverage and spousal negotiating power. Rosario's influence in further weakening patriarchal control could be seen when she overrode any idea that Evelyn, as a female, should not go away to college or leave the home until she got married, a traditional view of Latino parents, especially fathers, in the United States. While Rosario was at first ambivalent about Evelyn living away from home, in the end she supported her daughter and overcame any reluctance her husband felt. Evelyn notes that this support by her mother first manifested itself when Rosario agreed, despite her husband's objections, that Evelyn could spend weekends at UCLA rather than coming home. "Mami stopped calling, not because she didn't want to or didn't care. It was her way of telling me she believed I was doing the right thing and that she trusted my judgment."[26]

Hondagneu-Sotelo does not claim that all patriarchal relationships are fully diminished by the immigration and resettlement process, but she does believe that they are significantly modified: "Patriarchy is renegotiated through migration and resettlement in a variety of ways, and family power relations take many new forms. While it would be premature to hail the end of patriarchy in these families, it is significant that there is a general trend toward more egalitarian relations."[27]

X

Women are often key actors in the resettlement process, as Hondagneu-Sotelo stresses, and this was certainly true of Yamileth and Rosario. "While Mexican men often play an important part in initiating migration," Hondagneu-Sotelo notes of her study of Mexican immigrants, "women play an important part in solidifying settlement."[28] Both Yamileth and Rosario learned how to negotiate their new surroundings and systems. For example, Yamileth understood how to enter the United States more than once with just a travel visa and then overstay it. She became aware that she could easily purchase a fake green card and then use it to obtain a social security card. Her ultimate achievement in negotiating the immigration system was when she understood that she could get married to a U.S. citizen and in this way be eligible for permanent residence and able to get a driver's license.[29] Rosario on her several trips by herself to the United States also learned certain strategies to avoid being detected as undocumented by immigration officials. On one trip back to Washington, DC, via Miami, for example, immigration officials stopped her. Rosario showed them her temporary visa, but she was also prepared to be questioned, having already hidden inside her clothes any incriminating evidence, such as letters, that she had entered the United States not as a tourist but to work. Of course, Rosario more fully negotiated the system by researching and understanding the 1986 immigration law and how she and her family could successfully apply for amnesty and legal residence.[30]

Immigrant women further promote resettlement by integrating their children into the public school system. Yamileth, on her first trip to the United States, enrolled not only her son, Miguel, in school, but also her four nieces because her sister, Leticia, didn't know how. Neither did Yamileth, but she managed to do so, even though she couldn't speak English.[31] On one occasion, to avoid being charged for school meals for Miguel and her niece Nora, Yamileth went to the school and with her limited English negotiated not having to pay. "I told the principal some truth and some lies, and she gave the children food. For example, I told her that we hadn't been here long, that I didn't have work, and that we were alone. That right now I was helping a woman sell clothes but it didn't pay well, only one hundred dollars a month."[32] Miguel not only went to elementary and middle school but also completed high school. Yamileth believed that the greatest opportunity she could acquire from her undocumented life in LA was to provide an education for her son. "For me the future is thinking about tomorrow and preparing yourself for it," she stresses. "The only heritage a parent can leave is the intellectual preparation of a child, not a chair or a house that they can sell. An education allows them to fight for survival, wherever they go. No one can take that inheritance."[33] At the same time, as part of the educational integration of her son, Yamileth complained that the schools in the United States seemed less demanding than the ones in Nicaragua. She had hoped that Miguel could get a more challenging education. "I just wish they didn't make the work so easy here," she laments. "It'd be better if they pushed the students more."[34]

Rosario also believed in education, and even before she brought her family to the United States, she enrolled herself in a GED program in Washington, DC, and obtained her high school diploma. When she brought her entire family to the LA area, she made sure to enroll Evelyn and her siblings in public school. The only exception was her daughter Sonia, who as the oldest daughter first started working, but later returned to school. When Evelyn became a senior in high school and applied to UCLA, Rosario gave her daughter the money for the application, even though this might have exposed the family as being undocumented. Once Evelyn became a college student, Rosario and her husband contributed to their daughter's education. Like Yamileth, and most other immigrant parents, Rosario interpreted success not on her or her husband's terms but on those of their children.[35]

Learning English is another way immigrant women often seem to take the lead in the resettlement of their families. Yamileth not only enrolled in evening English classes in LA, but she encouraged Miguel and her nieces to learn it by buying them English-language books in addition to what they learned at school.[36] Rosario, on her first job in Washington, DC, bought an English textbook to teach herself English at night while also picking up some English in her domestic work. Over the eight years that she traveled by herself to the United States, she learned enough to teach her children some English in El Salvador before their family migration. Once across the border, she continued to encourage her children to learn English, not only at school, but also at home, where she had her English-speaking brothers teach them.[37] Learning English became a major step forward in the resettlement of Rosario and her family.

Acquiring new consumer tastes, learning how to use new household appliances in their domestic work, and even purchasing a house, as Rosario did in 1987, all contributed further to the two women's vanguard role in the resettlement process. At the same time, both employed what Alejandro Portes and Rubén G. Rumbaut refer to as "selective acculturation" in their study of contemporary immigrants and their children.[38] While Yamileth and Rosario underwent acculturation, or transculturation, as a result of their U.S. experiences, both maintained various homeland traditions and customs as well as the Spanish language. Yamileth, for example, besides her criticism of the schools also expressed concerns that children in the United States had too many freedoms that worked against family discipline. Living in South Central LA, with its gang culture, only increased her fears about Miguel becoming involved with gangs or being hurt by gangs.[39]

XI

Yamileth and Rosario also contributed to the resettlement of their families by initiating a sense of community, which fostered social integration. Of the role of immigrant women in promoting community, Hondagneu-Sotelo observes, "If men are community pioneers, it is women who are the community builders."[40] Immigrant community consists of engaging in immigrant community groups as well as in more informal family-related relationships. Neither Yamileth nor Rosario appears to have been part of immigrant self-help groups, but both women created community by nourishing their extended families, or doing "kin work," through collective living conditions, family gatherings, and special family occasions such as baptisms and birthdays.[41] Yamileth added to this family community when she operated her bakery by including several family members in her enterprise. Moreover, she and others in her family assisted Leticia in her beauty shop.[42] While in Oregon, Yamileth contrasted the lack of neighborhood community among white Americans there with her own Nicaraguan community-oriented culture. "What I've never understood, though, is that each person lives in his house but doesn't pay attention to anyone else, not even a neighbor," she tells Hart. "I don't know if it's that the other person's life has no importance or what. Here, if someone dies, so what? It's not us. We, on the other hand, are used to helping people. If someone on our block in Estelí [Yamileth's hometown] dies, we ask if we can help. Sometimes we make coffee or spend a night in the house with the dead person. What I see here is each person for himself."[43] Yamileth's and Rosario's visions of community were expanded from their Nicaraguan and Salvadoran backgrounds now that they lived in the LA area with other Latinos such as Mexicans. Although Yamileth criticized the behavior of some Latinos she witnessed during the LA riots in 1992, she began to identify as a Latina. "We're part of the family," she asserts. "We're all Latinos."[44]

XII

The necessity and capability of immigrant women to work outside the home as part of their U.S. experience appears to be a major factor in tempering and relaxing patriarchal ideology, which asserts that women should not work outside the home. In the United States, such an ideology among Latino immigrants, in most cases, is not feasible given the financial pressures on the family plus the more readily available work for immigrant women. In turn, receiving their own salaries to be used along with that of their husband's to pay household expenses is a key negotiating tool for Latina immigrant women. This financial contribution makes it possible to modify spousal relationships in some immigrant families, although not without vestiges of traditional patriarchy. Yamileth and Rosario became the main breadwinners in their families as they found employment outside the home. Yamileth had no choice as a single mother, and so for her, changing patriarchal relationships was not even a question. She lived without such influence. Rosario's initial trips to the United States to find work while her husband remained at home in El Salvador led to her earning more money than her husband, and her remittances back home were crucial in sustaining the family. This situation had already modified her relationship with her husband before the entire family finally migrated to Los Angeles, and after they did, Rosario was the first to find work while her husband remained jobless for some time. She remained the primary breadwinner, at one point holding three jobs at the same time: at a delicatessen, a military surplus shop, and a Jack in the Box, where she night managed.[45]

Able to work outside the home and being chiefly responsible for reassembling their families in the United States, immigrant women such as Yamileth and Rosario are key, as Hondagneu-Sotelo concludes, to the permanent resettlement of Latino immigrants. They may not be the only key, but they are a significant one. While immigrant men, especially as solos who leave their families in their homeland, are prone to engage in transnational migrations, going back and forth across borders, immigrant women, particularly married women who bring their families and single mothers like Yamileth, appear less likely to follow this pattern. Immigrant men and women both, at different levels, possess the dream of returning permanently to their homelands, what I call the "Mexican dream," and what in the context of this chapter's stories could be called the "Nicaraguan dream" and the "Salvadoran dream." Yet this longing seems to be gendered in that men appear to hold on to this dream longer than women do, even though for many it turns out to be no more than a dream. Immigrant women seem less wedded to these dreams, especially as they find work in the United States and begin to raise their children in their new American environment. Seeing the future in their children, immigrant women seem less willing to abandon their new homeland, which they perceive to have better educational, medical, and economic opportunities for their children. Yamileth and Rosario recognize that the needs of their children override parental nostalgia and any hopes of returning home. Reassembling families or creating new families in the United States almost ensures that they will permanently remain. After Yamileth's daughter is born from her affair with her Salvadoran lover, she recognizes this reality. "I've always had the idea of returning to Nicaragua," she muses, "but not right now, not tomorrow, nor the morning after. A reason to stay in the United States was to have had my daughter here."[46]

XIII

Immigration and resettlement are complex processes involving many social and personal factors. Gender is certainly one of these factors and, as Hondagneu-Sotelo argues, a major one. In the case of Latino immigration to the United States, both in the past and today, some men make the decision to migrate, often emigrating on their own. As the stories of Yamileth and Rosario reveal, however, women often share in the decision to migrate or play the decisive role. In either case, gender is an important determinant in personal and family decisions to uproot oneself from one's home country and migrate to another. But if immigration is the first step, resettlement is the second, and women are often vital to this critical process, as demonstrated by Yamileth and Rosario. In this dual undertaking, traditional patriarchy and gender relations are significantly transformed in certain instances, as these stories further reveal. Immigration is not a static social process, and neither are gender relationships as part of this process. In these gendered transitions, as Hondagneu-Sotelo concludes, women tend to be the beneficiaries. "[W]omen gain in the process of settlement while men lose," she stresses. "Women gain greater personal autonomy and independence, becoming more self-reliant as they participate in public life and gain access to both social and economic resources previously beyond their reach. Many women begin to participate in family decision making in areas where they previously had no say."[47]

By emphasizing gender in an analysis of immigration, we can more effectively, at least in the United States, address and combat common stereotypes about immigrants that are held by many Americans, especially the stereotypes suggesting that Latino immigrants, unlike earlier European ones, do not acculturate and integrate. Studying the role of immigrant women gives us a very different and dynamic view of Latino immigration, revealing gendered motives aimed not at ethnic separation but at a more nuanced ethnic integration. In the words of a common 1920s saying about Mexican immigrant women's greater predilection for Americanization, "Go after the women."[48]

PART II

THE NOVEL

6

HISTORY, LITERATURE, AND THE CHICANO WORKING-CLASS NOVEL

A Critical Analysis of Alejandro Morales's *The Brick People*

I

A HETEROGENEOUS PEOPLE and possessors of a long and complicated history, Chicanos, at least in their U.S. experience, have been predominantly a dispossessed working-class population, alienated from the fruits of their labor and of the very land they have worked on to enrich their Anglo bosses. Conquered, deprived of their lands, exploited for their labor, and positioned as second-class citizens following the U.S. annexation of the Southwest in the mid-nineteenth century, Mexicans in a new U.S.-sponsored capitalist environment underwent what Albert Camarillo calls "proletarianization" in his study of Santa Barbara's Mexican community.[1] Valued as essentially a cheap labor force, composed of both nineteenth-century Mexicans and, more importantly, thousands of immigrant workers from Mexico in the twentieth century, proletarianized Mexicans have also been subjected to racial, gendered, and cultural forms of discrimination, which together have produced a dual but unequal society in the region, characterized by more advantageous opportunities and rewards for whites and fewer ones for Mexicans, who became permanent minorities in the United States.

Within these institutionalized patterns of exploitation and oppression, Mexicans proved to be a labor catalyst for the impressive growth of an extractive economy in the Southwest. High birth rates plus consistent immigration from

Mexico to the present day have only increased the importance of Chicano workers to the region as well as elsewhere.[2] This central experience as workers dispossessed from their historical lands in the Southwest and in Mexico characterizes the Chicano saga. It is exactly these conditions and contributions that Alejandro Morales powerfully brings to life in his sweeping historical novel *The Brick People* (1988). A combination of the exhaustive historical novel, like James Michener's books, with their casts of hundreds, and the Latin American boom novel, with its stress on magical realism, *The Brick People* represents one of the most serious efforts by a Chicano novelist to come to grips with the historical evolution of Chicanos, especially as working-class people.[3] Because it confronts history and makes it central to the text, *The Brick People* is both a literary and a historical document and hence a text that obliges a critical review from literary critics and historians alike (a division that is disappearing in some academic circles, such as new historicism and intellectual history).

II

Morales's view of Chicano history, like that of most of his intellectual generation, is shaped by the Chicano movement of the late 1960s and early 1970s. The movement in its search for history and in its authentic hunger for memory stressed that the deep roots of the Chicano experience went back to the pre-Columbian epoch. Chicano history in its Indian, Spanish, and Mexican manifestations is filled with ironies and contradictions so well articulated in Corky Gonzales's epic poem *I am Joaquín* and in the seminal essays by Octavio Romano in *El Grito*.[4] Chicano history as interpreted by the *movimiento* is also a history of a people closely identified with the soil, the earth—*la tierra*—a people of the land: peasants, farmers, farmworkers, miners. It is also a history of a people in Mexico and in Greater Mexico (the borderlands, Aztlán, the Southwest) whose lives and cultures have been shaped by their affinity to the earth or, to use the more fashionable term, the environment. Yet that relationship to the land has likewise spurred its share of tragedies. Every person's land has also been someone else's desire. The pre-Columbians enslaved each other for the fruits of the land. The Spaniards, in turn, enslaved the Indians. The Mexicans enslaved Indians and themselves. The Anglos came, saw, and conquered the land. This almost cyclical history based on contestation for the land is at the heart of Morales's view of Chicano history. While influenced by pre-Columbian themes, Morales sees Chicano history, as Rodolfo Acuña does in *Occupied America*, as essentially commencing with the Anglo conquest.[5] Hence, for Morales, Chicano history has had three key periods: the Anglo conquest and subsequent subjugation of the Mexican in the post–Mexican War era; the capitalist expansionist period of the late nineteenth and early twentieth centuries, characterized by large-scale Mexican immigration to the Southwest; and what can be called La Reconquista in the more contemporary period, when Chicanos aspired to re-conquer what John Chávez calls the "lost land."[6] Morales's view of Chicano history here is largely consistent with the historical themes propounded by the Chicano Movement with its stress on internal colonization, a historical but lost homeland, and La Reconquista. Morales also deviates from this collectivist interpretation of history, however, to posit a somewhat more individualist conception of that history.

III

Set in Southern California, in the greater Los Angeles area, *The Brick People* first concerns the effects of the Anglo conquest on the resident Mexican population. By focusing on changes in land tenure and on the dispossession of the Mexicans, Morales adds to the Chicano critique of what Carey McWilliams labeled "the Spanish fantasy."[7] Promoted by turn-of-the-century tourism entrepreneurs, the Spanish fantasy ignored the Mexican contribution to California history and instead suggested an "authentic" and quaint Spanish or other European cultural presence in California, which Anglo tourists could enjoy upon visiting the Golden State. Instead of Indians, mestizos, mulattos, friars, soldiers, peasants, and landowners all living in relationship to each other in a harsh frontier environment, the Spanish fantasy romanticized their experiences by referencing only handsome Spanish dons and beautiful Spanish señoritas, always dancing, singing, and making merry. Into such a bucolic society, Anglos entered and easily resettled. No conquest, no dispossession of land, no racism, no exploitation exist in the Spanish fantasy. By contrast, in Morales's history, Anglos subjugate and steal the lands of the Mexicans—of the Californios. Anglos exploit and kill Indians and Asians. This is Manifest Destiny—it is God's country, but this god is white and only speaks English.

Employing magical realism rather than social realism, and clearly influenced by Latin American writers such as Gabriel García Márquez and Carlos

Fuentes, Morales critiques the Mexican loss of land. In doing so he sets out a dichotomy between what he believes, somewhat romantically, to be the Mexicans' organic ties to the land and the Anglo's alienation, exploitation, and destruction of the land. This separation is clearly portrayed when Joseph Simons, one of the Simons brothers who will construct a brick empire in Los Angeles during the early 1900s, asks a waiter about a photograph of a Mexican woman in the restaurant. The waiter, apparently Mexican, informs Simons that the woman was Doña Eulalia Pérez de Guillén, a prominent member of an old Californio family, who in the nineteenth century owned vast tracts of land in the Pasadena area, indeed, some of the land owned currently by the Simons family. Doña Eulalia died a tragic death. Land-hungry Anglos had murdered her husband and three sons in 1878. Upon discovering their bodies, which had been thrown into a pit, Doña Eulalia screamed "¡Mi Familia! ¡Mi Vida!" She fell on her knees, grabbed fistsful of earth, rubbed the earth on her body, ripped her dress, and exposed her body to nature before finally throwing herself into the pit with her family. Three weeks later the grave was discovered. The authorities plus hundreds of the curious descended on Doña Eulalia's land to witness the tragic deaths.

> No one was willing to touch the clothes. Finally one of the local roughnecks jumped into the hole and grabbed the dress and threw it out at his friends, whose faces suddenly communicated terror. The man in the pit looked at his feet and saw hundreds of indescribably large brown insects. The insects began to crawl up his pant legs. Many people were paralyzed. Horror choked the people as they watched the insects overtake them, spread out and cover El Rincón de San Pascual.[8]

The waiter also informs Simons about the mystery of Doña Eulalia's age. In the 1830s it was said that she was about 57; eight years later, however, she gave her age as 40. When the Anglo land-grabbers began to encroach on her property, her age was reported at about 155, and after her death, documents were discovered that indicated her age was 170! According to the waiter, many in the region believed Doña Eulalia was still alive and roamed the countryside. Rather than appearing as a woman in search of her children, however, as in the popular Mexican folk legend La Llorona, Doña Eulalia had taken on the appearance of millions of brown insects. "She understood the earth in a special way and possessed powers of the earth," the waiter concluded. "She is the soil and those insects are her."[9]

For Morales, Doña Eulalia symbolizes the dispossessed Mexicans who themselves become the earth and who will not rest until they have regained their domain and expelled the Anglo invaders. In the meantime, they are the brown insects, or what Oscar Zeta Acosta called the "Cockroach People" in writing about Chicanos in the 1970s.[10] Like cockroaches Chicanos can be killed, but they don't die. They survive and struggle for control of the earth. They are the earth.

IV

Having conquered the Mexican borderlands and, by the late 1800s, dispossessed the Californios of their richest lands, the new Yankee rulers set out to capitalize the mode of production by not only introducing new capitalist enterprises, but also creating an expandable pool of surplus labor in the form of the Mexican population. By the turn of the century, much of California and the rest of the Southwest had been transformed from a nineteenth-century semifeudal Mexican economy to a full-blown capitalist one based on Yankee capital and, in part, the exploitable conditions of Mexican labor. Morales seeks to recapture this history and, in so doing, correct what he calls the "historical amnesia" of California, which has all but swept Mexicans off the pages of history.

Representative of the capitalist transformation of Southern California is the Simons family. Beginning with a brick factory in Pasadena, the Simons brothers extended their holdings to include brick plants in Los Angeles, Santa Monica, and what would come to be called Simons, California, site of the biggest plant, located near Montebello, east of Los Angeles. To the Mexican workers, the Simons plant was known as El Hoyo—the hole. It was built at Rancho Laguna with land purchased from another California family, the Bartalos. Like Doña Eulalia, Doña Bartalo, who sells the land, represents to Morales the decline of the Californios and their reincarnation as creatures of the earth. As Doña Bartalo leaves the room where she has signed the deed letters turning her land over to the Simons family, "Joseph and Walter [one of the other brothers] notice that on the lace at the bottom of her full dress were two large brown insects."[11]

The success of the Simons's brick empire, especially of its key location at Simons, was based on the employment of hundreds of Mexican workers, mostly immigrants who had arrived in a chain migration from Guanajuato, the home state of Rosendo Guerrero, Simons's Mexican foreman, who kept the workers in line. The accessibility of cheap labor from Mexico allowed the Simons brothers to amass sizeable profits for themselves and to provide their workers with just enough to make them feel grateful for their jobs. Walter Simons, Joseph's younger brother, had visited Porfirio Díaz's Mexico and, while finding abhorrent Díaz's ruthless and bloody oppression of his people, was still impressed by the dictator's system of law and order, especially regarding the labor force. Yet Díaz's strong-arm tactics failed in the end and led to the Mexican Revolution of 1910. Learning from this experience, Walter hoped to import Díaz's law and order but maintain it through a patronizing relationship with the workers. This system of labor control replaced overt repression with a company town environment, which included cheap housing, a school, a church, and a company store—the *tienda de raya*, where liberal but burdensome credit was dispensed. Such provisions kept the workers content and, at the same time, in a form of debt peonage to Simons. The Simons brothers justified their structured and exploitative labor system with their racist views toward Mexicans, including the belief that all Mexicans were essentially lazy. In an interview concerning their Mexican workers, Walter's second wife, Edith Simons, notes that while she appreciates the loyalty of their workers, she also fears them as a potential menace. "I must confess a strange thought that just came to me," she tells her interviewer, "Mexicans, like cockroaches, are extremely adaptable. They will survive anything. Many might perish but there will always be survivors to propagate the race. They're just like cockroaches."[12] Walter expresses similar feelings when he admits to himself that perhaps Mexicans feel closer to the earth—the very earth that he exploits. "Mexicans were like the earth," Morales writes of Walter's feelings. "Mexicans were the earth, he often would say to himself alone."[13]

This underlying suspicion and fear of Mexicans proves to be not without validity as the specter of Doña Eulalia and of the victimization of the Mexican in the previous century comes to haunt and torment the Simons family. This is most graphically revealed in the death of Orin Elmer, one of the Simons brothers. Upon becoming feverish one evening, Orin Elmer stumbles into the kitchen:

> He found himself leaning into the sink where unwashed dinner dishes had been left. He reached for one dish and turned it to find hundreds of crawling insects. He looked again and now the insects had completely taken over the sink and were dispensing onto the counter. He turned both faucet handles to wash the crawling bugs away. But from the mouth of the faucet came a louder hiss, followed by silence and a stream of thousands of insects which enveloped the bottle of water

he held. He moved to protect the bottle. With each step he crushed hundreds of brown bugs. They now blanketed the floor, the walls, the ceiling.

Orin Elmer's delirious language became a terrifying scream. He staggered to his bedroom. The insects were taking over the house. His bed covered with creatures. He could not escape them. The beasts were now crawling onto his legs. They fell down from the ceiling. Orin Elmer crushed and pulled them from his hair as he screamed and struggled to exit their image.[14]

After Joseph and Walter find Orin Elmer and take him out of the house, they decide to burn down the structure to destroy the insects. Before doing so, however, the brothers notice that the insects have mysteriously disappeared. But the bugs have not left Orin Elmer alone. "The strangeness had burrowed itself in Orin Elmer, who throughout the daybreak hours gagged and coughed up pieces and at times whole brown insects that came from deep within his body."[15] Rosendo, the foreman, advises Walter that the only thing that can save his brother is a *curandero*—a Mexican folk healer. "Your brother is not ill with fever, nor is he poisoned. He is *hechizado*—cursed."[16] But Joseph refuses to have anything to do with what he considers Mexican superstitions. "I will never allow my brother to be treated by ignorant Mexican Indian doctors," he tells Walter, who is in favor of the curandero.[17] Instead, Joseph exclaims that Orin Elmer will receive the best and most modern American medical treatment available. But modern science proves to be no match for the power of the disinherited:

At eleven in the morning Orin Elmer drowned in a cocoon of brown insects. His engulfed body gave off putrid odors and ghastly popping sounds. His family was never able to brush the plague off his body. As his mother undressed him, the insects insistently clung to the skin and left his clothes immaculate. When Orin Elmer was placed in a casket, millions of bugs surrounded his corpse. Only when the box was closed forever did the multiplication of insects seem to subside.[18]

Some years later, in the early 1930s, Joseph is overcome by the brown insects. "Ever since 1929, when Joseph claimed to have seen millions of brown insects rise from a pit in a field near his home and devour a family of street people," Morales writes, "his mind had skipped slowly into itself until his words and actions became inside out, absurd."[19] As if recognizing that these creatures represented life more than he, Joseph begins to eat the insects. But he can't be saved. He has destroyed too much. One day Walter finds his brother dead, his skull split apart. "When Walter pushed his brother out of the blood, hundreds of brown insects scattered from underneath Joseph's back. Thousands more scurried away. Walter, infuriated with the beasts, crushed as many as he could under his shoes but the insects kept coming from someplace under his brother's body."[20]

Anglo capitalists, Morales suggests, can never really possess or dominate the land because they don't respect it. They only covet it for their own wealth. Only those who identify with the earth will ultimately live in peace with it. Perhaps not now, but in time. As more Mexican immigrants enter the old northern borderlands, resettle, and have offspring, this previously Mexican territory, through a form of biological reconquest, will revert once again into Mexican hands. This is illustrated in a dream that a Simons worker's daughter has one night at the same time as the great San Francisco earthquake in 1906. The dream relates the theme of reconquest through the employment of pre-Columbian religious symbolism, in particular the figure of Quetzalcoatl—the Plumed Serpent and the symbol of the greatness and humanity of the pre-Columbian world:

> The child got up from bed. She fell to the floor and her body contorted. She spoke in English and Spanish. She felt an enormous weight on her body and said it was tons of bricks, that a whole building had fallen on her. She saw the city destroyed before her eyes. She suffered great pain which caused her to see everything clearly. Her vision penetrated the earth itself. She witnessed fire consuming the city and she heard the screams of children who burned. The earth moved, El Eco [the daughter] told us, the earth shook. And then she stared at the earth and told us of a plumed serpent so large, so great, that it could not fit in our mind, but she saw it all. That serpent was an energy twisted and turned within the earth, causing great tremors. El Eco said that a part of the great serpent ran throughout the state, north and south. For a long time she did not move or speak and then it was as if she had died.
>
> Oh God, I [the father] said, and then she began to cry and all the children came into the room. And there we were, all of us, crying because El Eco had gone. Suddenly her body twisted violently as if it were burning and slowly she became tranquil. But before she slept peacefully, she told us that the great serpent would twist and turn until we as people would have the necessary children to reconstruct a homeland here in this place.[21]

But while the reconquest awaits, the Mexicans of Simons struggle to survive economically and culturally. Although exploited by Simons, the Mexicans take pride in their labor, belying the racist view of their inherent laziness. Morales's Mexicans instead are the "salt of the earth." "We are not afraid of hard work!" one worker exclaims.[22] Their adjustment to harsh working conditions is aided by the ability of families to remain together and by a sense of community among workers' families. Family and cultural preservation are a form of covert resistance. A few, like Malaquías de Leon, are fortunate enough to be able to save what they need to leave Simons and rent farmland. "For awhile I have been thinking about renting some land," Malaquías pronounces. "I am one of these ranchers who has to be up to his neck in earth to feel free. I don't feel free in Simons."[23] But most Mexicans are not as fortunate. They remain in debt to the company store and bound to the brick plant. They take pride in their hard work, but they are secretly unhappy. Like Malaquías, they hunger for a return to the land—their land. This unhappiness is noted after a photo is taken of the work crew upon celebrating the recognition of the Simons Brick Factory as being the largest in the world. Management provides the workers with copies of the photograph, which the workers with pride take home (the photo is the same one illustrated on the inside cover of the book). Milagros, the wife of Damian Revueltas, points out the photo's contradiction: "It is a photograph filled with repression. The men are stiff, tense, as if they were dead, all faces are faces of fear or hate. Very few of the men are smiling. It is a photograph of sad prisoners, of tired slaves, of men angered for being where they are at. As if they are forced to do what they do, not want to do."[24]

V

What alternatives for social change do the workers possess? How will they prepare themselves for La Reconquista? This is the problematic that Morales wrestles with through the eyes of Octavio Revueltas, the key Mexican protagonist in the novel. In tracing Octavio's personal history, Morales takes the reader through many of the changes that affected the Mexican communities in the United States during the early twentieth century, from arrival during the tense period of the Mexican Revolution to permanent settlement by the Roaring Twenties; then from the Great Depression, dislocation, and deportations of the 1930s to the U.S. entry into World War II, which younger Mexican Americans embraced as an opportunity to prove their patriotism, only to be reminded of their second-class status by racist outbursts such as the Zoot Suit Riots in Los

Angeles in 1943. Octavio and his family experience all these changes, but what unifies their experiences is Octavio's burning desire to rise above his lowly status as a brick worker in Simons. This ambition provides the drama for the lesson Morales weaves from history.

Having grown up in the United States, Octavio has no desire to return to Mexico, unlike his father, who grew up there. Octavio possesses not the Mexican dream of immigrants—the hope of return to a better life in Mexico—but the mythical American dream of individual success and a good life for himself and his family in the United States. In the meantime, Octavio works hard, saves his money, and acculturates like other Mexican Americans. He even refuses to donate part of his salary to his father, hoping to save enough by himself to build a home for his mother and his younger brothers and sisters. But like most children of immigrants—the Mexican American generation—Octavio recognizes that his future is in the United States.[25] "The United States, Octavio decided, was the place where he would build a house for his own family. Mexico retreated into fading images in his memory, and life in Simons and in Los Angeles became more exciting everyday."[26] When he marries Nana, daughter of Malaquías, he transfers these dreams into his own family. To add to his income, Octavio pursues his own form of private enterprise by becoming a successful gambler. Yet he does not fully control his own future. It is tied to the Simons Brick Factory. With the onset of the Great Depression, the factory begins to curtail production, and Octavio, sensing his vulnerability, recognizes that his hope for the future may be in jeopardy. A proud man, Octavio resents having to work for the gringos.

To protect himself and his family, Octavio begins to explore alternative strategies. He attends meetings of the militant Spanish-Speaking People's Congress in Los Angeles as well as the Confederación de Sindicatos de Campesinos y Obreros and the communistic Cannery and Agricultural Workers' Industrial Union. Octavio's own militancy is further spurred by inhaling the red dust connected with the brick factory. Fired up by his hatred of Walter Simons and of Anglo racism, Octavio rebels against the idea that Mexicans should continue to work faithfully in the hope of a future better life. Octavio rejects such hope, which he believes to be a form of false consciousness, and instead opts for workers taking their destiny into their own hands: "He disliked the word hope. Hope, he believed, was a concept of oppression used by the dominant society to rule the mass of people. Hope represented nonmovement, never advancing forward, never bettering the workers' economic state. Hope was a void, a holding zone used to control. Octavio would not be controlled. He rejected hope and searched for a plan of action against Walter."[27]

Like thousands of other American workers in the 1930s, Octavio and his coworkers at the brick factory turn to unionization as a viable strategy to protect themselves against the vicissitudes of the bosses. And like most unskilled and semiskilled workers of the period, they find a welcome haven in the new unions of the Congress of Industrial Organizations (CIO), which are heavily influenced by radicals, including members of the Communist Party. Mexican workers in California, for example, during the 1930s engaged in a number of unionizing drives and strikes. While some failed, others succeeded. Through Octavio's leadership, the brick workers join the Cannery and Agricultural Workers' Industrial Union and proceed to strike against the Simons plant. Whether based on actual events or not, Morales here possesses a writer's choice, to portray this labor action as a success or as a failure. He chooses the latter. By using black strikebreakers, who are unfairly portrayed as complicit with the Anglos against the Mexicans, Walter Simons breaks the strike. Octavio and the workers in their anger and despair become discouraged about collectivist action and blame the Anglo leadership of the union. They accuse the union of selling out the workers and of cheating them out of their strike benefits. Portrayed as one-dimensional leftwing ideologues, the Communist Party leaders pose an easy target for Morales to set up as straw people. At a union meeting, Octavio attacks the leadership for being as corrupt as the capitalists. "You are a bunch of sons-of-bitches. You're the same as old man Simons. Your only interest is in what you're going to gain. You're thieves and exploiters."[28] Of course, the real relationship between such Anglo CP leaders and the Mexican rank and file was much more complex, with many Anglo radicals working quite well and successfully with the Mexicans.[29] In Morales's novel, however, the workers reject the union, go back to work, and save some face when Simons agrees to replace the hated company store with a workers co-op. Unfortunately, Morales depicts the workers as naïve and greedy, and through their abuse of the credit system, they destroy the co-op.

At this crucial point in his novel, Morales channels it into what I would more properly call working-class literature, as distinguished from what was referred to in the 1930s as proletarian literature. What is the difference here? Working-class literature, in my view, is literature about workers, but not necessarily from a worker's point of view. It may, like most novels, convey middle-class values rather than aspiring to help create alternative working-class ones. Above all, it is literature that is not fundamentally committed to act as a political weapon. It is not written in the ambience of profound social change. On the other hand, proletarian literature as defined during the heyday of the Left in the United States, the 1930s, is not just about workers' lives; the writers, whether of working-class or middle-class backgrounds, are socially committed to the class struggle. Proletarian literature possesses what Waldo Frank in 1935 called a "revolutionary vision."[30] And as Walter Rideout notes, just as most novels reflected bourgeois values, the proletarian novel "would reflect proletarian values, would bring the worker to class-consciousness, steal him for the coming revolution, prepare him for the role he would play in the next stage of history. Art was a form of politics; it was a weapon in the class war."[31] Even Josephine Herbst, who decried the use of the term "proletarian literature," agreed that at least the novels of the 1930s, which concerned workers and the poor, "could be classified as vehicles for protest and engines for change."[32] To be sure, many of these proletarian novels were somewhat artificial, with stereotypical workers and romanticized visions of the class struggle; on the other hand, many were not, such as Jack Conroy's *The Disinherited*, and represented an innovative new realist novel form that broke from the more traditional and politically conservative modernist novel.[33] Whether artistically advanced or not, proletarian literature sought to promote class consciousness and the elimination of exploitative class relations characteristic of capitalism.

Of course, Mexican workers like their Anglo counterparts also met with defeat in the 1930s, which led to disillusionment and frustration. At the same time, however, many overcame their despair and continued to struggle for their rights as workers and as Americans. Some of my research, for example, explores the ability and tenacity of Mexican American workers to conquer adversities. Mexican American workers who joined the International Union of Mine, Mill, and Smelter Workers in the Southwest during the 1930s spearheaded successful drives that led to union recognition and the eventual elimination of so-called Mexican jobs and Mexican wages in unionized plants. While these efforts did not fundamentally alter class relations, they did advance the struggle of Mexican workers and extend protections for the first time to such workers.[34] It is this more inspiring history, however, that Morales chooses to ignore. Rather than at least showing the dialectic of Chicano labor history, based on both successes and failures, disillusionment and commitment, Morales provides only the side of collective defeat. Unlike the truly proletarian novels of the 1930s, Morales gives the reader no alternative model for social changes based on the collective interests of all workers.

Instead what Morales provides is a more individualistic and conservative model of social change founded on each worker's dream of achieving private home ownership. Not political group struggle, but individual mobility. Not a collective reconquest of the lost land, but individual homeownership. Hence the novel concludes with Octavio deciding that the only viable goal for him is to save his income and gambling profits to purchase a plot of land on which he can construct his home. This becomes particularly important to him since earlier efforts to rent homes in Anglo neighborhoods in Montebello met with racist housing covenants against Mexicans. But Octavio has also concluded that it is as futile to struggle against racism as it is to combat employers. The only viable alternative is to retreat into one's family, one's culture, and one's home. "Octavio disliked gringos," Morales writes. "They denied him shelter that he deserved, had earned, and could afford for his family. He felt less a man, a father, or husband; less in the eyes of his wife, children and friends. Octavio did not possess the power to overcome the gringo adversaries."[35] Octavio resents having to live in his parents' empty garage after his company-owned house burns down. He will not live like an insect. "He condemned himself for bringing his wife and children to living like cockroaches of the earth."[36] Octavio, in the end, does not identify with Acosta's "Cockroach People." No one, of course, would advocate that Mexicans should live like insects. What is missing here, however, is Morales's recognition that the struggle against poverty, inferior housing, racism, and worker exploitation cannot be an individualized effort. It has to be a collective one based on workers' interest as a class. No one should be against the promotion of individual talents, but Morales erroneously seems to believe that individuality can exist outside class and social relations, which, in fact, it cannot. As Victor Molina notes: "Individuality is precisely a *product* of the ensemble of social relations."[37] Or as Karl Marx observed in *Grundrisse*, "The human being is in the most literal sense a political animal, not merely a gregarious animal, but an animal which can individuate itself only in the midst of society."[38] Class, race, and gender exploitation and oppression can only be effectively contested by a community, such as those at Simons or in Smeltertown in El Paso, where the Mine Mill workers took on ASARCO and won. Octavio rejects this recognition of collective power. In its place, he retreats to the very American dream that he had earlier condemned.

As Octavio moves to pursue his own individualistic goals (for union workers have also achieved home ownership without necessarily betraying their communal struggles; indeed, these struggles have led to such material rewards), his adversary, Walter Simons, dies as his brothers did, at the hands of the brown insects. In Europe, Walter chokes to death when scores of brown insects inundate his mouth while he sleeps in a Paris hotel. Ironically, Simons succumbs not at the hands of his own workers, but at the specter of Doña Eulalia and the nineteenth-century Californios. Simons dies, his workers are faced with job loss as the Simons empire collapses, but Octavio dreams of his home while he works for Phelps Dodge. As if to provide a cultural veneer to such ironic consequences, Morales has a curandera save Octavio's life from a potentially terminal cancer. Octavio absorbs the American dream, but, so Morales tells us, still retains his culture. The problem in all this is not a dearth of Octavios in Chicano history, but that Morales is not really using Octavio's story to critique what I believe to be not only false consciousness (that everyone can pull themselves up by their own bootstraps) but a politically regressive strategy that pits a false sense of individualism against the collective interests of the working community. Morales takes no distance from Octavio and thus presents him as the model of La Reconquista. Moreover, he does not even present an alternative model, of which there have been many in Chicano history based on group struggles. Morales does not explore the contradictions and the dialectic. What might have become what I consider a proletarian novel, imbued with class consciousness and inspiration, in the end becomes only a novel about workers—but not for workers. *The Brick People* likewise breaks with the legacy of the Chicano Movement, which, despite its contradictions and ambivalences, still posited the value of collectivist struggles, which Morales seems to despair of, instead favoring individualized aspirations.

VI

Comment should also be made here of Morales's depiction of Mexican women. While showing the strength of women as wives and mothers in sustaining the family and in promoting Mexican cultural traditions, Morales regrettably does not provide his female characters with an alternative search for empowerment outside the traditional and patriarchal structures in which they live. They resent the sexist treatment they receive at the hands of their husbands—the double standard—but they do not rebel to overthrow such confining and oppressive relations. There is Pascuala, for example, whose husband, Gonzalo, the foreman, carries on an affair for years with his employee Amalia and has children by her. Morales says of Pascuala that she "tolerated this life, never admitting that her husband had another woman. Despite what was common knowledge in Simons, she never acknowledged the fact that Gonzalo fathered children other than with her. When she contemplated the pride and excitement her children had for their father, she did not complain."[39] Nana, Octavio's wife, rather than supporting Octavio's involvement with organizing the brick workers during the Depression, instead counsels noninvolvement. Nana's main goal, and ultimately Octavio's, is to own her own home. Her marital problems and Octavio's disregard for her are repressed. "In these years Nana became a solitary woman, a woman finding energy, inspiration and the will to endure from within herself."[40] But this energy, inspiration, and endurance are directed not toward her own liberation or that of other oppressed women in Simons, but toward surviving, keeping her family intact, and supporting her husband's ultimate search for the American dream. This is not to suggest that Morales should have depicted these women as feminists, but that, as with the workers, he might have provided alternative models of women who, despite the durability of patriarchy, have rebelled in various ways and have pursued alternative strategies. One is reminded here of the women of the famous Salt of the Earth strike in New Mexico and their struggle not only against patriarchy but against capitalist class exploitation.[41]

VII

All of this is not to disparage Morales's *The Brick People*. The book is an ambitious effort. It is engrossing. It is sweeping in scope. Like Ralph Ellison's *Invisible Man*, which symbolizes much of the history of African Americans in the United States, *The Brick People* symbolizes much of the Chicano experience. Morales is correct in interpreting this history as essentially one of Mexicans as the dispossessed: cheated and robbed of their nineteenth-century lands, and then cheated and robbed of the fruits of their labor in the twentieth century. It is a history of people in motion, of migration, of coming "north from Mexico," as Carey McWilliams put it, of working people, and of the major contributions of Mexicans to the building of California ("the brick people" is a metaphor for their fundamental contribution). Morales's novel is a history of dialectical tensions and change, of cultural retention and acculturation, of continuity and change between generations. It is all of this.

But what Morales's novel is not, and here it differs crucially from recent Chicano historiography, is a history of people's struggles—struggles that have not only manifested the grievances of Chicanos, but also given rich meanings to their lives. Yes, many have faced defeat and rejection, but even in defeat, many have been enriched by their feelings of solidarity with their *compañeros* and *compañeras*. As I write this, I can't help but conjure up the faces of Chicano workers I have interviewed, who in relating their victories and defeats never hinted at feelings of futility or hopelessness and never regretted their involvements in collective actions. I particularly recall my interview with Humberto Silex, a giant in Chicano labor history, who helped put together the Mine Mill movement in El Paso. Harassed, red-baited, blacklisted from jobs, threatened with deportation, and even abandoned by the union, Silex, over eighty years old and blind when I interviewed him, still displayed a vigorous enthusiasm for his history. Like Octavio, Silex also became a homeowner, but there was much more to Silex's life than owning a home, including his contribution to the struggle of Mexican workers in this country to overcome class, race, and gender discrimination. That and his memories of these efforts are more important to him than his material possessions.[42] In this sense—in my political reading of *The Brick People*—I believe Morales's novel, while highly important and of much value to historians, fails. It does not provide a vision of a truly better and more just world for all workers, a world achievable not by individual quest, but only by community struggle. It does not provide, to paraphrase Lenin, a lesson or even a hint of what is to be done.

7

THE MEXICAN AMERICAN
SEARCH FOR IDENTITY

Ruben Salazar's Unpublished Novel,
"A Stranger's House"

I

THE FIGURE OF RUBEN SALAZAR continues to fascinate. Killed forty-six years ago while covering the Chicano antiwar moratorium in East Los Angeles on August 29, 1970, for the *Los Angeles Times* and KMEX, the Spanish-language television station in LA, this Mexican American journalist remains a myth to many and a martyr of the Chicano Movement of those times. Publications, films, plays, symposiums, and commemorations on Salazar continue to be done.

The events surrounding his death are well known to Chicano studies scholars, and here I only summarize them.[1]

On August 29, 1970, organizers staged the largest antiwar demonstration in Chicano history. Aimed at protesting the U.S. military intervention in the civil war in Vietnam, the growing Chicano casualties in the conflict, and the draining of federal antipoverty funds from Chicano and other minority communities to pay for the war, somewhere around twenty thousand protestors, mostly Chicanos, demonstrated in East LA, the main Chicano barrio in Los Angeles.

It was a peaceful march that concluded at Laguna Park (later renamed Ruben Salazar Park). As the marchers streamed in by early afternoon, entertainment and speakers began the rally program. Soon, however, sounds of a commotion adjacent to the park were heard. Without notice, a large number of Los Angeles county sheriff deputies, supported by contingents of Los Angeles police officers, forced their way into the park, declaring the rally an "unlawful assembly." They shot tear gas into the assembled crowd and began to use their nightsticks on some Chicanos. Demonstrators would later call this a "police riot." Forced to vacate the park, Chicanos fled onto adjacent Whittier Boulevard, which became a war zone. Storefronts were broken, and cars and buildings were set on fire. Many were arrested, and unfortunately, three people were killed.[2]

One of these casualties was Ruben Salazar. After following the conflict in the park, Salazar with his KMEX crew retired later that afternoon to the Silver Dollar Café on Whittier Boulevard. Sometime after they arrived, deputy sheriffs also converged on the Silver Dollar. They would later claim they had been tipped off that an armed man was in the café; however, no evidence of a weapon was found on the premises. After forcing some people who were leaving the café back inside, one of the deputies fired at least two tear gas projectiles into the establishment. One hit Salazar in the head, instantly killing him.

News of Salazar's death quickly spread throughout the Chicano community and Los Angeles. Although Salazar was respected by Chicano Movement activists, they did not consider the politically moderate Salazar to be part of *la causa*—their cause. Salazar did not consider himself a movement activist. As a professional journalist and the most prominent Latino journalist in the United States at that time, Salazar did not consider it appropriate for him to be politically engaged while maintaining his objectivity as a journalist, though he was sympathetic to the political struggle.

Despite Salazar's self-chosen distance from the politics of the movement (he still reported on movement events), his death instantly elevated him to martyr status within the movement, which embraced him as one of its own. His image was almost immediately put on movement posters, leaflets, murals, and other materials. In time, libraries, public housing units, scholarships, and educational and media programs were named after the fallen journalist. In addition, the U.S. postal service issued a stamp in his honor. In death, Salazar became a Chicano hero and martyr. This status continues to perpetuate his memory and his historical standing.

Yet, as I attempted to demonstrate in my 1995 edited collection of the best of his journalism, to mark the twenty-fifth anniversary of his death, Ruben Salazar was much more than the guy who got killed at the Silver Dollar. To me, he should be chiefly remembered as a true pioneer in Latino journalism. What is important about the historical Salazar is his journalism. He was a first-rate reporter and a committed one. He possessed courage, principles, standards, and integrity—values not often seen today in the media.

Salazar achieved many goals in his life, but they weren't handed to him. They came as a result of his hard work to prove himself. Working in a predominantly Anglo journalist world, Salazar also bore the weight of his minority status. He struggled with this and his sense of ethnic identity all his life.

II

Ruben Salazar was born in 1928 in Ciudad Juárez to parents who were Mexican nationals. When his parents migrated across the border to El Paso, Texas, within a year after Salazar's birth, Salazar was naturalized as a U.S. citizen. He attended public schools and, shortly after graduating from high school, enrolled in the U.S. Army and was stationed in Germany. Upon release from military service in the early 1950s, Salazar used the recently enacted GI Bill of Rights to financially support attending the local Texas Western College in El Paso. He majored in journalism and wrote for the campus newspaper and literary magazine.

Upon graduation, he soon found his first stint as a journalist with the *El Paso Herald-Post*. In the two years he served on that staff, Salazar became almost a celebrity figure in his hometown because of a series of investigative pieces he wrote about horrid conditions in the city jail as well as on the drug culture of the border. For the city jail exposé, he actually impersonated a drunk in order to be arrested and get an inside view of jail conditions.

Apparently desirous of a more prestigious journalistic career, Salazar left for California, where he worked for a couple of years for newspapers in Santa Rosa and in San Francisco. By the late 1950s, he had migrated to Los Angeles, where he wrote for the *Los Angeles Herald-Express*. In this position, he came to the attention of the *Los Angeles Times*. It would become a fortuitous connection. In the early 1960s, the *Times* was undergoing a major overhaul from a second-rate paper into a first-class one. As part of these changes, new editors and reporters were being hired and recruited. Salazar became part of these new recruits. Wanting to improve its local coverage, including communities such as the Mexican American one not previously widely covered, the new *Times* editors saw in Salazar someone who could provide that reporting from East LA and other Mexican American areas.

Although never wanting to be stereotyped as a "Mexican reporter," Salazar saw a golden opportunity in moving to the *Times*. In the early 1960s, before the commencement of the Chicano Movement, Salazar was the sole journalist for a major English-language newspaper covering the Mexican American community.

And he did so with distinction. He wrote on Mexican American politics, educational issues, gangs, the border, the ending of the Bracero Program (the contract labor program with Mexico, begun in 1942), the state of the farm workers in California, and a major award-winning six-part series on East Los Angeles.

In 1965, Salazar was promoted to the prized position of foreign correspondent as a result of his recognized work. He was sent to cover the U.S. intervention in the Dominican Republic. Later that year he was dispatched as one of the *Times* reporters covering the growing U.S. military presence in Vietnam. Upon returning, he was sent in 1966 to Mexico City, where he was further elevated as bureau chief, covering Mexico, Central America, and the Caribbean.

In 1968, however, after covering the protests around the Mexico City Olympics, which had led to hundreds of students being killed by the Mexican army, in what became known as the Massacre at Tlatelolco, Salazar was recalled to Los Angeles. The *Times* valued his work in Mexico City, but another crisis convinced *Times* editors to bring Salazar home. This crisis was the growing protests surrounding the developing Chicano Movement in LA and throughout the Southwest, where the majority of Chicanos lived. The *Times* was taken aback, for example, when thousands of Chicano students staged walkouts of schools in East LA in spring 1968 to protest years of inferior education. Seeing itself without a veteran reporter to cover this major protest movement, the *Times* turned to Salazar.

Although reluctant to give up his prime job as a foreign correspondent and still leery of being typed a "Mexican reporter," Salazar as a good company man agreed to return. During the next two years, he provided extensive coverage of the movement in his articles and, by 1969, his weekly column on Chicano issues. In these pieces, Salazar attempted to explain the movement to *Times* readers and indirectly provide a voice for the movement in an establishment publication. Salazar gave even more attention and voice to the movement when he also became news manager of KMEX in 1970. He focused particularly on police abuse and brutality in East Los Angeles. This did not endear him to police officials and later gave rise to conspiracy theories surrounding Salazar's death.[3]

III

As a Mexican American who came of age prior to the Chicano Movement of the late 1960s and early 1970s, with its prescriptive identity based on Chicanismo, the ethnic and cultural nationalist ideology of the movement, Ruben

Salazar searched for the answer to what it meant to be a Mexican in the United States. Reading his journalism, particularly his later columns, you get some sense of Salazar's quest. For example, in one of his most quoted columns, he wrote, "A Chicano is a Mexican-American with a non-Anglo image of himself."[4]

Yet, as I noted in my book on Salazar, he never seemed to identify fully as a Chicano in the way that the militant movement defined Chicano. Salazar was proud of his Mexican American heritage, but a part of him still seemed to believe that the American system could be reformed to provide acceptance of Mexican Americans. This view differed significantly from Chicano Movement identity, which rejected acculturation, assimilation, and integration in favor of a more separate if nebulous identity and politics.

Although Salazar was, in my opinion, still grappling with his identity at the time of his death, it is his death that elevates him into a Chicano. He becomes immortalized as a Chicano. He becomes in death what he seemed not yet to be in life, or perhaps didn't want to be. We will never know.

In addition to his journalism, a new source previously unknown has surfaced that sheds considerable light on Salazar's confrontation with identity questions in the years before the Chicano Movement. This source, in a way, also illuminates the consciousness of other Mexican Americans of his generation—the Mexican American generation, those Mexican Americans who came of age, generationally and politically, in the pre–Chicano Movement years.[5]

This source is the unfinished novel entitled "A Stranger's House," which Salazar began writing in English apparently around 1958 and continued working on until about 1964. I was given access to it by his eldest daughter, Lisa, when I interviewed her for my book on Salazar. The only stipulation she made was that the entire manuscript not be published. "A Stranger's House" consists of six chapters of different lengths and states of completion, as well as at least a couple hundred unorganized pages as well.

The novel is obviously somewhat autobiographical and closely follows Salazar's coming-of-age years in El Paso. It is the story of the Márquez family. The father, Felipe, is a mestizo from Guadalajara who comes to the Mexican border town Cuidad Juárez, across the border from El Paso, as a young man in the 1920s. He is a jeweler by profession (as was Salazar's father) and ekes out a living on the Mexican side of the border. There he meets his future wife, Esperanza, who had migrated to Juárez from Monterrey. Unlike Felipe, Esperanza claims pure Spanish descent and is of the hacendado class overturned by the Revolution of 1910. Her father was killed by the revolutionaries. Married in Juárez,

Esperanza convinces Felipe that it would be better to raise a family in El Paso. He reluctantly agrees and is able, despite the onset of the Great Depression, to secure a job in a jewelry store on the other side.

In El Paso, Esperanza gives birth to her only child, Lorenzo, or Lencho, as they will call him. They first live in the large Mexican immigrant El Segundo Barrio, or Second Ward, in the southern part of the city, adjacent to the border. Disdaining living there, Esperanza in time is able to arrange for the family to move into a mixed neighborhood north of the railroad tracks, the dividing line between Mexican El Paso and Anglo El Paso. Esperanza's hope—her name symbolizes it—is that Lorenzo will grow up to be a successful and an accepted American. He is able to attend an American school, not the Mexican schools of the south side barrio. He learns English quickly and makes Anglo friends. In the seventh grade, however, Lorenzo encounters his first experience with Anglo racism. This forces him to recognize his difference as a Mexican American. It creates ambivalence about his identity, which is exacerbated by different views on ethnicity held by his parents and by his later high school friend José Contreras. Out of these conflicting perspectives, Lorenzo will arrive at some of his own conclusions. These conclusions are not closed ones, however, since the novel itself is not closed. In this sense, the novel unintentionally parallels Salazar's ongoing search for identity, which is cut off by his tragic death at age forty-two.

IV

In addition to being a narrative about Mexican American identity, "A Stranger's House" is an indictment of U.S. racism and, interestingly, Mexican racism as well. Salazar clearly had strong opinions on racism and the role it played in causing the Mexican American identity crisis. This is important to note because a body of historians and other Chicano studies scholars incorrectly suggest that the Mexican American generation was addicted to assimilation and shy about combating racism while straining to pass for white. One recent book on Chicanos and race, for example, makes a blanket charge that Mexican American leaders in the pre–Chicano Movement era all embraced the concept of whiteness for Mexican Americans.[6] Certainly, there were those who fit this pattern, but Salazar's generation was as diverse as the later Chicano generation. Ruben Salazar's testimony about the race question is evidence of more complexity and diversity than essentialism on this issue within both generations.

V

In the character of Esperanza, Lorenzo's mother, Salazar takes a distance and critiques the assimilationist model. As the story unfolds, he will reveal the contradictions of those like Esperanza, who, while well-meaning, cannot or will not see the obstacles to Mexican American assimilation into the U.S. system. Salazar clearly understood that assimilation is a two-way street. It's not enough for Mexican Americans to want to assimilate. The dominant population also has to want to assimilate them. In Esperanza's obsession with her son achieving a better life as a U.S. citizen, she ideologically blinds herself to the problems involved.

Esperanza's assimilationist ideology is first shaped by her contrast between Mexico and the United States. To her, the United States is truly the promised land and the land of opportunity, unlike Mexico, especially post-Revolutionary Mexico, which she sees as a land of barbarians who have taken over. There is no hope in Mexico. The future, at least for her children, will be *al otro lado*, or on the other side. This contrast between the two sides of the border she later passes on to the young Lorenzo. She says to him, "I used to go to the edge of the river and look at the American side. It looked wonderful, Lorenzo. With its bright lights, tall buildings and cars running around."[7] Esperanza admits to Lorenzo, however, that she did not achieve the American dream. But she will see to it that he does: "I didn't capture it [the dream], son. I ran away to Juárez and then to El Paso to escape the barbarians. I didn't succeed, Lorenzo. But you will. I swear to God you will."

For Esperanza, assimilation means turning your back on Mexico. She counters Felipe's continued attachment to Mexico and Mexican culture, as well as his pursuit of what I call the Mexican dream. This is the aspiration of those immigrants who believe that their stay in the United States will be only temporary until they can return to a better life in Mexico. Esperanza rejects this for her and her son. "Going back to Mexico would not be good for Lencho," she lectures her husband. "There is no future in Mexico. I have never heard of a boy in our circumstances getting ahead in Mexico. I have heard many stories about poor boys making good in the United States."

Esperanza promotes assimilation to Lorenzo not only by rejecting her homeland, but also by taking a racial and class distance from the poor working Mexican immigrants whom they have to live with at first in El Segundo Barrio. Here, Salazar critiques still another form of racism—Mexican racism. He understood through his own family and probably through his relations with other Mexican Americans who shared his mother's racist views toward non-white Mexicans that while the formation of racial identity among Mexicans was more fluid and less rigid than among Anglos, nevertheless Mexicans also accepted a racial hierarchy that prioritized light skin. Salazar's indictment of racism from both Anglo and Mexican sides reveals his rather sophisticated and nonethnic nationalist political views. To Salazar, all racism, irrespective of its source, was to be condemned.

Esperanza cannot deny her own Mexicanness, but she can suggest that she is different from other immigrants. Esperanza claims that she is of the *gente decente* of the upper classes of Mexico and that she is of pure Spanish descent, not Indian or mestiza. Salazar notes in the text, however, that Esperanza in fact possesses what he refers to as some "Indian blood," although her complexion is fair.

Esperanza stresses to Lorenzo that she and her family were not peasants but hacendados. Regrettably, the rabble took over Mexico during the Revolution. "Mexico became a land run by *pelados*, barbarians," she tells Lorenzo. As her father lay dying, his last words were "The barbarians are taking over." Esperanza's use of the term *pelado* resonates with Samuel Ramos, the post-Revolutionary Mexican philosopher, who also castigated the lower class with the derogatory term *pelado*. Salazar unlike Ramos, however, is critiquing Esperanza's pretensions and biases.

In Esperanza's opinion, the pelados are uncouth, but they are also inferior Mexican Indians, or mestizos. She tells Lorenzo that he is not like them: "*Eres Americano, mi hijo, no un pelado Indio Mexicano*. You are American, my son, not a nasty Mexican Indian." Esperanza sees all the Mexican immigrants in El Segundo Barrio as pelados and indios. "These Mexican Indians," she tells Lorenzo, "are worse than dogs. They are the vomit of Mexico, the vermin of the United States."

She contrasts herself not only with the immigrants, but with her own husband, Felipe. She observes that even though Felipe is a mestizo, she married him because she believed that he was more cultured than the rest, and besides, he was lighter. After they marry, however, she begins to despair of Felipe. She sees herself as the more appropriate role model for Lorenzo, not Felipe, who is, in her opinion, not very ambitious, too much given to drink, and too Mexican. By contrast, Esperanza humbles herself and works hard by taking in laundry for others, saving her earnings so the family can move out of the barrio. "All day long I'm breaking my back trying to make a decent home," she lambastes Felipe, "and all you do is slop up wine. You're worthless—just like all goddamn

Mexican Indians." When Lorenzo sees his father in a drunken stupor and tries to help him, Esperanza admonishes him: "Keep away from him ... you're never going to be like that. ... Look at him ... a goddamn drunken Indian."

Even Lorenzo is not immune from Esperanza's tirades concerning race and class. On one occasion, when Lorenzo gets into a fight at the American school and returns home with his clothes soiled, Esperanza goes into a fury and attempts to shame her son about his appearance. To her, a cultured white American does not act or look this way. "You're as dirty as an Indian," she shouts. "Haven't I taught you to say [sic] clean? Why do you think we moved away from el Segundo barrio[,] which is full of Mexican Indians? So you could have a chance to be decent and clean. Sometimes, though, I think that you're no better than your father. Look at you. As dirty as a Mexican Indian from Juárez."

Esperanza's assimilationist strategy for Lorenzo involves getting him out of the barrio, putting him in an American school, and having him accepted by the Anglos. For her, this is the only way her son will succeed in this country. She attempts to instill these ideas in him as soon as possible. "Drink your milk my son," she tells him one day. "[Y]ou must have lots of strength in this life. You're going to go to a good school and will have nice clothes and nice friends. And then some day you'll be a doctor or a lawyer or something like that. You won't have to be a Mexican. You'll be an American and can hold your head high."

Esperanza is pleased that after they move out of the barrio, and Lorenzo begins to attend Bailey Elementary School, that he develops friendships with Anglo kids. "It is good the way they're accepting Lorenzo," she tells Felipe. "My son will go far. He will be one of them in no time." And when Felipe questions this strategy and Esperanza's belief that their son can somehow pass as an American, she counters by proclaiming, "Lorenzo is an American. I know you don't want to accept that. But he is. He was born here and this is his country and he's as good as anyone in it. He's going to put everything that we are behind him."

VI

If assimilation was one tendency or influence that Salazar and other Mexican Americans faced, so too was the reality of being of Mexican descent, including having Spanish-speaking immigrant parents. One could not avoid this. While Esperanza represents one type, focused on Americanization, Felipe represents still another. He reflects those many Mexican immigrants who continue to look back to Mexico for their sense of identity. Indeed, for many immigrants, lo mexicano increased in importance on this side of the border. This was the *México de afuera* (Mexico of the Outside) promoted by the Spanish-language press in the United States and in the Mexican consulates. While Esperanza rejects Mexico and embraces the United States, Felipe does the contrary. As a result, Lorenzo grows up with these dual competing influences, which are very much a part of Mexican American culture and identity.

Felipe never accepts living in El Paso. He does it to please Esperanza, and of course, his job is there. His body is on this side of the border but not his soul. While Esperanza pursues the mythical American dream, Felipe pursues the mythical Mexican dream—the return to la patria that means for him Guadalajara. As a result, Felipe develops the theme of living in "A Stranger's House" that is, of course, the title of Salazar's novel. One gets the impression that Salazar sympathized more with his father's position than with that of his pretentious mother. This does not mean that Salazar accepted the Mexican dream. He did not, but he clearly felt for his father's longing and the pain of being separated from his homeland. At the same time, he also understands that his father was helpless to do anything about it. In Salazar's novel, Felipe is too weak to really challenge his wife, who dominates the Márquez household.

By using "A Stranger's House" as the title of the novel, Salazar takes his father's side but understands that for him as a Mexican American, this stranger's house is also his house. For Salazar, unlike Felipe, there is no possibility of returning to Mexico. It's not even a dream. Whether they liked it or not, Salazar and his Mexican American generation had no choice. As the Woody Guthrie song goes, this land is my land—for better or for worse.

But this is not the case for Felipe. As an immigrant, he does not feel comfortable and secure north of the border and hopes to return to Mexico. Esperanza's assimilationist ideology is countered by Felipe's Mexican nationalism. These represent two powerful strains in Mexican American political thought, and Salazar was obviously working through this in constructing his own identity.

Felipe's concept of a stranger's house is not just based on cultural differences. It is also steeped in racial and ethnic tensions. Immigrants were made to feel unwelcomed whenever they crossed the border into El Paso, even if, as in Felipe's case, they possessed the proper documents. Felipe feels this humiliation at one crossing, when he and other Mexican nationals are forced by U.S. immigration inspectors to be disinfected before being allowed entry into El Paso. They are taken off the streetcar and escorted into a bathhouse. When Felipe expresses dismay at such treatment, an Anglo official further humiliates him by saying, "O.K., Pancho . . . you *sabe baño?*" [Do you understand bath?] Before Felipe and the others shower, they are sprayed with Fleet, usually used to get rid of mosquitoes and other insects.

Living as a stranger in El Paso, especially when he ventures outside the barrio, Felipe whenever possible goes to Juárez, where at least temporarily he can feel more mexicano, especially with the aid of tequila and the nostalgic songs of the mariachis. One particular lyric sung at his favorite cantina expresses some of Felipe's sentiments:

Naci en la frontera, aca d'este lado
Por mas que la gente me juzgae texano
Yo les aseguro, que soy mexicano
I was born on the border, on this side
Despite people's attempt to see me as a *texano*
I can assure you that I am *mexicano.*

Yet Juárez and border culture do not fully satisfy Felipe. To him the real Mexico was not the frontera, or border area, which he felt was too Americanized, but the interior, such as his hometown of Guadalajara. He experiences alienation on both sides of the border. Unlike the romanticization of the border by later Chicano cultural critics, Felipe sees it as a hostile environment on one side and an aberration of the real Mexico on the other. "But to Felipe, a jeweler, El Paso was like an undersized ring which fits if you force it into your finger—but never comfortably. A Mexican in El Paso, except in *el Segundo barrio,* always felt like an intruder. And Juárez across the river was not Mexico, Felipe reminded himself. It's an American playground. They do all the things they are not allowed to do in El Paso, with Mexico playing the whore."

Even though Felipe, largely because of his alcoholism, is not strong enough to prevail over Esperanza, he does at times in the story challenge her assimilationist views. He represents a counternarrative to her melting pot model. For example, when Esperanza insists that Lorenzo is an American and not "*un pelado Indio Mexicano,*" Felipe unfortunately physically abuses her by slapping her, then asserting, "Don't ever say that again. He's a Mexican and we will soon go back to where we belong." And when Esperanza agrees with the principal of Lorenzo's school that her son should be punished for speaking Spanish at school, Felipe disagrees: "I would think that speaking Spanish—especially in a place where half the people are Mexicans and Mexico is just across the river—would make you as good if not better than anyone else."

Felipe goes further and challenges Esperanza's class and racial pretensions, which she is attempting to pass on to Lorenzo. Felipe believes that Mexicans should not pretend to be what they are not. "I know that one is what one is and you can't change that," he admonishes Esperanza. "I have never played that game and pretending to be something I'm not, Esperanza. I hope Lencho won't get hurt playing it." Felipe adds insult to injury when he directly disputes the airs that Esperanza tries to put on. "Just who do you think you are anyway?" he says. "You're a Mexican and I don't give a damn how much your *hacendado* father stole from other people. You're still one of us whether you like it or not. And we all belong in our home. Ours is Mexico—not this stranger's house."

Part of Felipe's alienation is his belief that assimilation, even if possible, will damage the Mexican spirit. He agrees with the Mexican philosopher José Vasconcelos that the United States is primarily a materialistic culture and not a humanistic one. He expresses concern that Esperanza is only interested in material success rather than human values. "What is this Americanism that Esperanza always talks about?" Felipe asks Don Alberto, one of his drinking buddies.

Where is its guts? How can I touch it, kiss it, hit it, feel it? It's got to be something besides just a shining new refrigerator my wife keeps talking about. Something I can love, hate, react to. Or is it just a state of mind in which one is rich without feeling? Comfortable without pride? Satisfied without effort? ... Show me where the guts of Americanism is—without the shiny refrigerator—and I'll drop my Mexicanism. But don't ask me or my son to replace our guts with a non-thing. Life must be more than a comfortable void.

Felipe's views are only reinforced when Lorenzo experiences rejection at his school. This further convinces Felipe that the only solution is to return to Mexico proper. "Lencho is unhappy among these Americanos," he tells Esperanza. "[A]re we going to let him suffer just because he's a Mexican—must we live in a country where we're not wanted?"

VII

Assimilation and Mexican cultural nationalism are not the only views on identity that Salazar introduces and that Lorenzo confronts. Salazar puts forth a third but less developed and somewhat confusing perspective in the character of

José Contreras, who, as his surname suggests, represents an oppositional figure. A friend of Lorenzo's later at El Paso High School, José stands for a type of cynicism among some Mexican Americans. He rejects both assimilation and Mexican cultural nationalism and forges his own self-serving identity based on pure individual pleasure. Rejecting the United States and Felipe's Greater Mexico, José adopts as his place the notorious border town of Juárez. He does so not because he feels pride in lo mexicano as Felipe does, but because he can fulfill his fantasies there.

José is a rich Mexican American whose mestizo father made lots of money as a labor contractor for the big cotton farms of West Texas. As in Latin America, where money whitens, José's father is accepted in Anglo circles as a "Spanish American." José rejects this false identity. Instead, he acts out the role of the "uppity Mexican," a type vehemently disliked by Anglos. José relishes this role because his father's money and social standing protect him.

Although a U.S. citizen, José has no illusions about this country accepting Mexicans. What is more, he doesn't care. To avoid being drafted as the winds of World War II gather, José acquires dual citizenship. He has no sense of country, no sense of social responsibility, and he rejects all ideologies, all commitments other than to himself.

In befriending Lorenzo, José taps into Lorenzo's ambivalence about his identity. José in effect tells him that all his concerns about where he fits in are nonsense. Americans will never accept him as a full-fledged American. The only thing he should be concerned about is getting the most out of life. José introduces Lorenzo to the notorious world of Juárez as well as to that of the Juárez upper-middle class, which José parties with. José's cynicism and his narcissism have some attraction for Lorenzo but at the same time do little to satisfy his quest for identity.

VIII

If through Esperanza, Felipe, and José we acquire insights into Salazar's views on Mexican American identity, we get even more through the character of Lorenzo, Salazar's alter ego. Through Lorenzo, Salazar works out his struggle for identity.

Part of this struggle is that while Esperanza wants to make Lorenzo into what he is not, Lorenzo early on discovers that he is something else. For example, he is from a Spanish-speaking family. He can't disguise this. It's perfectly natural to speak Spanish to his friend Juan at his elementary school. This is when Lorenzo is taken to the principal's office for speaking "Mexican."

Salazar uses the episode when Esperanza scolds her son for speaking Spanish to contradict the assimilationist model. "I thought you said that I am you," Lorenzo says to his mother. "Didn't you say once that I must tell myself that I'm as good as anyone?" Lorenzo exposes Esperanza's contradictions when he wonders why it is acceptable to speak Spanish at home but not at school.

There is no question that Salazar through Lorenzo rejects Esperanza's concept of assimilation. Salazar understands that Mexican Americans undergo acculturation, and that it is important to integrate into U.S society, but not at the expense of their cultural heritage. He also seems to understand, however, that the obstacles to assimilation and integration involve racism toward Mexican Americans and their marginalization as "the other."

In the most dramatic exposé of Esperanza's contradictory views, Salazar writes of Lorenzo in the seventh grade developing a crush on a pretty blonde Anglo girl, Betty. She is also the sister of his best friend, Harry. Lorenzo invites Betty to be his partner at the school's May Pole dance. Betty, who also has a crush on Lorenzo, accepts at first, only to be confronted by her girlfriend, Jay, who expresses shock at Betty's decision: "With a Mexican?" she asks Betty. "Why[,] they're not even white."

This sows doubts in Betty's mind, and she goes to her mother to sort it out, hoping that her mother will give her permission to go with Lorenzo. But her mother supports Jay's opposition. Lorenzo, she tells Betty, should "go with his kind and you with yours." Betty now racializes Lorenzo and turns on him for being a Mexican, something she had not been as conscious of before. She avoids him completely. When Lorenzo recognizes this, he approaches Betty and asks why the change. In a state of fury, Betty sticks a pencil in his neck and cries out, "Stay away from me, Mexican." At the same time, Lorenzo is attacked by two of Betty's friends, who taunt him by calling out "Mexican, Mexican!"

This incident, which is crucial to Salazar's narrative, signifies Lorenzo as different and shocks him. When called to the principal's office to explain what happened, Lorenzo says, "She called me a Mex-I-can." And Salazar adds of Lorenzo, "He found a new sound to an old familiar word, and the new meaning brought shame. He couldn't figure out why."

As a result of this traumatic encounter with racial prejudice, Lorenzo is startled into beginning to recognize that he is indeed seen as different from the Anglo kids. He is seen as a Mexican and not the American that his mother told him he was. Salazar underscores this pressure of knowing that you are seen as a stranger, as a foreigner, as un-American, and as nonwhite—the wound that Mexican Americans carry with them. It is his wound as well. Lorenzo reveals this injury when he later tells Harry, "I thought it didn't make any difference if a Mexican liked a girl, I didn't know it was wrong. The way Betty shouted 'Mexican!' was really bad. I didn't know I was different."

This shock of being marginalized is further reflected in his growing rejection of his mother's assimilationist strategy. When he returns home that afternoon with his clothes dirty from the fight and his mother scolds him for this and accuses him of being like a dirty Mexican Indian, Lorenzo angrily talks back: "You're right[,] mother. I'm a dirty Mexican . . . please never tell me again I'm going to be like an American. Because I'm not. Look at you and father. Why[,] you don't even speak English. We're Mexican."

As he encounters other forms of racial exclusion in El Paso, Lorenzo begins to quickly accept the idea that while Mexican Americans may make some progress, they will always be seen by many Anglos as Mexican and not American. Of this, Salazar writes, "Lorenzo in an American business suit still looked Mexican. Lorenzo jutterbugging [*sic*] still appeared Mexican. Lorenzo talking American slang still sounded Mexican."

The recognition of this racialized difference intended to subordinate Mexicans in El Paso to Anglos further moves Lorenzo to "becoming Mexican American," to use historian George Sánchez's concept.[8] To be Mexican American, Salazar proposes, is the result not only of growing up in dual cultures, but also of rejection by the dominant culture. For Salazar, the hyphen originally in "Mexican-American" rather than being a bridge between cultures is in fact a dividing line. This interpretation differs from that of integrationist Mexican American civil rights groups of the time, such as the League of United Latin American Citizens (LULAC). Salazar considered recognition of this separation and the tension associated with it to be the burden of being Mexican American.

Alienated from the assimilationist model and recognizing his marginalization in El Paso, Lorenzo begins to feel more comfortable with Felipe's promotion of lo mexicano. Yet here too, Lorenzo is not fully at ease. Through his father, he accepts his Mexican background but not Felipe's Mexican dream of returning to Mexico. For Lorenzo, Mexico represents his parents' homeland but not his. There is no going back for him. "My father tells me we're in a stranger's land and should go back home," Lorenzo tells his friend José. "What home? I have no other home."[9]

One aspect of mexicanidad that Lorenzo temporarily accepts, however, in order to deal with his ambivalence about identity, is the Juárez border culture that José Contreras introduces him to. José tells him to forget about his place in U.S. society and to instead indulge himself in the world of partying in the Mexican border city. Lorenzo for the moment agrees and accompanies José to Juárez. This is an antidote for Betty's rejection. (Salazar would later refer to San Francisco as "Juárez with class.")[10]

But partying in Juárez proves to be no solution for Lorenzo's search for himself and a secure identity. Juárez only makes it worse. It confirms the negative stereotype of being Mexican. Part of Lorenzo's disgust with Juárez border life is also the recognition that it represents no effective retreat or solution for the Mexican American's struggle for identity. The fact was that Mexican Americans, or Chicanos, were also not accepted by Mexican nationals, who looked down on them as pochos, or Americanized Mexicans. "Juárez society is a pretentious one," Salazar wrote. "They like to think of Americans as barbarians—'*sin cultura*'—but they reserve their greatest contempt for the Mexican-American —'*el pocho*.'"

Lorenzo's rejection of Juárez is also a rejection of what he considers to be the cynical world of José. Despite his alienation from both sides of the border, Lorenzo still believes that his life has meaning; he just has to find his way. "Cynicism is too easy, José," he tells his friend. "It's giving up before trying. It's talking without thinking. You know, José, you don't hate life. You're afraid of it."

IX

Not comfortable with Esperanza's assimilationist views, Felipe's Mexican dream, or José's cynical narcissism, Lorenzo attempts to come to his own sense of identity. This is where the novel becomes more complicated because the ending is not in finished form. What exists are incomplete sketches of different although somewhat related endings. Even further complicating the ending is that in a prologue written in more complete form, Salazar does bring closure to Lorenzo's story. The result of what almost amounts to a puzzle is that it's not clear what if anything Salazar has concluded about his own identity. Like the unfinished novel, his identity remains fluid, with various contradictions.

What are these different endings and what is in the prologue?

In one, Salazar has Lorenzo deciding that he has to go beyond narrow ethnic or even national identity and instead embrace a worldview centered on the common humanity of all people—a universal man. He endorses what he believes to be the ideals of the United Nations. Yet this ironically involves joining the U.S. military so he can go fight for the UN in Korea in the early 1950s. Lorenzo's lofty ideals are contradicted by the continued role of nationalism within the UN structure and the fact that although the UN sanctioned the so-called police action in Korea, it was primarily a U.S. intervention. So is this how the Mexican can resolve the identity question? It's not clear.

In a second ending, Lorenzo decides that he will not abandon the United States. It is his country. He will struggle to make it into a more tolerant society that accepts differences within unity. This is a particular pluralistic model. Lorenzo concludes that he will be his mother's American, but on his own terms, not hers or anybody else's. Here he can be proud of being Mexican American and not ashamed of having Spanish-speaking parents while still being an American. Certainly, this view seems to coincide with Salazar's more liberal political views, which he expressed in his journalism. But the problem in the novel is that Salazar doesn't stop here, nor does he prioritize this view.

Still another ending that Salazar was considering was making Lorenzo believe that the United States was in fact the beacon of democracy. Lorenzo begins to read Thomas Jefferson in earnest and concludes that Jeffersonian democratic ideals are his as well. At the same time, Lorenzo understands that his acceptance by other Americans still faces obstacles. In a variation of the first ending, Lorenzo comes to believe that the one American institution where he will be fully accepted is the U.S. military. He not only joins but also hopes to be sent to Korea to fight alongside other Americans. This, of course, was a sentiment shared by other Mexican Americans at that time. Here there is a connection with José Villarreal's novel *Pocho*, published in the late 1950s, which concludes with the main Chicano character joining the military.

But Salazar doesn't leave it at that. He goes back to José to introduce a counterview to Lorenzo's newly found patriotism. When Lorenzo tells José about his plans, José scoffs at them and points out the contradictions of finding identity in a conformist institution like the U.S. military that, rather than being democratic, embodied the worst of U.S. society, including racism. "You'll always be a Mexican in their eyes, Lencho," José tells him. "And getting your ass blown off isn't going to change this. You're not in the club, man. Can't you understand that? . . . There's only something more stupid than a Mexican fighting an American war—and that's a nigger fighting for gringos."

José's view is reinforced again in the prologue, which suggests only that Salazar like José remained skeptical about assimilation and the future of Mexican Americans in U.S. society. In the prologue, Lorenzo finds himself in Korea, believing that he is fighting for democracy against communism. Disregarding his own safety, Lorenzo is killed by a North Korean soldier. His body is returned in a flag-draped casket to El Paso, where his mournful parents and José pick it up. Salazar could have made this into a patriotic and assimilationist setup for the novel, but he doesn't. Though some can read this Americanism into the prologue, it is complicated again by José's voice. At the train station, José recalls some of Lorenzo's last words to him: "I do want so much to be an American. But they won't let me." And that is why he chooses to go to Korea, to prove himself as an American. José can't help but think now about Lorenzo, "He's an American now. A dead one. This they let 'em."

X

Whether Ruben Salazar's novel is ever published or not, it represents a new and significant source for attempting to understand his complicated and evolving struggle with issues of ethnic identity. It is a partial mirror into the pre–Chicano Movement struggle for identity by other Mexican Americans. What is interesting about the novel is that it reinforces what I believe to be Salazar's continued ambivalence about identity up to the moment of his death. In addition, the novel is also prophetic in that it foreshadows Salazar's own death. Lorenzo dies at a young age. Ruben Salazar dies at a young age. And they both die in a form of combat, participating in larger struggles other than their own individual ones. At a time when the role of strangers (Latino immigrants) in U.S. society is still a part of our national discourse, Salazar's "A Stranger's House" remains quite relevant.

8

¡RAZA SÍ! ¡GUERRA NO!

A Historical Perspective on the Chicano Antiwar Movement in Stella Pope Duarte's *Let Their Spirits Dance*

Is there ever a time when violence is the only way to deal with a situation? Then again, isn't that what war is about? Nations forget common sense, common interests, and make public enemies of each other.

—STELLA POPE DUARTE

But the thing about remembering is that you don't forget. You take your material where you find it, which is in your life, at the intersection of past and present.

—TIM O'BRIEN

I

THE CHICANO ANTIWAR MOVEMENT concerning the Vietnam War was one of the most significant manifestations of the Chicano Movement of the late 1960s and early 1970s. The movement, or El Movimiento, in turn, was the largest civil rights movement and empowerment struggle by people of Mexican descent in the history of the United States. It made Chicanos and by extension other Latinos into national political actors for the first time. Although the movement projected itself as being "revolutionary," in the end it achieved major reforms and new opportunities for Chicanos and other Latinos in education, the professions, business, skilled employment, the media, entertainment, and politics, not to mention a more confident and assertive ethnic pride that challenged the then-prevailing stereotypes of the passive, sleepy, and dirty Mexican, or the so-called sleeping giant. The roots of what is now being referred to as "Latino power," and evident in the 2012 presidential election, are found largely in the Chicano Movement.

Stella Pope Duarte's 2002 novel, *Let Their Spirits Dance*, is a Chicano Movement masterpiece. I say Chicano Movement novel not to essentialize what is a nuanced portrayal of the effects of war on human beings and families, but to historicize the story, which is set in part during the period of the movement and reflects its legacy as well as the role the Vietnam War played in the lives of that generation of Chicanos. I refer to the novel as a masterpiece because it is not only a major literary success by a powerful and sensitive writer, but also a major historical document, which historians of the Chicano Movement, of the Vietnam War, and of the so-called sixties can usefully employ to understand the effects of history on ordinary people. *Let Their Spirits Dance* is, to borrow from Howard Zinn, a people's history of the United States.

In the novel, Stella Pope Duarte, like a historian, analyzes some of the key themes of the Chicano antiwar movement and, like a revisionist historian, provides some new perspectives on this significant aspect of the Chicano Movement. The Chicano antiwar movement produced some of the largest and most vocal protests of the antiwar movement as a whole, highlighted by the massive Chicano antiwar moratorium march of August 29, 1970, in East Los Angeles, when more than twenty thousand people, mostly Chicanos, protested against the war in Vietnam. It was the largest protest of the movement and the largest antiwar protest by any minority group in the country. Unfortunately, this protest, like the Chicano Movement as a whole, has remained largely marginalized if nonexistent in the histories of this unprecedented era of political upheaval in the United States, including an equally unprecedented national antiwar movement. The Chicano Movement, including the Chicano antiwar movement, is part of American history but still largely excluded as such. Stella Pope Duarte joins Chicano historians in revising that history to include the Chicano experience.[1]

II

The Chicano antiwar movement focused on certain key themes that Duarte also picks up in her novel and expands on. The first is the large Chicano involvement in the war, way beyond the percentage of Chicanos in the U.S. population. Chicano movement activists considered this to be a racist exploitation of

Chicanos. Of course, Chicanos and other Latinos had always participated in America's wars, despite the racist view of them as nonpatriotic "illegal immigrants." In the twentieth century alone, hundreds if not thousands fought in World War I and, of course, in World War II.[2] In World War II alone, thirteen Chicanos won the Congressional Medal of Honor. They and the other brave and patriotic Chicanos were part of the "greatest generation" although excluded from this honor thanks to their neglect in the works of Tom Brokaw and Ken Burns.[3] In Korea, thousands more Chicanos fought and died for their country, and then again in Vietnam.

Duarte's novel is constructed around the death of Jesse Ramírez in Vietnam in 1968 and how almost thirty years later his still grieving mother, Alicia, is convinced that she hears Jessie's voice one night and that it calls to her to visit the Vietnam Veterans Memorial Wall in Washington, DC, to touch her son's name on it. Teresa, Jesse's younger and loving sister, narrates the story of how the entire family and some of Jesse's friends drive all the way from their barrio, El Cielito, in Phoenix to Washington, DC, in the early summer of 1997. They are going to the Wall to remember and honor not only Jesse but also those thousands of other Chicanos/Latinos, other minorities, and working-class whites who gave the ultimate for their country. In this narrative, Duarte first touches on the fact that disproportionate numbers of Chicanos served in the war. Of course, this was not surprising since Chicanos had always served in large numbers in the military, especially as foot soldiers. Indeed, Jesse's father was a *veterano* of World War II.

The novel also references other Chicanos from El Cielito who, like Jesse, were drafted or enlisted in the military and saw service in Vietnam, such as Leito, the nephew of Tortuga, a friend of Jesse's. Teresa notes that the military emptied the barrios during the war. This tradition of military service was exploited by the military even as later, President Richard Nixon, after his election in 1968, began to incrementally withdraw troops from Vietnam. Chris, Jesse's buddy, who also served in Vietnam, notes this when he tells Teresa on the way to Washington: "There were so many Chicanos over there, and even more when troops were being pulled out and only certain companies were left. We had front row seats. You know no Chicanos is gonna do the rear when his buddies are up front."[4] Ricky, a neighbor of the Ramírezes who likewise served in the war, observes when he arrives at the Wall with the family that 191,000 men of Latino descent served in Vietnam, and that this did not include those without Latino surnames.[5] Chicanos not only fought in large numbers in the war, but also fought bravely, as they had in other conflicts. Some received the Congressional Medal of Honor, and many others won other awards for bravery and dedicated service. Jesse was given posthumously a Silver Star, a Bronze Medal, a Purple Heart, a Good Conduct Medal, an Air Medal, and two medals from the South Vietnamese government.[6] While Duarte focuses on the key issue of the Chicano antiwar movement—that Chicanos in unjust numbers were cannon fodder for the war—she does not neglect that many other minorities, such as blacks, also served in large numbers in the conflict. Gates, a black resident of El Cielito and a close friend of Jesse's, also accompanies the family to Washington.[7]

III

A major reason Chicanos were such a large contingent of the troops being sent to Vietnam was that they were being disproportionately drafted to fight the war. This became a significant issue for the Chicano antiwar movement. The issue of disproportional draft rates for Chicanos gained attention because of what became known as the Guzmán report. Professor Ralph C. Guzmán, a political scientist at Cal State, Los Angeles, studied draft statistics and issued a report in 1967 and in 1969 showing that while Chicanos were 12 percent of the population of the Southwest, including California, where most Chicanos lived, they represented 19 percent of the casualties from this region.[8] In her novel, Duarte calls attention to this draft injustice.

One of the reasons for the draft imbalance had to do with the historical educational discrimination against Chicanos in what for years were called "Mexican schools." These segregated and inferior public schools for Mexican Americans failed over the course of the twentieth century to promote educational mobility, including college, for Chicanos. The only way to avoid the draft during the Vietnam War was if you continued your education beyond high school and went to college. Most Chicanos did not do so, not only because of the lack of encouragement from teachers and counselors, but also because many dropped out of school as a result of the racist treatment and inferior education they had received. In the East Los Angeles schools, for example, some high schools had dropout rates of 50 percent or more. Dropping out of school and not going on to college meant that these young men were prime targets for being drafted.[9] This type of drafting and similar pressure to join the military also affected other minorities as well as poor working-class people in general. Manuel, Teresa's friend, says in the novel: "Chicanos are another group who have been drafted left and right, along with the Blacks, and other minorities."[10]

Jesse Ramírez was one of those Chicanos who didn't go on to college or did so without graduating and instead joined the military. In the novel, when the family escorts Jesse to the Phoenix airport for his flight to Vietnam, his nana (grandmother) starts to wail and makes this connection: "Ay mijito ... Ay Dios, why didn't you stay in college? You're so smart!"[11] But Jesse didn't stay in college, and even more Chicanos didn't even go to college and therefore were drafted. Teresa notes that not only were Chicanos not encouraged to go to college, but most couldn't afford it anyway. The result was the disproportionate drafting of Chicanos and, as the Guzmán report indicated, a disproportionate number of Chicano casualties. Teresa says, "Coffins kept coming from Vietnam wrapped in American flags. We could have tolled death bells from one end of South Phoenix to the other. Our guys didn't stand a chance. Most of them didn't have money to go to college. They were sitting ducks for the draft."[12]

Teresa resents the fact that many white males escaped the draft because they went to college. This includes the white principal of the elementary school where she teaches, Mr. H., who objects to Teresa's teaching her students about the Vietnam War. "Little weasel," she thinks of him. "That's what he looks like. An albino weasel who stayed at home protesting the war when my brother was fighting in Vietnam to save his flabby ass!" From Vietnam, Jesse affirms his sister's views when he writes to her that even in the war, white soldiers often received more noncombat duties than Chicanos and other minorities did. He mentioned one case where a white soldier was shifted out of his unit because his mother knew a U.S. senator: "Los Chicanos don't have mommys who know senators and none of them I know of have more than high school education, if even that."[13]

Besides the lack of education increasing their draft pool, Chicanos in barrio schools were subject, as they still are today, to heavy military recruitment ("Be all you can be"). They were falsely told that if they joined the military, they would be able to learn skills that would help them get good-paying jobs later. In a powerful monologue, Duarte via Teresa makes a stinging indictment of this type of exploitation by the military:

By 1968, we were all drowning. La raza was submerged by mainstream America, a submarine drifting under a sea of politics, prejudice, and racism. Barrios like El Cielito, ignored by the U.S. government, suddenly appeared on Uncle Sam's map.

Chicanos who had never been thought about before were on the list of draftees. Uncle Sam's finger was pointing at them, ordering them across the ocean to war, a war that the President kept saying was a "conflict." Minorities always attract attention when there's a war, and Chicanos, descendants of Aztec warriors, have always made it to the top of the list. . . . This was a game that said, We're gonna pay you for being over there, and if you don't want to go, we'll draft you anyway. So why don't you join up and avoid all the trouble? You know you don't want to stay in school, anyway. And lots of guys didn't. They had families to support, they had buddies over there. They couldn't pack and run.[14]

Such recruitment was not just focused on U.S.-born Chicanos, but also targeted Mexican immigrant youth. Jesse in one of his letters to Teresa tells her of one such immigrant from Detroit, Tiny, who was killed. The son of migrant farm workers, Tiny was recruited to join the U.S. Army by a recruiter telling him the lie that enlisting would ensure he got a green card after his service. "That's the way they work to build up the Army, with lies," Jesse exclaimed. "Lies!"[15]

IV

Because of the high numbers of Chicanos being drafted and put in combat in Vietnam, they experienced high casualty rates, as the Guzmán report documented. Duarte notes this loss of Chicano lives as well as other forms of collateral damage from the war. Thousands of Chicanos were killed or maimed in Vietnam. "Los Chicanos are like ducks in a row in Nam," Ricky says in the novel, "waiting for the next bullet, Teresa."[16] This loss of lives is brought to readers' attention in a particularly powerful concluding section, in which Duarte re-creates the Vietnam Wall for us. Many readers have probably never been to the Wall, but Duarte compensates for this by providing us a literary version that is so effective, we feel as if we are actually there, seeing and touching the names—names such as Angel Luis Sánchez, Robert Cinosa González, Aurelio Garza Herrera, Pedro Caudillo, David Esequiel Padilla, Anibal Ortega Jr., Miguel Pagan, Ernesto Coto, Arturo Barriga, and on and on, including, of course, Jesse A. Ramírez.[17]

Chicano antiwar activists considered these high casualty rates to be the result of a form of genocide. In Rosalío Muñoz's public statement refusing his induction, he proclaimed: "I accuse the government of the United States of America of genocide against the Mexican people. Specifically, I accuse the draft, the entire social, political, and economic system of the United States of America, of creating a funnel which shoots Mexican youth into Viet Nam to be killed and to kill innocent men, women, and children."[18] This theme of genocide is also referenced in the novel. Teresa, for example, in seeing all those Spanish surnames on the Wall, says "This is a massacre, a travesty."[19] Antonio Fuentes, a Brown Beret member, is even more forceful in promoting the genocide theme in a speech Teresa attends in Phoenix. He shouts:

> PROTEST RAZA! PROTEST! Uncle Sam stole our land, now he's killing our boys in Vietnam. Two Latinos for every gringo! Is that justice? We're on the front lines, in artillery, blowing mines, the first to fire. We don't get soft jobs, in offices ... we can't get into fancy officer's clubs, we can't get no deferments.... NO! We're coming back in boxes, mi raza. They're wiping us out! My brother was killed over there ... to make some fucking white general look good![20]

El Cielito suffers its share of Chicano casualties. Faustino, son of Jesse's godmother, Irene, is killed in the war in 1967. Still others not mentioned lose their lives in the war—so many that Duarte, through Teresa, observes that La Llorona, the weeping maternal figure in search of her dead sons in Chicano folklore, looks no longer in El Cielito but in Vietnam: "Hearts in El Cielito were being plundered. La Llorona quit hunting El Cielito at night looking for her children. She flew over the Pacific to Vietnam and finally quenched her thirst for the children she had drowned so long ago. She wrapped her ghostly shroud around Chicanos and other Latinos who were being ripped apart from their bodies every day in the war and was satisfied at last."[21] These include Jesse, who prophesies his death on the way to the airport for his flight to Vietnam. He leans over in the car and tells his sister, "I don't think I'm coming back, Teresa. Take care of Mom." Even in death, Jesse continues to be a casualty when the military returns his body to the wrong address, mistaking him for another Ramírez killed in the war.[22]

Casualties of war, including the Vietnam War, are not just those killed in combat. Some become casualties after they return, suffering physically and even dying due to exposure to deadly toxins, such as Agent Orange, used by the United States in the war. On the outskirts of Washington, the Ramírez family meets a woman, Carmen Ybarra, who tells them that her husband, a Vietnam veteran, died years later of skin cancer probably caused by Agent Orange. He was only fifty-three and never saw his grandson. These casualties from the war were not publicly memorialized. "There are so many casualties of the Vietnam War," Teresa notes, "and lots of them aren't on the Wall." Teresa also reminds us that other such casualties died after the war from alcoholism and drugs.[23] Of course, thousands, including Chicanos, returned maimed, with lost limbs and other physically impairing injuries that would forever change their lives, as they continue to do today, returning from Afghanistan and earlier from Iraq. No one returns from a war without some injury, including psychological and emotional. One is never the same after being in combat. Duarte reminds us of this and expands the Chicano antiwar protests over Chicano casualties to include those who came back with nonphysical but emotional wounds. This form of wound is reflected in Chris, who becomes ill on the trip with the family as a result of his lingering trauma from being in the war. "It happens sometimes," he tells Teresa. "I guess my body's got the nights in Nam recorded like a history lesson." He further relates that he had even contemplated suicide: "I looked at myself in the mirror one day, and I couldn't stand what I saw. I was disgusted with myself because I couldn't get Nam out of my system. That was the day I almost turned a gun on myself. If it hadn't been for thinking about my two daughters, I probably would have done it."[24] Some sixty thousand Americans, including Chicanos, were killed in Vietnam. Many thousands more Vietnamese on both sides of the conflict also lost their lives, however, something that Americans often overlook in just lamenting the loss of American lives. To her credit, Duarte does not neglect this tragic fact. At the Wall, as Teresa confronts all those Chicano names and other American names, she can't help but think about Jesse's Vietnamese wife, son, and grandson, whom she had just met the night before: "I look at Thom and Lam and wonder if they have a wall in Vietnam to honor all of their victims. Mothers cry in the same language the world over."[25]

V

One aspect of the Chicano antiwar movement that the few scholars who have studied it have not paid much attention to is the antiwar sentiment among Chicano soldiers in Vietnam. By contrast, Duarte notes this opposition at various levels. For example, we know that in the war, American soldiers sometimes refused to obey their officers if following orders might mean a suicide mission. There were reports even of so-called grunts actually killing their officers under the guise of friendly fire. In the novel, Jessie challenges his commanding officer about a mission that Jesse believes, based on his experience as a sergeant, might lead to unnecessary casualties. "I told him [Major Cunningham] stop volunteering our platoon, *pendejo*, what do you want, to see us all dead?"[26] This type of almost insubordination also involved questioning the U.S. command's war strategies, including what was called the strategic hamlet policy, whereby American troops would establish defensive perimeters around South Vietnamese villages and provide economic support for the peasants. Jesse points out the shortcomings and contradictions of this strategy in a letter to his sister. "We're supposed to be helping the Vietnamese people with food and protection," he wrote, "but all I see us doing is scaring them and making their lives miserable."[27] Of course, given the very difficult task of fighting a guerilla insurgency in a war whose goals seem unclear, many soldiers apparently began to raise questions about the relevance of the war itself. What was this war all about and what exactly was their mission? To win the war? To force a stalemate? Who in fact was the enemy? Are U.S. soldiers really there to protect democracy against communism? Chicano soldiers may have thought no differently. In a powerful note to Teresa, Jesse clearly questions the relevance of the war: "Sis, this must be hell. What are we doing here anyway? Get this. Trucks here are made in Russia. They got Mitsubishi engines from Japan and Goodyear tires from the U.S. So what do you think this is all about? I look around and think the Vietnamese are right when they say 'Dogs go home!' It's all about money and land for rice. I'm sending you the gold of Asia in this letter, rice, what else?"[28]

Jesse's views are later bolstered by fellow soldier Chris, who tells Teresa on the way to the Wall: "I knew the war was sick—so sick, and we still kept fighting."[29] Through their perilous experiences, American soldiers saw the contradictions of the war just as the antiwar protestors at home were pointing them out. The difference was that the GIs were living these contradictions and dying because of them. What contradictions? Allegedly fighting for peace while destroying a country. Jesse, as almost an organic "grunt" intellectual but given his voice by Duarte, says in other letters to Teresa, "I've been thinking, sis, how the U.S. prays for peace, then turns around and arms itself to the teeth for war. Are we Legion?" He further observes, "So much of the country is destroyed by bombs, Agent Orange, and napalm. . . . It's like the U.S. can't make up their minds to kill them or let them live. I guess maybe that's peace to our country, that they can go to another country and take cover. In other words, let us destroy you, then we'll have peace."[30] The failed strategies of the Vietnam War, its relevance or irrelevance, and the contradictions of the war in turn elicited the issue of the morality or immorality of the conflict in Southeast Asia. Jesse ponders this: "I'm up for patrol. Search and destroy, that's our mission. I wouldn't want to meet Jesus Christ some night and have to explain what I was doing here. Do you think He would understand?"[31]

If some American soldiers, including some Chicanos like Jesse, could be accused of being antipatriotic, Duarte suggests that while such soldiers questioned the war, they did not question protecting each other in the battlefields. This was their patriotism. This was their version of the Chicano antiwar theme "La batalla está aquí" (the battle is here)—the war is not in Vietnam but in the barrios. For some Chicano soldiers, being in the war or in the barrio meant protecting themselves—that's what the war was for them. At the Wall, Teresa meets Tennessee, a Vietnam vet, whose life was saved by Jesse. In this very moving scene in the novel, Tennessee says to Teresa, "Jesse would have done it for whoever needed him. That's the way it was for the guys in Vietnam. They fought the war for one another."[32]

Of course, some vets who were fortunate enough to return home alive transferred their war experiences to the antiwar movement. This was powerful because these warriors for war had now become warriors for peace. Some Chicano vets joined the Chicano antiwar movement, as Ricky Navarro does in the novel. He marches on August 29, 1970, in the streets of East LA, where he encounters Teresa, who through her brother's death has come to see at a personal level the very questions about the war that her brother was conveying to her. Both Ricky and Teresa are at the Chicano Moratorium to provide an answer to why Jessie was killed and to take from his death the commitment to end a war to save other lives. "We're here to do something about Jesse's death, Teresa," he tells her. "We're here to remember our guys." To which Teresa responds, "Please do something for Jesse ... his life has to count, it just has to!"[33]

VI

One of the themes of the Chicano antiwar movement involved Chicanos identifying with the Vietnamese, whether revolutionaries or not. This theme originated in part with Luis Valdez and the Teatro Campesino, who in one of their *actos*, or skits, *Vietnam/Campesino*, at the time of the war emphasized that Chicanos had much in common with the Vietnamese, including that both were colonized peoples fighting for their liberation. This theme helped influence the Chicano antiwar movement by questioning the prowar ideology that the Vietnamese, specifically the "Communists" or "Viet Cong," were the enemies of the United States. Chicanos said no; they are like us, not enemies. This theme is picked up by Duarte and is illustrated in certain parts of her novel. For example, she stresses that Chicanos and the Vietnamese were very much alike physically, or racially. They looked like each other. Of course, because of the indigenous background of most Chicanos, linked by some to migration from Asia many centuries ago, they possess Asian genes. As such, to borrow from Danny Valdez's movement song, they are both "brown-eyed children of the sun." Teresa notes that Jesse "was fighting people who looked like people we knew." And in one of his letters to his sister, Jesse writes, "Some old man is waving at me. These people look at us los Chicanos like we're one of them. We look more Vietnamese than American, that's for sure."[34]

Borrowing from *Vietnam/Campesino*, Duarte also suggests that one experience linking Chicanos with the Vietnamese is their common backgrounds, for many of them, as farm workers—campesinos, or peasants. Both are people of the land—la tierra. "I tell the guys shoot, cover yourselves," Jesse writes to Teresa, "but it's hard when you look at the Vietnamese in the face. They're farm people, they look like a bunch of migrants bending over the rice paddies. They look so pathetic. Gabachos [whites] who have been here for a while say it's all cover. They push them around, beat them up, even the women. I can't, sis, it would be like hitting my nana [grandmother] or tata [aunt]." Chris corroborates this sentiment when he tells Teresa, "[W]e didn't go out of our way to beat up on the Vietnamese. How could we? Some of us came from migrant families. We saw them out in their little plots of land, and so help me God, they looked like our nanas and tatas. Some of us had come from the cotton fields to the foxholes of Nam, there was nothing in between."[35]

Not only did the Vietnamese look like Chicanos and come from campesino backgrounds, but aspects of their culture also resembled that of Chicanos. Jesse observes that the Vietnamese possess their version of Día de los Muertos, or Day of the Dead, celebrated by Mexicans on both sides of the border. "They have altars around here for the dead," he informs Teresa. Moreover, some, including a family that he came to know, were also Catholics, like many Chicanos. "Guess what?" he writes to his sister. "The mass's the same over here in Vietnam."[36] In fact, the family that Jesse came to know was that of Thom, the young Vietnamese woman he falls in love with. In the ultimate Chicano linkage with the Vietnamese, Jesse marries her, and Thom bears his son, giving birth to Lam Ramírez after Jesse is killed. Lam, in turn, fathers his own son, Jesse's grandson, Joshua Ramírez. In Washington, when the Ramírez family visit the Wall, there is a moving reunion of both families, who because of Jesse have become one family.[37]

VII

An additional critique of the Vietnam War articulated by the Chicano antiwar movement was that Chicanos had no stake in that war and that the real war should be at home, in the barrios, fighting against racism, injustice, and discrimination. This was the real battleground. Antiwar activists agreed with Muhammad Ali when, in refusing his induction, he proclaimed, "I have no quarrel with the Vietnamese. No Vietnamese have ever harmed me. But I can tell you who has harmed me. It's been white racists in Kentucky. If I'm going to fight anywhere, that's where I'll fight" or words to that effect. Although Chicanos had a long tradition of military service and often linked it to their machismo, the Chicano antiwar movement, as Lorena Oropeza notes, suggested that this machismo should be redefined and channeled to fighting for Chicano rights and Chicano power at home and not in Vietnam. It was an attempt, as Oropeza further observes, to revise Chicano masculinity.[38] Teresa seems to understand that war is not the result of Chicano machismo but of larger forces that exploit that machismo for their own ends:

> Jesse, a warrior? Perhaps. I don't believe that warriors are made in the womb. . . . There are plans, evil plans that take over the minds of men and search the deepest recesses of where hatred lurks, ready to spring. The beginning of a war may take place in an office building with windows overlooking the White House, or in the meanest hovel deep in the jungle. Soft, manicured hands can sign decrees of death and war, as can dirty, blood-crusted hands in villages where people no longer expect the sun to rise. War is the battleground of the human heart where avarice, hatred, greed for power, for money, for land, are allowed to thrive. The Godless man begins to sense that in the entire universe his right to live in the manner he chooses is the only way to live. The disorder in his soul is the beginning of war.[39]

Moreover, like Muhammad Ali, Chicanos didn't know any Vietnamese before the war. Vietnamese had never harmed them. Jesse's grandmother, Nana, in giving her departing grandson an *oración del Justo Juez* (the prayer of the Just God), says, "Keep it in your pocket. Don't forget the prayer. God will protect you. Your enemies won't even see you. Porque la guerra? I don't even know any Vietnamese. Why do you have to go there?"[40]

The Chicano antiwar movement further noted that Chicanos were already in a war zone in the barrios, much less having to go to war in faraway Vietnam. Battle Aztlán, the mythical homeland of Chicanos in the Southwest, was the real war. In the Chicano Moratorium march of August 29, 1970, one of the signs, as observed by Teresa, reads "Aztlán Si, Vietnam No!" In fact, that historic march literally became a war zone when the county sheriffs attacked the assembled rally, causing many casualties, including three deaths. Teresa, experiencing this at Laguna Park, notes, "All around me the world is a war zone. This is how Jesse must have felt in Vietnam—helpless, afraid, not knowing when the attack would stop, not knowing if he would live or die."[41]

Of the three Chicanos deaths, one was Ruben Salazar, the most respected Mexican American journalist in the country. Covering the moratorium, including the police attack, Salazar later went to the Silver Dollar Café, on Whittier Boulevard in East LA, to get a respite from the police riot. A squad of deputy sheriffs descended on the café and shot at least two tear gas projectiles into the restaurant, one of them striking Salazar and instantly killing him. Teresa observes that the sheriff "aimed directly at Salazar."[42] Her thoughts on this suggest the many conspiracy theories that followed Salazar's tragic death. The belief that the police had targeted him for assassination because of his hard-hitting coverage of police abuse has not abated, more than forty years after his death. Duarte seems to be suggesting that she believes in such a conspiracy as part of Battle Aztlán and the concept that *la batalla está aquí*.

VIII

Although Duarte's novel is a personal, family story about the Vietnam War, at the same time, the author pays homage to the significant Chicano antiwar movement by describing the events around the massive Chicano Moratorium in East Los Angeles. To gather information for this part of her novel, Duarte interviewed Rosalío Muñoz, the key organizer of the moratorium and the head of the National Chicano Moratorium Committee, as well as doing other research. Because of her research, Duarte provides one of the best accounts of that day, which is later reinforced by the work of historian Lorena Oropeza.[43] As part of Duarte's tribute to the moratorium committee, she mentions the names of key members, such as Muñoz, Ernesto Vigil, Roberto Elias, Gloria Arellanes, and David Sánchez, the prime minister of the Brown Berets.[44]

The Chicano Movement initially did not embrace the Vietnam War as part of its political agenda. As more Chicanos were killed and wounded in the conflict, however, and as Chicanos became more aware that educational and social programs were being cut to pay for the war, the movement began to realize that the war was a Chicano issue. Moreover, as noted earlier, Chicanos being primarily targeted for the draft also influenced opposing the war. But there were additional and very personal reasons some Chicanos, both men and women, came to oppose the war. This had to do with families who had lost loved ones in Vietnam, like the Ramírez family. In fact, one of Duarte's contributions to the history of the Chicano antiwar movement is focusing attention on this personal, family connection to the movement. Soldiers' family members, like Teresa, become antiwar not because of political or intellectual arguments but because they have lost a loved one. Why and for what did Jesse die? That alone made Teresa, and by extension many other Teresas, oppose the war. Through this process Teresa becomes Chicana and decides to go to the moratorium march. At the moratorium, to show her new identity, Teresa wears a T-shirt that says "Chicano Power." As she marches, she also notices that she, as a family member of a brother killed in the war, is not alone. She witnesses many other families in the march, along the route, and at Laguna Park, where the march concludes. "Lining the streets were newborn babies in their mothers' arms," she notes, "elderly men and women who looked like relics of the Mexican Revolution."[45]

Becoming Chicana and antiwar is further reinforced by the power of protest. She and thousands of others at the march are empowered by their numbers and their solidarity. This is the power of so-called direct action and mass protests, which characterized not only the Chicano Movement, but also the politics of the sixties. Alone, Teresa would probably not have publicly protested the war, but being joined by more than twenty thousand others empowers her to do so. This is people power. For Teresa and probably for others at the march who had lost a relative in the war, the mass protest was also part of their healing process. It was a way to release their grief along with others, which gave their grief a broader social meaning, to prevent other young Chicanos from being killed in the war by stopping the war. Teresa gives testimony to this feeling when she confesses,

I found out in 1970 that a protest is a living thing. It's not just a word. It's made up of people who are filled with pain, anger, despair. It's something that has a life of its own, something that lives and breathes, shouts, cries, and groans. . . . As we marched, I began to feel full inside, as if the very act of marching was food for my soul. The louder the shouts became, the fuller I felt. The whole world might have ended for me at that moment, and I would have died strong, unafraid, the aching in my heart over Jesse's death only a memory.[46]

Duarte concludes her history of the moratorium by graphically and powerfully describing the county sheriff's attack on the rally at Laguna Park (now Ruben Salazar Park). You cannot find a better and more powerful account of the attack than in her novel. In the documentary film *Requiem Twenty-Nine* and in the PBS series *Chicano! History of the Mexican American Civil Rights Movement*, particularly in part 1, "Quest for a Homeland," you see footage of the sheriff's attack. In one memorable scene, a deputy comes up behind a young Chicana and strikes her with full force across the back of her head. She immediately falls, and we then see someone from the march help her get up. That scene alone says it all with respect to the criminal and brutal police disruption of a peaceful demonstration. But who was that young Chicana? Drawing from this memorable image, Duarte provides the answer, at least fictionally; it is Teresa Ramírez. Here is Duarte's intertextual (film and novel) version of that scene as recounted by Teresa:

Everyone was running in between buses that were parked at one end of the park. Behind us, the police were pushing people up to tall chain-link fences, trapping them—everyone, men, women, babies. I saw an officer hit a boy on the side of the neck with his club. I ran up to the officer. "You fuckin' pig!" I yelled. He started chasing me, and I fell to the ground. He hit me once on the head, and I saw the world go black. Seconds later, I felt someone helping me up. It was Ricky. His head was split open on one side.[47]

IX

If young Chicano men like Jesse were casualties of the Vietnam War, so too— in a symbolic but nevertheless still real way—were families, la familia. Family members of those veterans killed in the war did not physically die in combat as their sons, brothers, and husbands did, but they died spiritually and emotionally from the loss of their loved ones. Suffering and grief was their Vietnam. Family casualties is an area that the Chicano antiwar movement did not focus on very much since the movement was more concerned with the actual deaths and maiming of Chicano soldiers. Scholars in this area have also neglected this theme. But Duarte does not neglect this area; in fact, it is the core of her story. This is her major contribution to our understanding of how the Vietnam War affected Chicanos.

Family suffering begins even before the loved ones have left for Vietnam. The fear that they won't return is already part of family members' suffering. They bemoan this departure, as we see with the Ramírez family. At home, Jesse's grandmother, Nana, has him kneel down as she extends her hand over him and blesses him: "I bless you in the name of the Father, and of the Son, and of the Holy Spirit. May God get you safely to Vietnam and bring you back home again!" Duarte through Teresa then describes the family reaction: "Her [Nana's] voice broke. She held him in her arms, his head on her lap. He was her baby, still. Mom and Dad knelt down with Jesse, crying, hugging him. I stood over them, tears falling, looking at the throbbing heart of *familia*."[48]

"Write to us, Jesse," his crying mother pleads with him before he leaves, "every day if you can, mijo." And at the airport, Teresa painfully tells her brother, "Jesse, please come back." Jesse's parents are the last to speak to him before he boards the plane, and their voices are already filled with suffering and grief. His mother says, "Ay mijito, my son . . . you're my world. Ay mijito, you have to come back to me! The war doesn't matter. It's you I want back in my arms! It's your voice I want to hear again!" Although Jesse's father, himself a veterano, puts on a staunch and macho attitude about his son going to war, all this breaks down at the airport, and his last words to Jesse are "I don't want no war hero. I want my son."[49]

The news of Jesse's death, of course, is the beginning of the second and real suffering and grief, as it is for all families who are told that their loved ones were killed in action. There is no way anyone, much less a parent, can prepare for such a moment. Teresa recalls exactly when she and her mother learned that Jesse had been killed. They were in church rehearsing the music for that Sunday's Mass, and her mother was the lead singer. Father Ramón walked in with a man in military uniform. Her mother knew that Jessie had died:

> My mother's voice ripped the silence apart. "MIJO! NO! NOT MY SON! NOT MY SON! PLEASE GOD, NOT MY SON!" Once, twice, many times . . . so many times, "NOT MY SON! PLEASE GOD, NOT MY SON!" I put my

hands over my ears. I thought I saw the saints on the stained glass windows do the same. My mother's voice made me cringe. "JESSE'S GONE! YOU TOOK MY SON! GOD, WHY DID YOU TAKE MY SON?" I arched my back to hold in the pain. Her cries bounced off everything at the same time, making one loud echoing shout. Yolanda grabbed my mother and held her up to her huge breasts like she was a baby. The pigeons on the rooftop cooed wildly. Who can stand to hear the sound of a mother who knows her son is no more?[50]

Thirty years have passed and still the Ramírez family suffers and grieves Jesse's death. La familia is a casualty of war. "I was in my own Vietnam anyway," Teresa says of her life after her brother's death, "whether anyone knew it or not." For her mother, the death of her son is even worse, and she lives with it every day. When Teresa asks her mother if she can take Jesse's medals to her class to show her students, her mother expresses her grief: "Here mija, take the medals before I get them all wet with my tears. Show them to the children, tell them what a good person your brother was. Tell them that when a son dies, his mother's heart goes with him."[51]

Family suffering and grief, however, is a long-term process. Just as veterans who survive a war can never forget their combat experiences and even develop emotional and psychological traumas, surviving families are similarly affected. They cannot forget their loved ones killed in battle, and they suffer every day. Thirty years after the Ramírezes received the news of Jesse's death, they are still grieving. When Teresa teaches her students about the Vietnam War and about the death of her brother, one of her students says to her, "Wow! That was almost thirty years ago, Mrs. Alvarez [Teresa's married name]." "Yes, Brandon," Teresa responds, "but it seems like yesterday. When you lose someone you love as much as I loved Jesse, the years are nothing. Nothing."[52] Teresa's grief includes a sense of guilt that she could not have been there when Jesse was hit by the bullet, so that perhaps she might have helped him and perhaps even prevented his death. But guilt also shifts to anger at a military and a government that she believes treated her brother as just another statistic and not as a real human being. Guilt and anger are part of Teresa's grief and part of her memories and even nightmares. These feeling overtake her while she is teaching her students about the war, and she has to leave her class in charge of her aide while she races to the bathroom. She is overtaken by her thoughts of Jesse:

Your mouthpiece, Jesse. Your mouthpiece—where was it? Did you fall and break all of your teeth? And me nowhere near to help you. Oh, Jesse—where was the wound? The wound that took your life? The hole in your body that made you bleed to death. Where were the medics, the bandages, the helicopter? Why didn't they move fast enough? Saved my brother. MY BROTHER fighting for political monsters who could give a shit if he lived or died. MY BROTHER brought back in a sealed coffin with a plastic lid. Your body all swollen, your face disfigured. Too many days. So sorry. He was sent to the wrong family. Can you believe the bastards didn't even get our address right! So sorry. The U.S. Army apologizes for such a tragic error. APOLOGIZES! What a trip! They should have gotten on their fuckin' knees and begged our forgiveness. And don't ever let me find out it was friendly fire, that some asshole from our side murdered MY BROTHER! Oh, God, I can't take this anymore.[53]

What Duarte is correctly suggesting is that a study of the casualties of the Vietnam War has to encompass both the veterans and their families. Both are part of this tragic story. Her novel is her way of historicizing especially the role of family in this saga. She tellingly connects the two when veterano Chris and Teresa are reunited in Albuquerque on the way to the Wall. Chris says to Teresa, "We're replicas of the '6os, a movie that's been on pause for thirty years. God forgot us and now He's remembering us again. It's hard to find words to say to each other when the script we knew was buried with Jesse. There's a volume between us, *The History of the Vietnam War*. We're casualties. Our photos should be in the book with captions, 'Survivors of the Chicano Bloodbath in Nam,' words that would tell people we had our own holocaust in Vietnam."[54]

But if Teresa suffers and grieves for her brother, the weight of suffering and grief, of course, is especially borne by her mother. She can never forget the loss of her son. What mother could? As she says, "The war has never ended for me!" There is no compensation for the loss of Jesse. Nothing that the government can give her can replace her son. "They never brought him back!" she exclaims. "These men, what did they know? Pendejos! They said, here, take these medals in place of your son. What were they thinking? I never wanted the medals. I wanted my son!" Alicia, Jesse's mother, suffers but she finds some compensation in her faith, which tells her that suffering is part of that faith. Hence, she is linked with Our Lady of Sorrows as part of her suffering. She, like Our Lady, bemoans the loss of her son.[55]

Despite the weight of suffering and grief that accompanies the death of loved ones in war, some families eventually find healing. From the pain comes a vision and a path to making something positive out of their loss. Hope arises out of this despair. This is very much the Christian message and the meaning of the passion and resurrection, and Duarte, in a novel that is filled with Catholic images and allusions, pursues this path. Jesse's death (the passion) will lead in time to the personal resurrection of his family. They will heal by giving meaning to Jesse's life, by remembering and passing on to others the memory of the Vietnam War and why there should be no more Vietnams. Jesse guides the way by seemingly appearing to his mother and leaving her with a belief that her son needs to tell her something, which at first Alicia cannot understand. Somehow, she begins to imagine that Jesse wants her and his family to visit the Vietnam Wall in Washington, DC, and touch his name as a way to heal and no longer grieve for him. Alicia makes a *manda*—a promise—to God and Jesse that she will do this. Almost as if by a miracle, Alicia and her family are aided in keeping her promise when the U.S. military grants them more than ninety thousand dollars in back restitution for having sent Jesse's body to the wrong address thirty years earlier. With this money, the family is able to afford the trip to the Wall, including other friends and Jesse's fellow veterans. But this is more than a trip; it is a peregrinación—a spiritual pilgrimage. Others join the family as their driving caravan receives national attention and becomes a way not only for the family to heal but also for the nation to heal from the tragedy of Vietnam. "We wouldn't be on the road if it weren't for war and suffering," Teresa reflects. "We're part of some unearthly plan to balance the scale of suffering, to release a spring in our souls that will free us from the fear of suffering."[56]

Because of the national attention the trip receives, Alicia becomes the embodiment of what we might call the Vietnam Moms. She represents all of those still surviving mothers who lost a son in Vietnam. They, like Alicia, have been suffering all these years, but now in Alicia they see hope and healing. They too will make something worthwhile of their sons' deaths. They will also remind others of the pain of war and why such wars have to stop. This will be their response to their sons' wishes in the night. Alicia becomes the symbol of this awakening. Espi, Teresa's friend in Phoenix, tells Teresa that her mother is being called the first Nana hero the country has ever known—the first grandmother hero. Teresa can't believe it. "What makes her a hero?" she asks Espi, who responds, "Are you kidding me? She's taking her life into her own hands by making the trip. She's answering her son's call to get to the Wall. This is a life-and-death situation. Then there's the whole thing about the money. How many other families did the government cheat? Poor families, minority families, victimized. That's what the stories are saying. Your mom's a symbol of all the other moms who lost their sons in Vietnam." The Wall thus becomes a symbol of this healing process that affects not only the family but the nation. Not all can get there, and tragically Alicia does not quite make it, but she is healed by the process and by meeting, literally on her death bed, Jesse's Vietnam family. Jesse lives in them, and the peregrinación to the Wall has made this meeting possible. She passes on Jesse's wish that his name be touched to Teresa, who will fulfill the manda. As she finds Jesse's name and touches it, Teresa says, "Hello, I've missed you ... hello, I love you. We made it. You called us, and we're here."[57]

X

So what is the legacy of Duarte's story? What does it all mean? I think there are several parts to this legacy. First, it is a reminder for us not to forget the tragedy of the Vietnam War so that there will be no more Vietnams, although unfortunately, as a country, it seems we have not learned that lesson, with the more recent wars in Iraq and Afghanistan. Yet Duarte wants us still to remember Vietnam and how it tore this country and families apart. We need to teach about Vietnam and learn the lessons of such a war. In the novel, Teresa attempts to do this even with her second-grade students, when she puts together a lesson plan on the war that includes telling Jesse's story. It is never too early to teach this lesson. "I tell the children about my brother, Jesse," she reflects. "Real name Jesús Antonio Ramírez. He always went by Jesse. He was killed in the middle of a battle right outside Saigon. I point to Saigon, Ho Chi Minh City, on the map. It was when all the crazy fighting was going on in 1968 after Tet, Vietnam's New Year holiday."[58]

Part of teaching about Vietnam, Duarte suggests, is to prevent future "wars of choice," meaning wars that are not necessary and that only benefit the American empire and ruling elites, not the American people. The United States cannot be the policeman of the world, she seems to say. The use of violence and force only demeans us as a society and perpetuates more force and violence. Teresa gives voice to this after the family caravan is racially harassed by a highway patrolman in Kansas. "We're victims of the lust for violence and power," she warns, "that led this nation to the madness of Vietnam." At the same time, Duarte tries to impress on us that only we have the power and the means to stop such madness, but we have to be aware of this power and use it. At the Wall, Teresa chastises herself and all of us when she laments: "Why did we let this happen?"[59]

But above all, *Let Their Spirits Dance* is a tribute to the Chicano Vietnam veteranos who were sent to fight this useless war and became casualties of it by being killed or returning physically and emotionally wounded. These veteranos were not responsible for this war. They were eighteen, nineteen, or twenty when drafted or "encouraged" to enlist. They were not warriors but victims of war. This tribute to the vets is an important corrective to the fact that the Chicano antiwar movement, like the general antiwar movement, was not sensitive to the plight of the veterans and blamed them for the war. By contrast, Duarte is welcoming them back home and giving them the honor and tribute that they deserve, not because they fought for their country but because they fought for each other and were torn from their families. Duarte welcomes them back to their familias. Their deaths are not in vain, she says. They are the voices that we need to listen to if we are to prevent future Vietnams. In her dedication in her novel, Duarte speaks to this at both a personal and a public level:

DEDICATED TO THE MEMORY OF
SGT. TONY CRUZ AND ALL LA RAZA
WHO DIED IN VIETNAM.

We hear you . . .

Jesse's mother put this tribute to her son and to the other Chicano vets who died in the war more bluntly. When told that President Clinton wants to use the Ramírez family visit to the Wall to pay a special acknowledgement to "Hispanics" who served in Vietnam, she says "Era hora," it's about time.[60]

Duarte, through her alter ego, Teresa, concludes her novel by stating that Jesse's death is the conduit to allow the story of the Chicano Vietnam veteranos to be told, including the effects of this tragic episode on their loving families. "It's OK that I knew my brother wasn't coming home," Teresa ends her story. "I was supposed to. It got me to write this book, to tell his story to the world."[61]

XI

Stella Pope Duarte has written a moving and powerful novel around the tragedy of the Vietnam War. The art of a creative writer is the ability to touch our hearts and souls. Duarte does this, and in this chapter, I can't do justice to its emotional impact. When I assigned the novel to my graduate seminar on history and narrativity, I asked my students: "How many of you cried in reading this novel?" Every single hand went up, including my own. There is no question about Duarte's skill as a novelist. I propose, however, that she is also a historian in that her novel is an analysis of the different themes of the Chicano antiwar movement, including proposing some that were not as focused on during the period of the Chicano Movement. The most important new theme that she introduces or at least highlights is that of the family as a Vietnam casualty. We have correctly centered our attention on the veteranos who were killed or maimed in the war, but we have not paid as much attention to the suffering and grief of their families, especially their mothers and sisters, as Duarte stresses. They too are victims. Yet, they are not helpless victims, as the novel proposes. In time, they use their suffering and grief not only to remember the war but to stop future Vietnams. They don't want other families to suffer as they have. Unfortunately, this has not always succeeded, as the U.S. wars in Iraq and Afghanistan reveal. Yet, these suffering families, like the Ramírez family, are also using their grief to call attention to these unnecessary wars and to attempt to stop them and other future wars of choice, including possibly in Syria. "Let their spirits dance" is not just a title of a novel but a clarion call to listen to the casualties and stop the madness of war. In the end, Duarte has produced a syncretic text, bringing together a family story with a historical context. In my opinion, she succeeds in this effort. She has produced believable characters that we can all identify with and even love. Frankly, I have personally fallen in love with Teresa—not once but the three times I have read this story. Therefore, I conclude this chapter with the code that Jesse used to sign off his letters to his sister, but I address it to Stella Pope Duarte:

SWAK (Sealed with a kiss)

EPILOGUE

MARIO, WHY DON'T YOU COME to the Chicano literature conference in Spain?"

This question was posed to me more than once by my colleague at UC Santa Barbara Professor María Herrera-Sobek a few years ago. María was one of the early Chicano literature professors along with my other colleague at UCSB, Professor Francisco Lomelí, who in the 1990s began to attend such conferences sponsored by the Instituto Franklin in Spain.

Chicano literature in Spain?

Yes, Spanish literary scholars, including graduate students, began to discover and study Chicano writers, men and women, as Chicano literature became better known and acknowledged in the United States, especially with the popularity of writers such as Rudolfo Anaya, Sandra Cisneros, Ana Castillo, and Richard Rodriguez, among others. Many of these Spanish scholars are professors or graduate students in American studies and therefore approach Chicano literature from this perspective. Given the historical links of Chicanos (Mexican Americans) and other Latinos in the United States to Spain, it is almost natural that Spanish critics would be interested in Chicano/Latino literature. Moreover, as Spain and other countries in western Europe experience third world migrations, including from Latin America, Spanish and other European intellectuals are attracted to the Chicano/Latino experience in the United States with respect to issues such as multiculturalism, bilingualism, transculturation, and racialization. The result has been a series of biannual conferences in Spain on Chicano literature, more recently expanded to include Latino studies.

Scholars such as Herrera-Sobek and Lomelí were on the ground floor for these gatherings and encouraged other Chicano and Latino literature professors to likewise attend. Many have over the years. They tried, as noted, to interest me in also participating, even though I am not a literary scholar but a historian of the Chicano experience. Still, the idea of attending conferences in Spain appealed to me. As an aside, it is curious and even ironic that more and more Chicano studies academics are discovering Spain, as opposed to the Chicano Movement period, when Spain was anathema to Chicanos as part of the legacy of colonialism, along with U.S. imperialism, as it affected indigenous people in Mexico and others of Mexican descent. Spain was the white European colonizer, and anything to do with Spain was rejected. By contrast, Mexico was rediscovered as the mother country, and many Chicanos during the movement made the cultural pilgrimage to Mexico. Today that has changed, and many Chicanos are now making another cultural pilgrimage, but this time to father Spain. I have no problems with this. The Chicano Movement exalted the mestizo heritage of Chicanos but in so doing stressed only the indigenous side and not the Spanish. But you can't embrace mestizaje without encountering the other side of the legacy, which is that of Spain. Hence, it is important that Chicano scholars are finally confronting the totality of mestizaje.

"But what can I contribute to these conferences?" I asked myself.

It's not that I'm not interested in literature, including Chicano literature. I'm always reading fiction, and this includes that of many Chicano and Chicana writers. In fact, I use some of this writing in my Chicano history classes as well as in the large (400–500 students) Introduction to Chicano Studies class that I also teach. In addition, I am the founder and organizer of the annual Luis Leal Award for Distinction in Chicano/Latino Literature at UC Santa Barbara, which is now in its thirteenth year. The award has been given to such writers as Oscar Hijuelos, Rudolfo Anaya, Denise Chávez, Helena María Viramontes, Pat Mora, Alejandro Morales, Graciela Limón, Jimmy Santiago Baca, Demetria Martínez, Hector Tobar, John Rechy, Stella Pope Duarte, and Reyna Grande. The award is named in honor of the late professor Luis Leal, one of the early pioneers of Chicano literary criticism and champion of Chicano literature.[1] Chicano literature is not foreign to me. In addition, I also teach an undergraduate seminar on Chicano/Latino autobiography and history. My interest in autobiography, in part, has to do with my many years of doing oral history, including testimonios of various historical subjects, such as Bert Corona, Frances Esquibel Tywoniak, Luis Leal, Sal Castro, Raúl Ruiz, Gloria Arellanes, and Rosalío Muñoz.[2]

Hence, in finally taking up Herrera-Sobek's invitation to participate in one of the conferences in Spain, I decided that my entryway into a literary event would be based on connecting my training and experiences as a historian with my interest in literary narratives, including fiction and autobiography. The result was that I not only went to my inaugural conference on Chicano literature in León, Spain, but I have now gone to two others, in Toledo and Oviedo. In addition, I have given papers in Chicano literature symposiums in Ireland and in a Spanish conference on American studies in the Canary Islands. Most of the studies that are included in this volume have their genesis in these papers, in which I did historical readings and analysis of narratives in fiction and autobiography. These presentations and now this volume represent my border crossing between the disciplines of history and literature.

The selection of these subjects has much to do with me. Edward Hallett Carr correctly observes that to know history is to know the historian.[3] The selection of different narratives examined in this book says something about me. My chapter on Professor Ruiz is an obvious connection with my own history; Ruiz was my mentor at UC San Diego, where I received my PhD in history. Fran Esquibel Tywoniak is the aunt of one of my students, who wrote a short oral history of Fran for one of my undergraduate classes in Chicano history. I was so amazed by Fran's story that I engaged with Fran to do her coming-of-age story as a testimonio. I was drawn to Mary Helen Ponce's autobiography because of my own work on the Mexican American generation of the 1930s and 1940s, where her story is contextualized. Moreover, in my generational studies, I have been particularly interested in the processes of acculturation and transculturation and found wonderful examples of such changes in Ponce's narrative. With Richard Rodriguez, I have admired his writing for many years, and I have never accepted how he was blacklisted from Chicano studies curriculum; I personally invited him to speak to a large audience at UCSB, and it was my pleasure to introduce him. I have never bought into Chicano studies political correctness and therefore was further drawn to Rodriguez for his unjust marginalization. John Rechy was born and raised in El Paso as I was, and this has given me a personal affinity to Rechy. I always when possible attempt in my work to make an El Paso connection. This is what also drew me to Ruben Salazar, also from El Paso. In addition, I at one point considered a journalistic career and have written many newspaper columns and many blog entries. With Alejandro Morales I share an interest in Chicano working-class history and have written on Chicano workers and struggles, most prominently in my testimonio of Bert

Corona, longtime labor and community leader in Los Angeles, beginning in the 1930s and 1940s, which connects with the period in part of Morales's *The Brick People*. In my history classes, I now attempt to integrate when possible the experiences of other Latinos, such as Central Americans, and as a result have used the Central American autobiographies that I study in this volume. Finally, my historical generation is the Vietnam War generation, so I was naturally drawn to Stella Pope Duarte's magnificent novel of that generation. Most scholarly work possesses an autobiographical connection, and much of mine has certainly had this, including this book.

I want to conclude by coming back to my thesis, which is that historians can benefit from historical readings of literary narratives, such as autobiographies and novels. Literary texts have a history because the writers are not outside history but inside it. They present the more personal side of history that historians tend to overlook because these insights are often not in the documents we research. Hence, literary narratives are historical documents because they shed light on history, especially in the case of Chicano/Latino history, by providing certain views of the past from the bottom up, that is, the more personal and grassroots experiences. Historical writing at one point in the pre-twentieth-century era was considered literature, and my point is that to a certain extent it still is, but that literature is also history; it is a dialectic. The historian can learn history from literature. I don't expect everyone to agree with me, but at least consider it.

NOTES

INTRODUCTION

1. See Didier Coste, *Narrative as Communication* (Minneapolis: University of Minnesota Press, 1989), 4.

2. Louis Gerard Mendoza, *Historia: The Literary Making of Chicana and Chicano History* (College Station: Texas A&M University Press, 2001).

3. Rigoberta Menchú, *I, Rigoberta Menchú: An Indian Woman in Guatemala*, ed. Elisabeth Burgos-Debray, trans. Ann Wright (London: Verso, 1984). Also see Gillian Whitlock, *Postcolonial Life Narrative: Testimonial Transactions* (New York: Oxford University Press, 2015); and John Beverly, *Testimonio: On the Politics of Truth* (Minneapolis: University of Minnesota Press, 2004).

4. Mario T. García, *Memories of Chicano History: The Life and Narrative of Bert Corona* (Berkeley: University of California Press, 1994); Mario T. García and Sal Castro, *Blowout! Sal Castro and the Chicano Struggle for Educational Justice* (Chapel Hill: University of North Carolina Press, 2011).

5. See Oscar Martínez, "On the Size of the Chicano Population: New Estimates, 1850–1900," *Aztlán* (Spring 1975): 43–67; Richard Griswold del Castillo, *The Treaty of Guadalupe Hidalgo: A Legacy of Conflict* (Norman: University of Oklahoma Press, 1990); Laura E. Gómez, *Manifest Destinies: The Making of the Mexican American Race* (New York: New York University Press, 2007); and Ian F. Haney López, *White by Law: The Legal Construction of Race* (New York: New York University Press, 1996).

6. See Mario T. García, *Desert Immigrants: The Mexicans of El Paso, 1880–1920* (New Haven, CT: Yale University Press, 1981); Albert Camarillo, *Chicanos in a Changing Society: From Mexican Pueblos to American Barrios in Santa Barbara*

and Southern California, 1848–1930 (Cambridge, MA: Harvard University Press, 1979); Ricardo Romo, *East Los Angeles: History of a Barrio* (Austin: University of Texas Press, 1983); and George J. Sánchez, *Becoming Mexican American: Ethnicity, Culture, and Identity in Chicano Los Angeles, 1900–1945* (New York: Oxford University Press, 1993), among other studies of the immigrant generation.

7. On the 1930s deportations and repatriations, see Francisco Balderrama and Raymond Rodríguez, *Decade of Betrayal: Mexican Repatriation in the 1930s* (Albuquerque: University of New Mexico Press, 1995); Abraham Hoffman, *Unwanted Mexican Americans in the Great Depression: Repatriation Pressures, 1929–1939* (Tucson: University of Arizona Press, 1974); and Natalia Molina, *Fit to Be Citizens: Public Health and Race in Los Angeles, 1879–1939* (Berkeley: University of California Press, 2006).

8. On the Mexican American generation, see Mario T. García, *Mexican Americans: Leadership, Ideology & Identity, 1930–1960* (New Haven, CT: Yale University Press, 1989); Richard A. Garcia, *Rise of the Mexican American Middle Class: San Antonio, 1929–1941* (College Station: Texas A&M University Press, 1991); and Sánchez, *Becoming Mexican American.*

9. Sánchez, *Becoming Mexican American.* Also see Gabriela F. Arredondo, *Mexican Chicago: Race, Identity, and Nation, 1916–39* (Urbana: University of Illinois Press, 2008); and David G. Gutiérrez, *Walls and Mirrors: Mexican Americans, Mexican Immigrants, and the Politics of Ethnicity* (Berkeley: University of California Press, 1995).

10. On the Chicano Movement, see Ernesto Chávez, *Mi Raza Primero! Nationalism, Identity, and Insurgency in the Chicano Movement in Los Angeles, 1966–1978* (Berkeley: University of California Press, 2002); Ignacio M. García, *United We Win: The Rise and Fall of La Raza Unida Party* (Tucson: MASRC, University of Arizona, 1989); Ernesto B. Vigil, *The Crusade for Justice: Chicano Militancy and the Government's War on Dissent* (Madison: University of Wisconsin Press, 1999); George Mariscal, *Brown-Eyed Children of the Sun: Lessons from the Chicano Movement, 1965–1975* (Albuquerque: University of New Mexico Press, 2005); Lorena Oropeza, *Raza Si! Guerra No! Chicano Protest and Patriotism during the Viet Nam War Era* (Berkeley: University of California Press, 2005); Maylei Blackwell, *Chicana Power! Contested Histories of Feminism in the Chicano Movement* (Austin: University of Texas Press, 2011); Randy J. Ontiveros, *In the Spirit of a New People: The Cultural Politics of the Chicano Movement* (New York: New York University Press, 2014); Lee Bebout, *Mythohistorical Interventions: The Chicano Movement and Its Legacies* (Minneapolis: University of Minnesota Press, 2011); García and Castro, *Blowout!*; Mario T. García, *The Chicano*

Generation: Testimonios of the Movement (Oakland: University of California Press, 2015); Mario T. García, ed., *The Chicano Movement: Perspectives from the Twenty-First Century* (New York: Routledge, 2014); Juan Gómez-Quinones and Irene Vásquez, *Making Aztlán: Ideology and Culture of the Chicana and Chicano Movement, 1966–1977* (Albuquerque: University of New Mexico Press, 2014); and Marc Simon Rodriguez, *Rethinking the Chicano Movement* (New York: Routledge, 2014).

11. Mario T. García, *The Latino Generation: Voices of the New America* (Chapel Hill: University of North Carolina Press, 2014). Also see Matt Barreto and Gary M. Segura, *Latino America: How America's Most Dynamic Population Is Poised to Tranform the Poltics of the Nation* (New York: Public Affairs, 2014).

12. On racialization, see Michael Omi and Howard Winant, *Racial Formation in the United States: From the 1960s to the 1980s* (New York: Routledge, 1986).

13. Luz María Gordillo, *Mexican Women and the Other Side of Immigration: Engendering Transnational Ties* (Austin: University of Texas Press, 2010).

14. See García, *Desert Immigrants*; and García, *Mexican Americans*.

15. On the history of the Mexican schools, see García, *Desert Immigrants*, 110–26; Gilbert G. González, *Chicano Education in the Era of Segregation* (Philadelphia, PA: Balch Institute Press, 1990); Guadalupe San Miguel, Jr., *"Let All of Them Take Heed": Mexican Americans and the Campaign for Educational Equality in Texas, 1910–1981* (Austin: University of Texas Press, 1987); Carlos Kevin Blanton, *The Strange Career of Bilingual Education in Texas, 1836–1981* (College Station: Texas A&M University Press, 2004); Carlos Kevin Blanton, *George I. Sánchez: The Long Fight for Mexican American Integration* (New Haven, CT: Yale University Press, 2014); and John D. McCafferty, *Aliso School: "For the Mexican Children"* (Santa Barbara, CA: McSeas Books, 2003).

16. Camarillo, *Chicanos in a Changing Society*.

17. See Sánchez, *Becoming Mexican American*; García, *Mexican Americans*; and Frances Esquibel Tywoniak and Mario T. García, *Migrant Daughter: Coming of Age as a Mexican American Woman* (Berkeley: University of California Press, 2000).

18. See García, *Mexican Americans*; García, *Memories of Chicano History*; García and Castro, *Blowout!*; and García, *The Chicano Generation*.

19. See, for example, Vicki L. Ruíz, *Cannery Women, Cannery Lives: Mexican Women, Unionization, and the California Food Processing Industry, 1930–1950* (Albuquerque: University of New Mexico Press, 1987); and Tywoniak and García, *Migrant Daughter*; and Mario T. García, ed., *A Dolores Huerta Reader* (Albuquerque: University of New Mexico Press, 2008).

20. Edward Hallett Carr, *What Is History?* (New York: Vintage Books, 1961), 54.

21. García, *The Chicano Generation*; Richard Griswold del Castillo, *La Familia: Chicano Families in the Urban Southwest, 1848 to the Present* (Notre Dame, IN: University of Notre Dame Press, 1984).

22. Mario T. García, *Católicos: Resistance and Affirmation in Chicano Catholic History* (Austin: University of Texas Press, 2008); Charles M. Tatum, *Chicano Popular Culture: Que Hable el Pueblo* (Tucson: University of Arizona Press, 2001); Michelle Habell-Pallán and Mary Romero, eds., *Latino/a Popular Culture* (New York: New York University Press, 2002).

23. See Emilio Zamora, ed., *The World War I Diary of José de la Luz Sáenz* (College Station: Texas A&M University Press, 2014).

24. See Raul Morin, *Among the Valiant: Mexican Americans in WWII and Korea* (Alhambra, CA: Borden Publishing, 1966); Maggie Rivas-Rodríguez, ed., *Mexican Americans and World War II* (Austin: University of Texas Press, 2005); Maggie Rivas-Rodríguez and Emilio Zamora, eds., *Beyond the Latino World War II Hero: The Social and Political Legacy of a Generation* (Austin: University of Texas Press, 2010); and Maggie Rivas-Rodríguez and B. V. Olguín, eds., *Latina/os and World War II: Mobility, Agency, and Ideology* (Austin: University of Texas Press, 2014).

25. See Roy P. Benavidez with John R. Craig, *Medal of Honor: A Vietnam Warrior's Story* (Washington, DC: Brassey's, 1995).

26. See Ignacio M. García, *Chicanismo: The Forging of a Militant Ethos among Mexican Americans* (Tucson: University of Arizona Press, 1997).

27. See Oropeza, *Raza Si! Guerra No!*; and García, *The Chicano Generation*.

28. See García, *Católicos*.

29. See William V. Flores and Rina Benmayor, *Latino Cultural Citizenship: Claiming Identity, Space, and Rights* (Boston: Beacon Press, 1997); and Renato Rosaldo, *Culture and Truth: The Remaking of Social Analysis* (Boston: Beacon Press, 1993).

CHAPTER 1

1. Ramón Eduardo Ruiz Urueta, *Memories of a Hyphenated Man* (Tucson: University of Arizona Press, 2003), 236.

2. My work includes books such as *Desert Immigrants: The Mexicans of El Paso, 1880–1920* (New Haven, CT: Yale University Press, 1981); *Mexican Americans: Leadership, Ideology & Identity, 1930–1960* (New Haven, CT: Yale University Press, 1989); *Memories of Chicano History: The Life and Narrative of Bert Corona*

(Berkeley: University of California Press, 1994); coauthored with Frances Esqui-bel Tywoniak, *Migrant Daughter: Coming of Age as a Mexican American Woman* (Berkeley: University of California Press, 2000); *Luis Leal: An Auto/Biography* (Austin: University of Texas Press, 2000); and *Católicos: Resistance and Affirmation in Chicano Catholic History* (Austin: University of Texas Press, 2008).

3. Jeremy D. Popkin, *History, Historians, and Autobiography* (Chicago: University of Chicago Press, 2005). See Kevin R. Johnson, *How Did You Get to Be Mexican? A White/Brown Man's Search for Identity* (Philadelphia, PA: Temple University Press, 1999).

4. Popkin, *History, Historians*, 4.

5. Quoted in ibid., 59.

6. Ibid., 60.

7. Ibid., 3–48.

8. García, *Desert Immigrants*. Also see George J. Sánchez, *Becoming Mexican American: Ethnicity, Culture, and Identity in Chicano Los Angeles, 1900–1945* (New York: Oxford University Press, 1993); Ricardo Romo, *East Los Angeles: History of a Barrio* (Austin: University of Texas Press, 1983); Juan R. García, *Mexicans in the Midwest, 1900–1932* (Tucson: University of Arizona Press, 1996); David G. Gutiérrez, *Walls and Mirrors: Mexican Americans, Mexican Immigrants, and the Politics of Ethnicity* (Berkeley: University of California Press, 1995).

9. Ruiz Urueta, *Memories*, 4.

10. Ibid., 6.

11. García, *Desert Immigrants*.

12. Ibid.

13. Ruiz Urueta, *Memories*, 13–14.

14. Ibid., 16–19.

15. Ibid., ix. On the Mexican American generation, see García, *Mexican Americans*. Also see Richard A. Garcia, *Rise of the Mexican American Middle Class: San Antonio, 1929–1941* (College Station: Texas A&M University Press, 1991); Benjamin Márquez, *LULAC: The Evolution of a Mexican American Political Organization* (Austin: University of Texas Press, 1993); Vicki L. Ruíz, *Cannery Women, Cannery Lives: Mexican Women, Unionization, and the California Food Processing Industry, 1930–1950* (Albuquerque: University of New Mexico Press, 1987); Douglas Monroy, *Rebirth: Mexican Los Angeles from the Great Migration to the Great Depression* (Berkeley: University of California Press, 1999).

16. Ruiz Urueta, *Memories*, 39–40. On the "Mexican schools," see García, *Desert Immigrants*, 110–26. Also see Gilbert G. González, *Chicano Education in the*

Era of Segregation (Philadelphia, PA: Balch Institute Press, 1990); Guadalupe San Miguel, Jr., *"Let All of Them Take Heed": Mexican Americans and the Campaign for Educational Equality in Texas, 1910–1981* (Austin: University of Texas Press, 1987).

17. Ruiz Urueta, *Memories*, 27. On the 1930s deportations and repatriations, see Abraham Hoffman, *Unwanted Mexican Americans in the Great Depression: Repatriation Pressures, 1929–1939* (Tucson: University of Arizona Press, 1974); and Francisco E. Balderrama and Raymond Rodríguez, *Decade of Betrayal: Mexican Repatriation in the 1930s* (Albuquerque: University of New Mexico Press, 1995).

18. On Mexican Americans and World War II, see Maggie Rivas-Rodríguez, ed., *Mexican Americans and World War II* (Austin: University of Texas Press, 2005); Richard Griswold del Castillo, ed., *World War II and Mexican American Civil Rights* (Austin: University of Texas Press, 2008).

19. Ruiz Urueta, *Memories*, 92.

20. Ibid., 177.

21. Ibid., 179.

22. Ibid., 184.

23. Ibid.

24. Ibid., 183.

25. Ibid., 190.

26. Ibid., 201.

27. Ibid., 196.

28. Ibid., 196–219. On the Chicano Movement, see Ernesto Chávez, *Mi Raza Primero! Nationalism, Identity, and Insurgency in the Chicano Movement in Los Angeles, 1966–1978* (Berkeley: University of California Press, 2002); Carlos Muñoz, Jr., *Youth, Identity, and Power: The Chicano Movement* (London: Verso Press, 1989); Alma M. García, ed., *Chicana Feminist Thought: The Basic Historical Writings* (New York: Routledge, 1997); Lorena Oropeza, *Raza Si! Guerra No! Chicano Protest and Patriotism during the Viet Nam War Era* (Berkeley: University of California Press, 2005); George Mariscal, *Brown-Eyed Children of the Sun: Lessons from the Chicano Movement, 1965–1975* (Albuquerque: University of New Mexico Press, 2005); Mario T. García, *The Chicano Generation: Testimonios of the Movement* (Berkeley: University of California Press, 2015); Mario T. García and Sal Castro, *Blowout!: Sal Castro and the Chicano Struggle for Educational Justice* (Chapel Hill: University of North Carolina Press, 2011); and Mario T. García, ed., *The Chicano Movement: Perspectives from the Twenty-First Century* (New York: Routledge, 2011).

29. Ruiz Urueta, *Memories*, 199.
30. Ibid., 203.
31. Ibid., 211.
32. García, *Mexican Americans*.
33. Ruiz Urueta, *Memories*, 199.

CHAPTER 2

1. See Shari Benstock, ed., *The Private Self: Theory and Practice of Women's Autobiographical Writings* (Chapel Hill: University of North Carolina Press, 1988).
2. Carolyn G. Heilbrun, *Writing a Woman's Life* (New York: Norton, 1988).
3. Mario T. García, *Memories of Chicano History: The Life and Narrative of Bert Corona* (Berkeley: University of California Press, 1994).
4. Rigoberta Menchú, *I, Rigoberta Menchú: An Indian Woman in Guatemala*, ed. Elisabeth Burgos-Debray, trans. Ann Wright (London: Verso, 1984).
5. Mary G. Mason, "The Other Voice: Autobiographies of Women Writers," in *Life Lines: Theorizing Women's Autobiography*, ed. Bella Brodzki and Celeste Schenck, 19–44 (Ithaca, NY: Cornell University Press, 1988).
6. Werner Sollors, *Beyond Ethnicity: Consent and Descent in American Culture* (New York: Oxford University Press, 1986).
7. I borrow the concept of polyphonic voices from the Russian literary critic Mikhail Bakhtin. See Katerina Clark and Michael Holquist, *Mikhail Bakhtin* (Cambridge, MA: Belknap Press, 1984).
8. Benedict Anderson, *Imagined Communities: Reflections on the Origin and Spread of Nationalism* (London: Verso, 1983).
9. The oral history interviews that form the basis of Frances Esquibel Tywoniak's narrative were conducted during the summers of 1990 and 1991. At this time, both the audiotapes and the transcripts remain in my possession.
10. As quoted in Carolyn G. Heilbrun, "Non-Autobiographies of 'Privileged' Women: England and America," in Brodzki and Schenck, *Life Lines*, 62.
11. All Fran quotations are from the interviews I conducted with her in 1990 and 1991.
12. W. E. B. Du Bois, *The Souls of Black Folk* (Chicago: McClurg, 1903).
13. See Doris Sommer, "'Not Just a Personal Story': Women's Testimonio and the Plural Self," in Brodzki and Schenck, *Life Lines*, 107–30.
14. Heilbrun, *Woman's Life*, 24.
15. Richard Rodriguez, *Hunger of Memory: The Education of Richard Rodriguez—An Autobiography* (Boston, MA: Godine, 1982).

16. See Gloria Anzaldúa, *Borderlands/La Frontera: The New Mestiza* (San Francisco, CA: Aunt Lute, 1987).

17. Heilbrun, *Woman's Life*, 48. See Mario T. García, *Mexican Americans: Leadership, Ideology and Identity, 1930–1960* (New Haven, CT: Yale University Press, 1989); Richard A. Garcia, *Rise of the Mexican-American Middle Class: San Antonio, 1929–1941* (College Station: Texas A&M University Press, 1991).

18. See Mario T. García, *Mexican Americans: Leadership, Ideology & Identity, 1930–1960* (New Haven, CT: Yale University Press, 1989); Richard A. Garcia, *Rise of the Mexican-American Middle Class: San Antonio, 1929–1941* (College Station: Texas A&M University Press, 1991).

19. As quoted in Susan Stanford Friendman, "Women's Autobiographical Selves: Theory and Practice," in Benstock, *Private Self*, 43.

20. Heilbrun, *Woman's Life*, 111–12. See Frances Esquibel Tywoniak and Mario T. García, *Migrant Daughter: Coming of Age as a Mexican American Woman* (Berkeley: University of California Press, 2000).

CHAPTER 3

1. See Mario T. García, *Desert Immigrants: The Mexicans of El Paso, 1880–1920* (New Haven, CT: Yale University Press, 1981); and Mario T. García, *Mexican Americans: Leadership, Ideology & Identity, 1930–1960* (New Haven, CT: Yale University Press, 1989).

2. Oscar Handlin, *The Uprooted: The Epic Story of the Great Migration that Made the American People* (Boston: Little, Brown, 1951).

3. Mary Helen Ponce, *Hoyt Street—An Autobiography* (Albuquerque: University of New Mexico Press, 1993), x.

4. Mary Louise Pratt, *Imperial Eyes: Travel Writing and Transculturation* (New York: Routledge, 1992), 6.

5. Fernando Ortiz, *Cuban Counterpoint: Tobacco and Sugar* (New York: Knopf, 1947; Durham, NC: Duke University Press, 1995). Citations refer to the Duke edition.

6. Ibid., 102–3.

7. Clifford Geertz, *The Interpretation of Cultures: Selected Essays* (New York: Basic Books, 1973).

8. Interview with Mary Helen Ponce in Karin Rosa Ikas, *Chicana Ways: Conversations With Ten Chicana Writers* (Reno: University of Nevada Press, 2002), 185.

9. I borrow the term "reconciliation" from Terry Huffman, "Resistance Theory and the Transculturation Hypothesis as Explanation of College Attrition and

Persistence Among Culturally Traditional American Indian Students," *Journal of American Indian Education* 40, no. 3 (2001): 29.

10. Ibid., 30.

11. George J. Sánchez, *Becoming Mexican American: Ethnicity, Culture, and Identity in Chicano Los Angeles, 1900–1945* (New York: Oxford University Press, 1993).

12. García, *Mexican Americans*.

13. Ponce, *Hoyt Street*, 8.

14. Ibid., 71, 121, 208, 266, 330.

15. Ibid., 112.

16. Ibid.

17. Ibid., 318.

18. Ibid., 35.

19. Ibid., 180.

20. Ibid., 319, 311, 322.

21. Ibid., 35.

22. Ibid., 220.

23. Ibid., 220, 311.

24. Ibid., 199.

25. Ibid., 160, 208, 269–71.

26. Ibid., 15–42.

27. Ibid., 293.

28. Ibid., 293, 329–30, 176, 267, 337.

29. Ibid., 303–5.

30. Ibid., 305.

31. Ibid., 15–42.

32. Ibid., 267.

33. Ibid., 176.

34. Ibid., 144.

35. Anthony Macías, *Mexican American Mojo: Popular Music, Dance, and Urban Culture in Los Angeles, 1935–1968* (Durham, NC: Duke University Press, 2008).

36. Ibid., 25–26, 210, 213–19.

37. Ibid., 208–9.

CHAPTER 4

1. W. E. B. Du Bois, *The Souls of Black Folk* (Chicago: McClurg, 1903; Boston: Bedford Books, 1997), 38. Citations refer to the Bedford edition.

2. See Mario T. García, *Desert Immigrants: The Mexicans of El Paso, 1880–1920* (New Haven, CT: Yale University Press, 1981); and Mario T. García, *Mexican Americans: Leadership, Ideology & Identity, 1930–1960* (New Haven, CT: Yale University Press, 1989).

3. Emma Pérez, *The Decolonial Imaginary: Writing Chicanas into History* (Bloomington: Indiana University Press, 1999).

4. George Mariscal, *Brown-Eyed Children of the Sun: Lessons from the Chicano Movement, 1965–1975* (Albuquerque: University of New Mexico Press, 2005).

5. Beth Hernández-Jason, "The Act of Reading John Rechy: Transnational and Transcultural Intertexts and Readers" (PhD diss., University of California, Merced, 2014).

6. Richard Rodriguez, *Hunger of Memory: The Education of Richard Rodriguez—An Autobiography* (Boston, MA: Godine, 1982); and John Rechy, *About My Life and the Kept Woman: A Memoir* (New York: Grove Press, 2008).

7. See Gilbert G. González, *Chicano Education in the Era of Segregation* (Philadelphia, PA: Balch Institute Press, 1990).

8. Rodriguez, *Hunger of Memory*, 4.

9. Ibid., 70.

10. Ibid., 9.

11. Ibid., 10.

12. Ibid., 23.

13. Ibid., 56.

14. García, *Mexican Americans*.

15. Rodriguez, *Hunger of Memory*, 27.

16. Ibid., 3.

17. Ibid., 4.

18. For the Mexican schools in El Paso, see García, *Desert Immigrants*, 110–26. Also see Rechy's 1958 essay "El Paso del Norte," published in John Rechy, *Beneath the Skin: The Collected Essays of John Rechy* (New York: Carroll and Graf, 2004).

19. García, *Desert Immigrants*, 110–26.

20. Rechy, *About My Life*, 50.

21. Ibid., 88–89.

22. Ibid., 65.

23. Ibid., 52.

24. Ibid., 90.

25. José Villarreal, *Pocho* (New York: Doubleday, 1959).

26. Rechy, *About My Life*, 152.

27. Rodriguez, *Hunger of Memory*, 55.

28. Ibid., 19.

29. Ibid., 15.

30. Ibid., 29.

31. Ibid., 3. For Rodriguez's struggle with ethnic identity, see Michael Nieto García, *Autobiography in Black and Brown: Ethnic Identity in Richard Wright and Richard Rodriguez* (Albuquerque: University of New Mexico Press, 2014).

32. Rechy, *About My Life*, 63.

33. Ibid., 69.

34. Ibid. 93.

35. Ibid. 95.

36. Ibid., 62.

37. Ibid., 87.

38. Ibid., 110.

39. Ibid., 111.

40. Ibid., 112.

41. Ibid., 115.

42. Rodriguez, *Hunger of Memory*, 135.

43. Ibid., 141, 146.

44. Ibid., 136.

45. Ibid., 140.

46. Ibid., 137.

47. Ibid., 139.

48. Ibid., 200.

49. Rechy, *About My Life*, 46.

50. Ibid., 108.

51. Ibid., 109.

52. Ibid., 144.

53. Mariscal, *Brown-Eyed Children*.

CHAPTER 5

1. See Dianne Walta Hart, *Undocumented in L.A.: An Immigrant's Story* (Wilmington, DE: SR Books, 1997); and Evelyn Cortez-Davis, *December Sky: Beyond My Undocumented Life* (Altadena, CA: In Xochitl In Cuicatl Productions, 2005). On the Central American migration to the United States, see María Cristina García, *Seeking Refuge: Central American Migration to Mexico, the United States, and Canada* (Berkeley: University of California Press, 2000); Sergio Aguayo and Patricia Weiss Fagen, *Central Americans in Mexico and the*

United States: Unilateral, Bilateral, and Regional Perspectives (Washington, DC: Hemisphere Migration Project, Center for Immigration Policy and Refugee Assistance, Georgetown University, 1988); Elizabeth G. Ferris, *The Central American Refugees* (New York: Praeger, 1982); Nora Hamilton and Norma Stoltz Chinchilla, *Seeking Community in a Global City: Guatemalans and Salvadorans in Los Angeles* (Philadelphia, PA: Temple University Press, 2001); Cecilia Menjívar, *Fragmented Ties: Salvadoran Immigrant Networks in America* (Berkeley: University of California Press, 2000); and Rossana Pérez with Henry A. J. Ramos, *Flight to Freedom: The Story of Central American Refugees in California* (Houston, TX: Arte Publico Press, 2007).

2. Pierrette Hondagneu-Sotelo, *Gendered Transitions: Mexican Experiences of Immigration* (Berkeley: University of California Press, 1994).

3. Ibid., 2.

4. Ibid., 192.

5. See Hart, *Undocumented in L.A.*, 137.

6. See Cortez-Davis, *December Sky*.

7. Hondagneu-Sotelo, *Gendered Transitions*, xxiv.

8. Ibid., 6.

9. See Hart, *Undocumented in L.A.*, xvi, xvii, xxv.

10. See Cortez-Davis, *December Sky*, 7–8, 17, 22, 24, 29.

11. Hart, *Undocumented in L.A.*, 102.

12. Ibid., 5. 7, 11, 61.

13. Cortez-Davis, *December Sky*, 33–34.

14. Hondagneu-Sotelo, *Gendered Transitions*, 27.

15. See Hart, *Undocumented in L.A.*, 9, 39–40, 64; and Cortez-Davis, *December Sky*, 49–52.

16. Hondagneu-Sotelo, *Gendered Transitions*, 39.

17. Ibid., 96.

18. Hart, *Undocumented in L.A.*, xi.

19. Cortez-Davis, *December Sky*, 61, 71. It cost Rosario and her husband five thousand dollars to pay the coyotes for transporting them into the United States.

20. Ibid., 5–6.

21. Hart, *Undocumented in L.A.*, 101.

22. Cortez-Davis, *December Sky*, 43.

23. Hart, *Undocumented in L.A.*, 64.

24. Ibid., 65.

25. Ibid., 66–67.

26. Cortez-Davis, *December Sky*, 137.

27. Hondagneu-Sotelo, *Gendered Transitions*, 146.

28. Ibid., xxiv.

29. Hart, *Undocumented in L.A.*, 82, 123–24, 135.

30. Cortez-Davis, *December Sky*, 49, 123.

31. Hart, *Undocumented in L.A.*, 30.

32. Ibid., 63.

33. Ibid., 70.

34. Ibid., 71.

35. Cortez-Davis, *December Sky*, 48, 101, 124, 127, 128.

36. Hart, *Undocumented in L.A.*, 112, 119.

37. Cortez-Davis, *December Sky*, 47, 60.

38. Alejandro Portes and Rubén G. Rumbaut, *Legacies: The Story of the Immigrant Second Generation* (Berkeley: University of California Press, 2001).

39. Cortez-Davis, *December Sky*, 125; also see Hart, *Undocumented in L.A.*, 41, 59, 71, 95.

40. Hondagneu-Sotelo, *Gendered Transitions*, 174.

41. Ibid., 179.

42. Hart, *Undocumented in L.A.*, 62, 85.

43. Ibid., 42.

44. Ibid., 120–21.

45. Cortez-Davis, *December Sky*, 99.

46. Hart, *Undocumented in L.A.*, 95.

47. Hondagneu-Sotelo, *Gendered Transitions*, 146.

48. George J. Sánchez, *Becoming Mexican American: Ethnicity, Culture, and Identity in Chicano Los Angeles, 1900–1945* (Berkeley: University of California Press, 1993), 98.

CHAPTER 6

1. Albert Camarillo, *Chicanos in a Changing Society: From Mexican Pueblos to American Barrios in Santa Barbara and Southern California, 1848–1930* (Cambridge, MA: Harvard University Press, 1979)

2. See Mario T. García, *Desert Immigrants: The Mexicans of El Paso, 1880–1920* (New Haven, CT: Yale University Press, 1981); Lawrence A. Cardoso, *Mexican Emigration to the United States, 1897–1931: Socio-economic Patterns* (Tucson: University of Arizona Press, 1980); Mark Reisler, *By the Sweat of Their Brow: Mexican Immigrant Labor in the United States, 1900–1940* (Westport, CT: Greenwood Press, 1976); Ricardo Romo, *East Los Angeles: History of a Barrio* (Austin: University of Texas Press, 1983); and Vicki L. Ruíz, *Cannery Women,*

*Cannery Lives: Mexican Women, Unionization, and the California Food Process-
ing Industry, 1930–1950* (Albuquerque: University of New Mexico Press, 1987).

3. Alejandro Morales, *The Brick People* (Houston, TX: Arte Publico Press, 1988);
Bruce-Novoa, "History as Content, History as Act: The Chicano Novel,"
Aztlán 18, no. 1 (1987): 29–44.

4. Octavio Ignacio Romano V, "Minorities, History, and the Cultural Mystique,"
El Grito (Fall 1967): 5–11; Romano, "The Anthropology and Sociology of the
Mexican Americans: The Distortion of Mexican American History," *El Grito*
(Fall 1968): 13–26; Romano, "The Historical and Intellectual Presence of Mex-
ican Americans," *El Grito* (Winter 1969): 32–46; and Romano, "Social Science,
Objectivity and the Chicanos," *El Grito* (Fall, 1970): 4–16.

5. Rodolfo Acuña, *Occupied America: The Chicano's Struggle Toward Liberation*
(San Francisco, CA: Canfield Press, 1972).

6. John R. Chávez, *The Lost Land: The Chicano Image of the Southwest* (Albuquerque: University of New Mexico Press, 1984).

7. Carey McWilliams, *North from Mexico: The Spanish-Speaking People of the
United States* (Philadelphia, PA: Lippincott, 1949).

8. Morales, *Brick People*, 11.

9. Ibid.

10. Oscar Zeta Acosta, *The Revolt of the Cockroach People* (San Francisco, CA:
Straight Arrow Books, 1973).

11. Morales, *Brick People*, 47.

12. Ibid., 126.

13. Ibid., 142.

14. Ibid., 78.

15. Ibid., 79–80.

16. Ibid., 80.

17. Ibid., 81.

18. Ibid.

19. Ibid., 185.

20. Ibid., 186.

21. Ibid., 55.

22. Ibid., 54.

23. Ibid., 102.

24. Ibid., 19.

25. See Mario T. García, *Mexican Americans: Leadership Ideology & Identity, 1930–
1960* (New Haven, CT: Yale University Press, 1989); and Richard A. Garcia's

Rise of the Mexican American Middle Class: San Antonio, 1929–1941 (College Station: Texas A&M University Press, 1991).

26. Morales, *Brick People*, 106–7.

27. Ibid., 188–89.

28. Ibid., 226.

29. See García, *Mexican Americans*; and Ruíz, *Cannery Women*.

30. As quoted in the introduction to David Madden, ed., *Proletarian Writers of the Thirties* (Carbondale: Southern Illinois University Press, 1968), xviii.

31. Ibid.

32. Ibid., xix.

33. Ibid.; Erling Larsen, "Jack Conroy's 'The Disinherited,'" in Madden, *Proletarian Writers*, 85–95.

34. See García, *Mexican Americans*.

35. Morales, *Brick People*, 271.

36. Ibid., 272.

37. Víctor Molina, "Notes on Marx and the Problem of Individuality," in *On Ideology*, ed. entre for Contemporary Cultural Studies (London: Hutchinson, 1978), 235.

38. As quoted in ibid.

39. Morales, *Brick People*, 120.

40. Ibid., 215.

41. See Herbert Biberman, *Salt of the Earth: The Story of a Film* (Boston, MA: Beacon Press, 1965); Michael Wilson, with commentary by Deborah Silverton Rosenfelt, *Salt of the Earth* (Old Westbury, NY: Feminist Press, 1978); Jack Cargill, "Empire and Opposition: The 'Salt of the Earth' Strike," in *Labor in New Mexico: Unions, Strikes, and Social History Since 1881*, ed. Robert Kern (Albuquerque: University of New Mexico Press, 1983), 183–267.

42. See Frank Arnold, "Humberto Silex: CIO Organizer from Nicaragua," in *Southwest Economy and Society* (Fall 1978): 3–20. Also see Monica Perales, *Smeltertown: Making and Remembering a Southwest Border Community* (Chapel Hill: University of North Carolina Press, 2010).

CHAPTER 7

1. For a history of Salazar, see my edited book, Ruben Salazar, *Border Correspondent: Selected Writings, 1955–1970*, ed. Mario T. García (Berkeley: University of California Press, 1995).

2. For more on the Chicano Moratorium, see Ernesto Chávez, *Mi Raza Primero!* *Nationalism, Identity, and Insurgency in the Chicano Movement in Los Angeles, 1966–1978* (Berkeley: University of California Press, 2002).

3. For Salazar's reporting during his career, see my edited volume of his writings, *Border Correspondent*.

4. See Salazar, "Who Is a Chicano? And What Is It the Chicanos Want?" *Los Angeles Times*, Feb. 6, 1970, reproduced in *Border Correspondent*, 235–37.

5. See Mario T. García, *Mexican Americans: Leadership, Ideology & Identity, 1930–1960* (New Haven, CT: Yale University Press, 1989).

6. See Ian F. Haney López, *Racism on Trial: The Chicano Fight for Justice* (Cambridge, MA: Harvard University Press, 2003).

7. All quotations herein come from Salazar's unfinished novel "A Stranger's House." No page numbers are attributed because of the unfinished and disorganized nature of the manuscript.

8. George J. Sánchez, *Becoming Mexican American: Ethnicity, Culture, and Identity in Chicano Los Angeles, 1900–1945* (New York: Oxford University Press, 1993).

9. This and all subsequent quotations are from Salazar, "A Stranger's House," n.p.

10. Salazar to Cesar Castillo, May 12, 1957, letter in author's possession.

CHAPTER 8

1. See Lorena Oropeza, *¡Raza Sí! Guerra No! Chicano Protest and Patriotism during the Viet Nam War Era* (Berkeley: University of California Press, 2005).

2. Ibid.

3. Ibid.

4. Stella Pope Duarte, *Let Their Spirits Dance* (reprint, New York: Harper Perennial, 2003), 19, 23, 115–16, 231; quotation on 231.

5. Ibid., 304.

6. Ibid., 76.

7. Ibid., 73.

8. On the Guzmán report, see Mario T. García, *The Chicano Generation: Testimonios of the Movement* (Berkeley: University of California Press, 2015), and the section on Rosalio Muñoz, the key organizer of the Chicano antiwar movement.

9. See Mario T. García and Sal Castro, *Blowout! Sal Castro and the Chicano Struggle for Educational Justice* (Berkeley: University of California Press, 2011), 110–32.

10. Duarte, *Let Their Spirits Dance*, 289.

11. Ibid., 20.

12. Ibid., 57.

13. Ibid., 63, 233.

14. Ibid., 56.

15. Ibid., 205.

16. Ibid., 8.

17. Ibid., 308–9.

18. *La Raza*, December 10, 1969, 6.

19. Duarte, *Let Their Spirits Dance*, 309.

20. Ibid., 169.

21. Ibid., 56.

22. Ibid., 21, 36.

23. Ibid., 238.

24. Ibid., 230, 232.

25. Ibid., 307.

26. Ibid., 52.

27. Ibid., 206.

28. Ibid., 136.

29. Ibid., 202.

30. Ibid., 252.

31. Ibid., 206.

32. Ibid., 307.

33. Ibid., 174.

34. Ibid., 53, 252.

35. Ibid., 52, 261.

36. Ibid., 138.

37. Ibid., 298–99.

38. See Oropeza, *¡Raza Sí! Guerra No!*

39. Duarte, *Let Their Spirits Dance*, 37.

40. Ibid., 20.

41. Ibid., 179.

42. Ibid., 182.

43. See Oropeza, *¡Raza Sí! Guerra No!*

44. Duarte, *Let Their Spirits Dance*, 175.

45. Ibid., 168–69, 171.

46. Ibid., 170, 176.

47. Ibid., 178–79.

48. Ibid., 211.

49. Ibid., 20, 25, 26.

50. Ibid., 135–36.
51. Ibid., 40, 80.
52. Ibid., 61.
53. Ibid., 85.
54. Ibid., 202.
55. Ibid., 276, 79, 50.
56. Ibid., 112.
57. Ibid., 216, 309.
58. Ibid., 61.
59. Ibid., 250, 309.
60. Ibid., 290.
61. Ibid., 312.

EPILOGUE

1. On Luis Leal, see Mario T. García, *Luis Leal: An Auto/Biography* (Austin: University of Texas Press, 2000).
2. Ibid.; Mario T. García, *Memories of Chicano History: The Life and Narrative of Bert Corona* (Berkeley: University of California Press, 2004); Frances Esquibel Tywoniak and Mario T. García, *Migrant Daughter: Coming of Age as a Mexican American Woman* (Berkeley: University of California Press, 2000); Mario T. García and Sal Castro, *Blowout! Sal Castro and the Chicano Struggle for Educational Justice* (Chapel Hill: University of North Carolina Press, 2011); and Mario T. García, *The Chicano Generation: Testimonios of the Movement* (Berkeley: University of California Press, 2015).
3. Edward Hallett Carr, *What Is History?* (New York: Vintage Press, 1961).

INDEX

ABOUT THE AUTHOR

Mario T. García is a professor of Chicano studies and history at the University of California, Santa Barbara. He is the author or editor of nearly twenty books, including *The Chicano Generation: Testimonios of the Movement*, and he has received awards from Southwest Books of the Year and the El Paso Writers' League. García is a past recipient of a Guggenheim Fellowship.